Young People a

This book examines the political engagement of young people in the Anglo-American democracies.

The commonly held view is that young people don't vote, they do not trust politicians and have low levels of political interest. But is this true, where is it true and to what extent? Examining voter turnout, political trust, political interest, electoral and non-electoral forms of participation and Internet use, this book provides a comprehensive account of political engagement among the young in the US, Britain, Canada and Australia. It shows young people's political engagement is much more complicated than many of the stereotypes suggest (in both good and bad ways) and challenges the conventional wisdom on a number of fronts. This book demonstrates how young people, while disengaged in some areas, are becoming more discerning about how and when they participate in politics and, as a consequence, political behaviour and political attitudes are becoming more volatile and unpredictable. In this way, this book provides a report card on young people's political engagement in the twenty-first century.

Young People and Politics will be of interest to students and scholars of political science, comparative politics, public policy and sociology, particularly those with a focus on young people and politics, political participation and public opinion.

Aaron J. Martin is a Lecturer in the School of Social and Political Sciences at the University of Melbourne, Australia.

Routledge research in comparative politics

1 **Democracy and Post-communism**
Political change in the post-communist world
Graeme Gill

2 **Sub-state Nationalism**
A comparative analysis of institutional design
Edited by Helena Catt and Michael Murphy

3 **Reward for High Public Office**
Asian and Pacific Rim States
Edited by Christopher Hood and B. Guy Peters

4 **Social Democracy and Labour Market Policy**
Developments in Britain and Germany
Knut Roder

5 **Democratic Revolutions**
Asia and Eastern Europe
Mark R. Thompson

6 **Democratization**
A comparative analysis of 170 countries
Tatu Vanhanen

7 **Determinants of the Death Penalty**
A comparative study of the world
Carsten Anckar

8 **How Political Parties Respond to Voters**
Interest aggregation revisited
Edited by Kay Lawson and Thomas Poguntke

9 **Women, Quotas and Politics**
Edited by Drude Dahlerup

10 **Citizenship and Ethnic Conflict**
Challenging the nation-state
Haldun Gülalp

11 **The Politics of Women's Interests**
New comparative and international perspectives
Edited by Louise Chappell and Lisa Hill

12 **Political Disaffection in Contemporary Democracies**
Social capital, institutions and politics
Edited by Mariano Torcal and José Ramón Montero

30 Political Leadership, Parties and Citizens
The personalisation of leadership
Edited by Jean Blondel and Jean-Louis Thiebault

31 Civil Society and Activism in Europe
Contextualizing engagement and political orientation
Edited by William A. Maloney and Jan W. van Deth

32 Gender Equality, Citizenship and Human Rights
Controversies and challenges in China and the Nordic countries
Edited by Pauline Stoltz, Marina Svensson, Zhongxin Sun and Qi Wang

33 Democratization and the European Union
Comparing Central and Eastern European post-Communist countries
Edited by Leonardo Morlino and Wojciech Sadurski

34 The Origin of Electoral Systems in the Postwar Era
A worldwide approach
Krister Lundell

35 The Globalization of Motherhood
Deconstruction and reconstructions of biology and care
Edited by Wendy Chavkin and JaneMaree Maher

36 Parties, Elections, and Policy Reforms in Western Europe
Voting for social pacts
Kerstin Hamann and John Kelly

37 Democracy and Famine
Olivier Rubin

38 Women in Executive Power
A global overview
Edited by Gretchen Bauer and Manon Tremblay

39 Women and Representation in Local Government
International case studies
Edited by Barbara Pini and Paula McDonald

40 The Politics of Charity
Kerry O'Halloran

41 Climate Policy Changes in Germany and Japan
A path to paradigmatic policy change
Rie Watanabe

42 African Parliamentary Reform
Edited by Rick Stapenhurst, Rasheed Draman and Andrew Imlach with Alexander Hamilton and Cindy Kroon

43 The Politics of International Law and Compliance
Serbia, Croatia and The Hague tribunal
Edited by Nikolas Rajkovic

44 The Funding of Political Parties
Where now?
Edited by Keith Ewing, Joo-Cheong Tham and Jacob Rowbottow

13 Representing Women in Parliament
A comparative study
Edited by Marian Sawer, Manon Tremblay and Linda Trimble

14 Democracy and Political Culture in Eastern Europe
Edited by Hans-Dieter Klingemann, Dieter Fuchs and Jan Zielonka

15 Social Capital and Associations in European Democracies
A comparative analysis
Edited by William A. Maloney and Sigrid Roßteutscher

16 Citizenship and Involvement in European Democracies
A comparative analysis
Edited by Jan van Deth, José Ramón Montero and Anders Westholm

17 The Politics of Foundations
A comparative analysis
Edited by Helmut K. Anheier and Siobhan Daly

18 Party Policy in Modern Democracies
Kenneth Benoit and Michael Laver

19 Semi-Presidentialism Outside Europe
A comparative study
Edited by Robert Elgie and Sophia Moestrup

20 Comparative Politics
The principal-agent perspective
Jan-Erik Lane

21 The Political Power of Business
Structure and information in public policymaking
Patrick Bernhagen

22 Women's Movements
Flourishing or in abeyance?
Edited by Marian Sawer and Sandra Grey

23 Consociational Theory
McGarry and O'Leary and the Northern Ireland conflict
Edited by Rupert Taylor

24 The International Politics of Democratization
Comparative perspectives
Edited by Nuno Severiano Teixeira

25 Post-communist Regime Change
A comparative study
Jørgen Møller

26 Social Democracy in Power
The capacity to reform
Wolfgang Merkel, Alexander Petring, Christian Henkes and Christoph Egle

27 The Rise of Regionalism
Causes of regional mobilization in Western Europe
Rune Dahl Fitjar

28 Party Politics in the Western Balkans
Edited by Věra Stojarová and Peter Emerson

29 Democratization and Market Reform in Developing and Transitional Countries
Think tanks as catalysts
James G. McGann

45 Parliamentary Oversight Tools
A comparative analysis
*Riccardo Pelizzo and
Frederick Stapenhurst*

46 Inclusion and Exclusion in the Liberal Competition State
The cult of the individual
Richard Münch

47 New Challenger Parties in Western Europe
A comparative analysis
Airo Hino

48 Metropolitan Governance and Policy
Jen Nelles

49 Rewards for High Public Office in Europe and North America
Edited by B. Guy Peters & Marleen Brans

50 International Security, Conflict and Gender
'HIV/AIDS is another war'
Hakan Seckinelgin

51 Young People and Politics
Political engagement in the Anglo-American democracies
Aaron J. Martin

Young People and Politics
Political engagement in the
Anglo-American democracies

Aaron J. Martin

LONDON AND NEW YORK

First published 2012
by Routledge
2 Park Square, Milton Park, Abingdon, Oxfordshire OX14 4RN

Simultaneously published in the USA and Canada
by Routledge
711 Third Avenue, New York, NY 10017

First issued in paperback 2014

Routledge is an imprint of the Taylor & Francis Group, an informa business

© 2012 Aaron J. Martin

The right of Aaron J. Martin to be identified as author of this work has been asserted by him in accordance with sections 77 and 78 of the Copyright, Designs and Patents Act 1988.

All rights reserved. No part of this book may be reprinted or reproduced or utilized in any form or by any electronic, mechanical, or other means, now known or hereafter invented, including photocopying and recording, or in any information storage or retrieval system, without permission in writing from the publishers.

Trademark notice: Product or corporate names may be trademarks or registered trademarks, and are used only for identification and explanation without intent to infringe

British Library Cataloguing in Publication Data
A catalogue record for this book is available from the British Library

Library of Congress Cataloging-in-Publication Data
Martin, Aaron J., 1928–
Young people and politics : comparing Anglo-American democracies / Aaron J. Martin.
　p. cm. – (Routledge research in comparative politics ; 51)
　Includes bibliographical references and index.
　1. Youth–Political activity–English-speaking countries. 2. Political participation–English-speaking countries. 3. Democracy–English-speaking countries. I. Title.
　HQ799.2.P6M365 2012
　305.235017'562–dc23
　　　　　　　　　　　　　　　　　　　　　　　　2011052174

ISBN 13: 978-0-415-69691-3 (hbk)
ISBN 13: 978-1-138-82599-4 (pbk)

Typeset in Sabon
by Wearset Ltd, Boldon, Tyne and Wear

Contents

List of figures xi
Acknowledgements xiii

Introduction 1

PART I
Voter turnout 19

1 Is turnout declining among the young? 21

PART II
Political attitudes 37

2 Political trust: the not particularly less trusting young 39
3 Political interest among the young 55

PART III
Political participation beyond voting 67

4 Electoral engagement: a disengaged youth 69
5 Non-electoral forms of participation: a brighter picture? 87
6 The Internet: emerging new forms of participation 102

PART IV
What can be done? 119

7 Policy reforms 121

Conclusion 135
Appendix: note on data sources and analysis 144

Notes 146
Bibliography 149
Index 164

Figures

1.1	Voter turnout in the US (1952–2008)	25
1.2	Voter turnout in Canada (1965–2008)	27
1.3	Voter turnout in Britain (1964–2010)	29
1.4	Would vote 'if not compulsory' in Australia (1996–2010)	30
1.5	Civic duty in the Anglo-American democracies	33
2.1	Trust in government in the US (1964–2008)	45
2.2	Trust/confidence in government in Canada (1965–2008)	47
2.3	Trust in political parties in Britain (1987–2005)	48
2.4	Trust in government in Australia (1969–2010)	50
2.5	Agree democracy is the best form of government	52
3.1	Interest in government and public affairs in the US (1960–2008)	59
3.2	Interest in politics in Canada (1965–2008)	60
3.3	Interest in politics in Britain (1974–2010)	61
3.4	Interest in politics in Australia (1967–2010)	62
4.1	Non-party identifiers in the US (1952–2008)	72
4.2	Non-party identifiers in Canada (1965–2008)	73
4.3	Non-party identifiers in Britain (1964–2010)	75
4.4	Non-party identifiers in Australia (1967–2010)	76
4.5	Party membership in the US	77
4.6	Party membership in Canada (1988–2008)	78
4.7	Party membership in Britain (1964–2010)	79
4.8	Party membership in Australia	80
4.9	Contacted a politician or civil servant in past year	81
4.10	Contacted by a political party in the US (1956–2008)	82
4.11	Contacted by candidates or a party in Canada (1965–2006)	83
4.12	Contacted by a party at home in Britain (1964–2005)	84
5.1	Attended a demonstration in past year	91
5.2	Signed a petition in past year	93
5.3	Boycotted consumer products in past year	94

6.1 Participated in political activities over the Internet 104
6.2 Joined a political forum or discussion group on the Internet in past year 106
6.3 Forwarded political messages on the Internet 107
6.4 Visited website of political organization or candidate 108

Acknowledgements

A number of people have made extremely generous contributions to my research for which I am very grateful. Thanks to André Blais, Colin Campbell, Keith Dowding, David Gow, Edith Gray, Kasper Hansen, John Langmore, Lawrence LeDuc, Gerry Matte, Philomena Murray, Juliet Pietsch, Larry Saha, Alfred Stepan, David Tucker, my ANU honours class and the staff at the Australian Data Archive and the Interuniversity Consortium for Political and Social Research (ICPSR). I would also like to thank the Australian National University (my former employer) and the University of Melbourne (my current employer) for providing an excellent institutional base to do this research. The Australian National University generously provided funding for travel which assisted my research. In particular, I would like to make a special note of thanks to Ian McAllister for his generous assistance over many years (as well as agreeing to read a draft manuscript) and Simon Jackman for facilitating my visit to Stanford in 2008 and then proving to be a tremendous host when I arrived. The usual disclaimer applies.

It would be remiss of me not to thank the thousands of people who took time out of their days to respond to the various surveys in this book.

My last and deepest thanks go to my family for, well, everything, and Laura for her endless love and support.

Introduction

Around the Anglo-American world, democracy is said to be in a state of ill health. This is typified in a 2005 American Political Science Association/ Brookings Institution report which argued:

> American democracy is at risk. The risk comes not from some external threat but from disturbing internal trends: an erosion of the activities and capacities of citizenship. Americans have turned away from politics and the public sphere in large numbers, leaving our civic life impoverished. Citizens participate in public affairs less frequently, in fewer venues, and less equally than is healthy for a vibrant democratic polity.
>
> (cited in Dalton, 2011a, 2)

This is no case of 'American exceptionalism.' In fact, there is widespread concern that citizens in many advanced democracies have become disengaged from politics (see Norris, 2001, 217). These concerns are not altogether new. In the eighteenth century Rousseau complained that 'we no longer have citizens' and in 1924 Arthur M. Schlesinger and Erik M. Erikson wrote of 'the vanishing voter' and bemoaned a lack of civic obligation among citizens (Schudson, 1998, 190, 295). Nevertheless, these concerns are thought to have become particularly acute of late. Around the Anglo-American democracies the nature of political engagement seems to be changing and for many commentators these trends are deeply alarming.

Alarm about this perceived problem has stretched well beyond the academy. Elites have also been troubled by what they see as a retreat from active citizenship. For example, in his autobiography former Prime Minister of Britain Tony Blair (2010, 686) wrote that there is a 'general malaise about politics which is a real problem in Britain and elsewhere.' In the US Chief Justice Breyer has also expressed his concern about 'indifference and cynicism because indifference means nonparticipation and cynicism means the withdrawal of trust ... without trust and participation, the constitution cannot work' (cited in Dalton 2004, 202). In Canada the then Minister of Finance (soon to be Prime Minister) Paul Martin gave a speech in which he pointed to low turnout 'as a symptom of more fundamental problems in our democratic system' (cited in Tanguay, 2009, 222).

When it comes to assigning blame for this problem young people are often singled out. Many analysts believe that young people today have become increasingly disengaged from political participation 'reflecting, it is feared, a broader disenchantment and disconnect with representative democracy' (Norris, 2003, 16). In the US Zukin *et al.* (2006, 3) write that the 'gradual disengagement of the American citizenry from public life, and especially from traditional political participation … has been greatest among the youngest Americans.' In Britain, young people are also depicted as disengaged from conventional politics and are commonly depicted in the media as the 'disaffected' generation (Fahmy, 2006, 1, 9). In Australia and Canada concerns have also been expressed about young people's political engagement (see Vromen, 2003; Howe, 2010; Milner, 2010).

This book examines these claims by conducting a 'stock-take' of young people's political engagement in the Anglo-American democracies (i.e. Australia, Britain, Canada and the US).[1] In doing so this book outlines the contours of young people's political engagement across the Anglo-American world. What constitutes political engagement? Zukin *et al.* (2006, 9) suggest that we start 'from the premise that there are many ways citizens can and do participate in the democratic life of the nation.' In line with this argument this book takes a broad view of political engagement in order to understand the wider contours of young people's political engagement. Political engagement is understood to take in both behavioural and psychological indicators of engagement. Political engagement in this book is taken to include voter turnout, political trust, political interest, electoral engagement, non-electoral participation and Internet use. I examine these factors over time, using, for the most part, each country's national election study (see Appendix for note on data sources and analysis). In this way, this book provides a report card on young people's political engagement in the twenty-first century.

The literature cited above suggests that the disengagement of young people from politics is a major challenge facing the Anglo-American democracies in the twenty-first century. Yet, as Miller and Shanks (1996, 34) and Milner (2010, viii) point out, surprisingly little research has been done on this subject and the different facets of young people's political engagement are not well understood—this is especially true of the Anglo-American democracies taken as a whole. This is surprising because young people 'are the ones who react to new conditions. Older people are, on the whole, too set in their ways to be responsible for social or political change, so most long-term change comes about by way of generational replacement' (Franklin, 2004, 216). Therefore, central to understanding political engagement in the Anglo-American democracies at the aggregate level is understanding political engagement among the young.

Examining young people's political engagement over time

Generational versus lifecycle effects

Central to this book are generational and lifecycle effects. These two effects have very different implications for levels of political engagement over time. The different assumptions of lifecycle and generational effects provide a lens through which political engagement should be analysed. If low levels of political engagement among the young are a product of the lifecycle effect, by which young people eventually come to be more politically engaged as they age, political engagement at the aggregate level should not decline over time. The lifecycle pattern is linked to the responsibilities of adulthood. Young people are engaged in a number of activities in early adulthood such as getting a licence, going to university, entering the workforce and are often very mobile, none of which is conducive to being politically engaged. This is referred to as a problem of 'start up' (see Verba and Nie, 1972, 139; Highton and Wolfinger, 2001). However, as the young age, and grow into the more stable adult roles of their late 20s and beyond, the lifecycle effect predicts that young people will change their political behaviour and attitudes accordingly.

According to the lifecycle effect the 'youth rebellion' is not to be taken seriously because as young people grow older they will 'come to their senses' and adopt the behaviour of previous generations (Hellevik, 2002, 293–4). The lifecycle effect is a caution against seeing the youth of today as different from the youth of yesterday. It is also worth remembering that young people have long been the target of complaints. Young people have been criticized for their lack of civic virtue as far back as the eighth century BC when Hesiod complained that he saw 'no hope for the future of our people if they are dependent on the frivolous youth of today, for certainly all youth are reckless beyond words' (cited in Levine, 2007, xiii). We hear echoes of this, albeit less dramatic ones, in the work of Putnam (2000). But a possible refrain is 'perhaps young people were always like that.' Lifecycle effects take this view into account. Evidence of lifecycle effects then should temper any concerns that the nature of young people's political engagement is changing in a dramatic way.

Generational effects predict an altogether different pattern. This explanation holds that experiences during adolescence and early adulthood make a lasting imprint on young people's attitudes and behaviour and these orientations will remain with young people as they age. This is connected to the work of Karl Mannheim who contended that 'when an age group enters social life, its formative experiences produce a distinct and lasting perspective' (Whittier, 1997, 761). These changes are caused by historically specific experiences whose effects the young will retain throughout the lifecycle. Therefore, once these changes develop they become a vehicle for further mobilization and transmission of change,

4 *Introduction*

which Mannheim saw as a harbinger of discontinuity in the social process (Wuthnow, 1976, 851). Generational change, then, is 'an ongoing process that continuously transforms the electorate' (Abramson, 1983, 308). Generational effects also bring into question political socialization (as discussed in more detail below) by which attitudes and behaviours are transmitted from parent to child.

Generational change is important because it is a potentially powerful mechanism for change at the aggregate level. For example, in the US between 1952 and 1992 (a shorter period than the American data covered in this book) the voting age population increased by 80 per cent. The number of people eligible to vote grew from 100 million to 180 million while 40 million of the 100 million eligible for the 1952 election died by 1992, and those 40 million were replaced by about 120 million newly eligible voters (Miller and Shanks, 1996, 23). In Britain, 80 per cent of those on the electoral register in 1945 were dead by 1992 and half of those on the 1992 register could not vote before 1970 (Butler, 1995, 64). These numbers point to the potential for generational change to be a powerful driver of aggregate change. Accordingly, we should pay more attention to generational effects as the consequences of generational replacement over time could be quite significant.

Putnam versus Inglehart and Welzel

According to different scholars these generational effects play out in different ways. Three of the most important scholars examining generational effects in regards to political engagement are Robert Putnam, Ronald Inglehart and Christian Welzel. In his famous work *Bowling Alone* Putnam (2000, 31) argues that 'the character of Americans' involvement with politics and government has been transformed over the past three decades.' Putnam (2000, 35) writes that:

> declining electoral participation is merely the most visible symptom of a broader disengagement from community life. Like a fever, electoral abstention is even more important as a sign of deeper trouble in the body politic than as a malady itself. It is not just from the voting booth that Americans are increasingly AWOL.

Putnam (2000) attributes much of this to generational change which, he argues, has played a lead role in depleting social capital and with this a decline in many forms of political participation and associational activity. He attributes generational change to an exceptionally civic generation being replaced by 'postcivic' cohorts. According to Putnam (2000, 261) young people today feel less guilty about not voting than older generations, are less interested in politics, are less likely to attend a public meeting, less likely to contact public officials or be involved in a community project. In other words, young people are much less politically engaged than older people. Putnam (2000, 260) sees this as coupled with young people valuing material wealth over being politically engaged. Putnam's views are very much in line (and have in some cases informed) many of the negative depictions of young people that are cited in this book.

Putnam argues that on almost every measure young people's political engagement has declined. But what about the non-electoral forms of participation that are covered in Part III of this book (as outlined below)? Putnam (2000, 252) disagrees with those who argue that political participation is evolving (see Norris, 2002; Inglehart and Welzel, 2005; Dalton, 2008) by pointing to evidence which shows that American citizens have *not* become more likely to be engaged in non-electoral participation such as signing a petition and that this trend is even more pronounced among young people. The one area where Putnam is less scathing of the young is in regards to political trust where Putnam (2000, 261) finds the young to be no less trusting of politicians and parties than older cohorts. Therefore, 'a key theme in much of the international literature is that young people's lack of social capital has resulted in their tendency to drop out of participatory politics altogether' (Fieldhouse *et al.*, 2007, 812). Taken as a whole Putnam makes a number of statements in *Bowling Alone* which we can test in the US and the other Anglo-American democracies in relation to young people's political engagement.

The arguments made by Putnam stand in stark contrast to those made by Inglehart and Welzel. According to Inglehart and Welzel's (2005, 19) revised version of modernization theory the process of socioeconomic development has a clearly delineated causal effect on political participation and attitudes:

> Socioeconomic development starts from technological innovations that increase labor productivity; it then brings occupational specialization, rising education levels, and rising income levels; it diversifies human interaction, shifting the emphasis from authority relations toward bargaining relations; in the long run this brings cultural changes, such as ... changing attitudes towards authority ... broader political participation, and more critical and less easily led publics.

According to this view socioeconomic modernization, largely due to the rise in education levels, 'reduces constraints on human choice by increasing people's material, cognitive, and social resources' making them more independent and able to act autonomously (Inglehart and Welzel, 2005, 25).

These arguments have clear implications for the young. All of the Anglo-American democracies are industrialized and rich and, at least up until recent years, have experienced high levels of economic growth. Therefore, that today's young people have been raised in such prosperous economic conditions means that generational effects should be present in terms of young people's political engagement. Indeed, Inglehart and Welzel (2005, 118) argue that increases in non-electoral forms of participation reflect generational change that 'is bringing a shift towards increasingly self-assertive and expressive publics.' Therefore, if the modernization process works in the way that Inglehart and Welzel (2005) argue that it does, young people will be found to be engaged in politics in a very different way to older people.

Inglehart and Welzel (2005, 4) argue:

> New forms of political self-expression extend the boundary of politics from the narrow domain of elite-led electoral campaigns into increasingly autonomous forms of public self expression.... Contrary to often-repeated claims that social capital and mass participation are eroding, the publics of postindustrial societies are intervening in politics more actively today than ever before; however, they are changing the ways in which they participate. Elite-led forms of participation are dwindling. Mass loyalties to long-established hierarchical political parties are weakening. No longer content to be disciplined troops, the public has become increasingly autonomous and elite challenging.

Inglehart and Welzel argue that these trends are most pronounced among the young, due to the generational effects outlined above. Accordingly, they argue that elite led activities like voting and joining a political party are *less* common among the young while non-electoral forms of participation such as attending a demonstration and signing a petition are *more* common among the young. This is cognizant with the view that

> traditional theoretical and conceptual frameworks derived from the literature of the 1960s and 1970s and even what we may call 'political participation,' need to be revised and updated to take account of how opportunities for civic engagement have evolved and diversified over the years.
>
> (Norris, 2002, 188)

However, despite Inglehart and Welzel (2005, 118) arguing that generational change is 'bringing a shift towards more self-assertive and expressive publics,' largely absent from the book which makes these claims is data on political participation disaggregated by age. Furthermore, as I argue in Chapter 5, the World Values Survey (that Inglehart and Welzel rely on throughout their work) is not well suited to analysing non-electoral participation among the young. In order to better test the predictions that Inglehart and Welzel make Parts I and III of this book examine whether 'mass participation has taken on a new character' (Inglehart and Welzel, 2005, 43) by disaggregating various data sources.

In relation to political trust Inglehart and Welzel (2005, 43) argue that, due to increases in education, 'Respect for authority is eroding.' This means that young people in particular are less likely to be trusting of elites. However, they argue that 'the decline in confidence in institutions does not pose a threat to democracy' but rather 'reflects the emergence of less deferential, more elite-challenging publics in modern societies which we interpret as conducive to democracy' (Inglehart and Welzel, 2005, 253). Furthermore, Inglehart and Welzel (2005) argue that support for democracy has not eroded.

Therefore, Inglehart and Welzel and Putnam have different views as to how generational effects should play out. Putnam is very pessimistic in arguing that young people's political engagement is declining on a number of fronts. Inglehart and Welzel, by contrast, argue that it is changing, and for the better. Throughout this book I will examine these claims in relation to young people's political engagement.

Socialization theory

Socialization theory is an important component of the theories outlined above. Socialization theory deals with 'the acquisition of prevailing norms and modes of behavior' and the process by which they are transmitted from one generation to another (Jennings and Niemi, 1974, 5)—how attitudes and behaviours are disseminated, in other words. Early studies (Almond and Verba, 1963) saw socialization as a key component through which the political culture of a nation is transmitted and attributed the stability of political attitudes and orientations to socialization (see also Easton and Dennis, 1969, 6). In the 1950s and 1960s socialization theory did a good job at explaining the stability of the political system by which young people acquired the voting habits and supportive political attitudes of their parents. The success of socialization theory in explaining the stability of the political system led Greenstein (1970, 969) to note that 'political socialization is a growth stock.'

However, the arguments put forward by both Putnam and Inglehart and Welzel suggest (in different ways) that the socialization process is breaking down and that young people are no longer inheriting the political attitudes and behaviours of their parents and grandparents. In other words, norms and behaviours are no longer being transmitted from parent to child in the way they once were. This is supported by much of the data in this book. That some of the habits of political engagement are not being acquired by younger cohorts has significant implications for political engagement. If, for example, young people are no longer acquiring the habit of voting then this suggests that young people are no longer being socialized into becoming regular voters. This has worrying consequences because for previous generations acquiring the habit of voting has kept turnout relatively high whereas for young people this appears to be changing (see Chapter 1).

8 Introduction

There are other examples in this book of the socialization process breaking down. Party identification is a good example of this. Early studies such as *The American Voter* found that 'party identification in essence is a non-political attitude formed mainly by socialization during childhood and adolescence. Thereafter party identification is supposed to be immune to politics and economic change' (Holmberg, 2007, 563). In *The Voter Decides* about two in three respondents remembered their parent's party identification which was very closely aligned with their own party identification and voting in their first and subsequent elections (Campbell *et al.*, 1954, 106). But party identification is declining among the young (see Chapter 4) bringing into question the process by which the young are socialized into the partisanship of their parents.

Evidence that the young may be turning away from electoral engagement towards non-electoral forms of political action (see Part III) also suggests that the young are becoming more immune to acquiring the behavioural habits of their parents. As for political trust, cultural accounts have traditionally emphasized the durability of norms acquired early in life through the socialization process and the limited impact of external situations (Jackman and Miller, 1995, 478). However, Chapter 2 shows trust to be much more variable than would be expected from these accounts. In other words, political trust seems to be much more of an evaluation of the political system rather than an unquestioned norm received through the socialization process.

Today's young seem to be changing the way the socialization process operates. Rather than following the behavioural and attitudinal patterns of their parents the young seem to be making their own calculations as to how they interact with the political world. This seems to be leading to different modes of activity and therefore greater instability and variation than the original socialization model would imply. Early socialization studies explained the persistence of political attitudes and behaviour quite well. But today we seem to understand less about the transmission process and how this changes over time. This all brings into question Jennings and Niemi's (1974, 4) claim that 'Value constellations and behavioral patterns would seem to emanate in large part from what one generation learns from the other.' If this learning process is no longer occurring this could have important implications for political engagement in the future. Accordingly, this book tests, albeit indirectly, how the socialization process is working among today's young.

Methodology

The methodology of this book has been guided by being able to examine generational and lifecycle effects and through these effects explore the socialization process. Studying age groups (as I do in the analysis throughout the book) as opposed to generations allows greater analytic leverage in terms of examining how young people's political engagement has been changing over time. For example, if this study examined generations (e.g. baby boomers and Generation X) there would be a limited period over which the latter generations (Generations X and Y) could be observed. This would prohibit us from examining generational versus lifecycle effects in as much detail as the methodology employed in this book allows. In contrast, looking at (where data allows) young people in the 1950s as compared to young people in the 2000s allows us to see how young people's political engagement has been changing over time. Using this method we can say, a young person today is (or is not) different from a young person 50 years ago. The value of this method is that in assembling disaggregated across-time data we can get a reasonably complete picture of young people's political engagement and how this has changed over time. This is a superior method in many regards to examining young people at one period in time (for example, Norris, 2003) or looking at specific generations (for example, Zukin et al., 2006).

It is also worth saying something about the age groups I have decided to analyse. It is common in studies of young people to define young people as aged between 18 and 24, even though there is no universally agreed definition of youth (see Fahmy, 2006, 29). However, because young people are often delaying getting married, getting a mortgage and having children into their late 20s and early (or even mid) 30s, I classify young people as being aged between 18 and 29. Furthermore, sampling error is likely to be smaller when the N is larger which is the case in regards to defining young people as aged 18–29 as opposed to 18–24. Therefore, in this study the term 'young people' refers to those aged 18–29. The term 'middle-aged' refers to those aged 30–59 and the term 'older people' refers to those aged 60 and over. I recognize that these age classifications are quite rough but this study is primarily concerned with how 'young people' are different from 'older people,' broadly defined, and the implications of this for political engagement over time.

Rather than looking at young people in one country this study examines young people (as compared to older people) across the Anglo-American democracies.[2] This comparative approach has been adopted for several reasons. As stated above, young people are thought to be politically disengaged across the Anglo-American democracies. Therefore, studying more than one country is an appropriate research strategy. As Milner (2010, 78) argues: 'Comparison is the *sine qua non* of meaningful analysis.' However, in employing the comparative method it is recognized that as useful as it can be 'it can necessarily lead to no more than partial generalizations' (Lijphart, 1994, 13).

There is a more pragmatic reason for studying the Anglo-American democracies as well. All of the Anglo-American democracies have run national elections studies over time stretching back to the 1960s, and the 1950s in the US (the exception is New Zealand which is not included in this book for this reason).[3] Many of these national election studies have asked the same questions over time which allows us to get a picture of how young people's political engagement has changed over time.

Studying young people's political engagement over time does however pose challenges in terms of identifying causal links. Because of the scope of this book I do not link specific events (which vary greatly across countries) causally to attitudes and behaviour. Rather, I prefer to employ the more cautious language of 'these things may be linked.' In their exhaustive study of generations in the US Miller and Shanks (1996, 24) admit to their failure to account for generational differences by stating that 'It is much more difficult to explain why the generations differed in the way they did ... we have no more than circumstantial evidence concerning' the origins of generational differences. However, Miller and Shanks (1996) argue that not being able to account for the causes does not prohibit them from accounting for the consequences of generational change. The problem of not being able to establish causal links afflicts other studies of generations (e.g. Zukin *et al.*, 2006) in which events are often linked to attitudes and behaviour without these links being empirically proven. Therefore, where generational differences show up that we cannot account for causally (because of the different variables that have been included in the national election studies) we can offer some tentative explanations. As in the work of Miller and Shanks (1996), this book can account for the consequences but not the causes of generational effects.

The plan of this book: political engagement in four parts

Part I (Chapter 1)

Part I of this book examines voter turnout over time. The message coming out of much of the literature is that young people don't vote. Book titles such as *Is Voting for Young People?* (Wattenberg, 2006) typify the tenor of much of the literature on voter turnout among the young. In this literature 'the half empty ballot-box is taken as the most common symptom of democratic ill-health' (Norris, 2011, 220). Accordingly, this problem has not escaped the attention of those such as former president Jimmy Carter who remarked in 2001 that non-voting among the young 'is something that is just as bad as the difference in ethnic groups or minorities not voting' (cited in Wattenberg, 2002, 102).

Part I examines these claims in regards to young people in the Anglo-American democracies. In doing so I show that patterns of turnout among the young are more volatile than much of the literature would lead us to expect. The two most recent American elections (2004 and 2008) have seen turnout among the young increase and turnout has also increased in recent years in certain elections in Canada and in the 2010 British election. Supplementary data cited in Chapter 1 suggests that this volatility is owing to low levels of civic duty among the young. Absent the civic duty that propels older people to the polls young people seem to be voting or abstaining depending on whether an election captures their attention or not. This chapter shows that young people would be better characterized as volatile voters rather than non-voters.

Nevertheless, that many young people are markedly absent in some elections is a cause for concern. Taken together with the findings of Chapter 4, the turnout and civic duty data cited in Chapter 1 suggests that electoral politics is becoming a less important permanent feature of young people's political engagement. This is troubling because, as I argue throughout this book, voting (and the parties that compete in elections) are central to democracy. No matter which other forms of political activity become more common among the young, voting and parties remain the essential ingredients in the political world.

Part II (Chapters 2 and 3)

Part II of this book examines young people's psychological engagement with politics in terms of their political attitudes. Political attitudes have been regarded as an important part of political engagement beginning with the early literature on voter behaviour (Almond and Verba, 1963). Indeed, 'Citizens' beliefs, attitudes and opinions lie at the heart of democratic theory and practice' (Kornberg and Clarke, 1992, 61). It is important to examine young people's psychological engagement with politics in particular because 'at the core of anxieties about the political disaffection of young people are concerns about young people's attitudes towards the political system itself' (Fahmy, 2006, 71). Accordingly, Part II examines political trust (Chapter 2) and political interest (Chapter 3) by drawing again from the national election studies which have asked roughly comparable questions over a long period of time.

Political trust has been a prominent theme beginning with the early literature on voter behaviour (Stokes, 1962; Almond and Verba, 1963). In fact, 'Trust among citizens in those who govern them has been a consistent theme in political philosophy, going back as far as antiquity' (McAllister, 2011, 71). Political trust has become an even more important topic of late with the perceived decline in trust in many advanced democracies capturing more and more attention among scholars and policy makers alike. This concern has arisen because of clear evidence 'of a general erosion in support for politicians and government in most advanced industrial democracies' (Dalton, 2004, 30). Pharr and Putnam (2000, 11) note that 'almost everywhere, it seems, people are less deferential to political leaders and more sceptical of their motives.' Declining levels of political trust have also caught the attention of elites such as President Carter who in 1979 warned that declining trust in government 'was a fundamental threat to American democracy' (cited in Dalton 2004, 1). Yet, although a lot has been written

12 Introduction

about political trust much of this research examines political trust at the aggregate level. There is very little empirical research on political trust among young people over time. Chapter 2 shows that while young people are generally less trusting than their elders young people's level of trust tends to be in synch with that of the broader population. The problem of low levels of political trust in the Anglo-American democracies affects the young and old alike. Therefore, rather than asking why young people aren't politically trusting we are better off asking why citizens of all ages lack political trust.

Chapter 3 turns to political interest. Dalton and Klingemann (2007, 4) write that 'One of the enduring debates of political behaviour research involves basic questions about the public's political abilities—the public's level of knowledge, understanding, and interest in political matters.' Along with political trust, the early political culture literature (Almond and Verba, 1963) held political interest and attention to public affairs to be an integral part of a successful and healthy political culture (Jackman, 1987, 417). But research following this has shown a public generally uninterested in political affairs (Erikson et al., 2002, 78). But how does all of this apply to the young? Where research (much of it cross-sectional) has been done, young people have been shown to have very low levels of political interest in the US (Lyons and Alexander, 2000; Putnam, 2000; Zukin et al., 2006, 7), Canada (Gidengil et al., 2003; Blais et al., 2004; Howe, 2010) and Britain (Pattie et al., 2004, 92). Chapter 3 examines young people's political interest over time and shows that political interest is not in secular decline among the young in the Anglo-American democracies. Young people have, however, become less interested in politics relative to older people.

Part III (Chapters 4 to 6)

Part III returns to behavioural indicators of political engagement by examining political participation beyond voting. The late twentieth century saw an expanding array of political activity beyond electoral forms of political participation such as voting or joining a political party. We need then to distinguish electoral forms of political engagement from non-electoral forms of political participation and ask whether young people are turning their backs on the electoral world to engage in non-electoral forms of participation such as attending demonstrations, signing petitions and participating in politics via the Internet (see note explaining use of terms).[4] Accordingly, Part III examines the broader dimensions of young people's political participation.

In Chapter 4 I examine what I term electoral engagement. Electoral engagement refers to both psychological engagement with electoral politics (identifying with a party) and behavioural measures of electoral engagement (such as joining a political party and contacting a politician). Chapter 5 goes beyond electoral engagement to look at non-electoral forms of participation (such as attending a demonstration or signing a petition). In Part III I move away from relying predominantly on the national election studies and use a broader range of data sources in order to be able to account for the various types of political participation that young people are engaged in. For the reasons spelt out in Chapter 5 the best data source to examine young people's levels of non-electoral participation is the International Social Survey Programme (ISSP). Chapter 6 goes further again by looking at political engagement on the Internet using two unique data sources.

In the literature young people are depicted as disengaged from electoral politics across the Anglo-American democracies (see Putnam 2000; Blais *et al.*, 2002, 8; Fahmy, 2006, 1; Zukin *et al.*, 2006, 189). However, missing from these analyses is a thorough investigation of electoral engagement among different age groups over time using the same data sources. In Chapter 4 I examine electoral engagement using, for the most part, each country's national election study. This chapter shows young people across the Anglo-American democracies to be very disengaged. This is particularly the case in regards to party identification which is concerning 'because party identification has been central to theories of mass political behaviour for more than four decades' (Dalton *et al.*, 2002, 37). This is occurring alongside a decrease in the number of young people who are members of political parties and low levels of contact between young people and politicians, parties and civil servants.

This negative picture of young people's electoral engagement is said to be offset by young people being more engaged in non-electoral forms of participation. Norris (2002, 222) writes that while young people are disengaged from traditional channels of participation, such as parties, young people are more likely to channel their energies through non-electoral forms of participation. Similarly, Zukin *et al.* (2006, 3) argue that citizens in the US

> are participating in a different mix of activism from in the past, and that is due largely to the process of generational replacement. We believe the volume of citizen engagement has not declined so much as it has spread to a wider variety of channels.

(see also Vromen, 2003; Pattie *et al.*, 2004, 110; O'Neill 2007). Therefore, depending on what types of political engagement we focus on young people may be found to be more engaged than the literature and data cited in Chapter 4 suggests. For instance, Norris (2002) argues that non-electoral forms of participation such as protesting, signing a petition and boycotting are often overlooked giving an unduly pessimistic picture of political participation. Taking into account these views Chapter 5 shows that young people are *more* likely than older people to be engaged in non-electoral forms of participation such as signing a petition and attending a demonstration.

14 Introduction

If we take the findings of Chapter 4 and Chapter 5 together we can see that while electoral forms of engagement are becoming *less* popular among the young non-electoral forms of activity seem to be becoming *more* popular. It seems then that young people in particular are increasingly willing to use a wide range of political actions in order to express their political voice. Chapter 4 and Chapter 5 show that this is particularly true of young people. Accordingly, the data cited in Part III is more in line with the optimism of Inglehart and Welzel as compared to the pessimism of Putnam.

The arrival of the Internet has added a further layer to these debates and 'has been viewed as both saviour and executioner of the current political system and its organizational infrastructure' (Ward and Gibson, 2009, 28). To optimists 'Digital technologies hold promise as a mechanism facilitating alternative channels of civic engagement ... revitalising mass participation in public affairs' but others hold more pessimistic views in regards to the Internet's potential to activate political engagement (Norris, 2001, 13). It is important to look at the Internet in relation to the young because

> New forms of mass communication traditionally have had a great appeal for younger people. Not only are the younger generation less likely to have established long-standing habits of media use, but they also are more willing to experiment with new technologies and formats.
> (Owen, 2006, 20)

Accordingly, Chapter 6 examines whether young people are more likely to be engaged in politics on the Internet through various means. Because of the lack of data, the analysis in Chapter 6 is confined to Australia and the US as comparable questions have been asked in these countries (in the 2011 ANUpoll in Australia and the 2006 Citizenship, Involvement, Democracy (CID) survey in the US). In this chapter I show that young people are more likely to be engaged in politics on the Internet. Yet, while the Internet is showing some potential to increase political engagement among the young this is likely to benefit the 'resource rich.'

Underpinning the chapters that make up Part III of this book are concerns about participatory inequalities. Research has shown that political participation is biased towards those of higher socioeconomic status (see Verba *et al.*, 1995). However, while we expect some differences in participation rates between social strata 'too large a gap implies that certain groups are excluded from the political process' (Dalton, 2006, 56). This is concerning in relation to non-electoral participation because those who participate in non-electoral forms of participation tend to be drawn from more advantaged groups (Barnes and Kaase, 1979, 526; Verba *et al.*, 1995, 2; Pattie *et al.*, 2004, 109). Therefore, while many types of political participation seem to be increasing 'ironically, overall increases in political involvement may mask a growing social-status bias in citizen participation and influence, which runs counter to democratic ideals' (Dalton, 2006, 74). I explain this in Chapter 5 as the dark side of modernization theory.

The change in styles of participation among the young away from electoral engagement and more towards non-electoral participation is, historically, a big shift. Traditionally, parties have mobilized those with fewer resources of whom many, if the resource model dominated, would not get involved in politics. For instance, in the US low socioeconomic status blacks with few resources have been mobilized into the political process by way of 'group consciousness' (Verba and Nie, 1972, 158–60). Therefore, if electoral forms of engagement (that are more equal) are declining and non-electoral forms of political participation (that are the most unequal) are increasing, this could see resource inequalities exacerbated in the future. Furthermore, political activism may be becoming even more elitist as it moves further away from representing class interests and more towards new issue priorities of the highly mobilized and informed. 'In other words, political voice may be in the center of a virtuous circle of capabilities for those advantaged in a society, but a vicious circle of capabilities for the disadvantaged' (Verba, 2003, 666). This is a real concern in regards to political equality.

Elections and the parties that take part in them serve an unparalleled good in helping represent majority, as opposed to niche, interests. Citizens project an

> extraordinary (and often conflicting) range of demands and interests upon politicians and the parties are required to broker all of this into some kind of politically manageable and coherent form. This is an absolutely vital function. It is also why some of the attacks on party are badly misplaced.
>
> (Wright, 2003, 77)

Given the centrality of parties to political society it is concerning that so 'many analysts downplay the role of political parties and other traditional types of political organizations' (Milner, 2010, 5). In Chapter 1 I argue that voting alone matters more than any other single activity. In Chapter 5 I argue that the political parties that contest elections provide a vital link between the citizen and the state. Elections and the parties that contest them have a great influence on the lives of many individuals. For this reason the optimistic tone of much of the literature which celebrates the expansion of political participation is somewhat misplaced. While the expansion of political participation is a positive development many analysts should be more concerned than they are about the volatile voting patterns, low levels of civic duty and the decline in electoral engagement that this book shows to be particularly acute among the young.

16 *Introduction*

Another theme running through Part III is the constraints we have in terms of data available. Because many of the forms of participation examined in Part III are new these have not been included in the main national election studies that this book relies on. As Fields (2011, 60) argues, 'We need to renovate our research methods to make them more sensitive to new trends in political participation.' But this is very challenging because many of the types of political participation covered in this part of the book are ephemeral and therefore difficult to capture and measure over time. As such, some important forms of engagement may be missed. Survey researchers are going to have to think about how to deal with these problems in the future.

Part IV (Chapter 7)

The final chapter (Chapter 7) examines what can be done to increase young people's political engagement. It offers policy recommendations in terms of better engaging young people in the political process. This chapter concentrates on increasing voting, electoral engagement more generally and political interest among the young. Particular attention is paid to increasing voter turnout because voting is the *sine qua non* of political activity in aggregating interests in a democratic way and reducing participatory inequalities. I look at four possible reforms aimed at the young; civic education reforms, elite mobilization, easing registration requirements and changing the electoral system as well as briefly considering other possible reforms. In terms of the most effective reforms a well designed civic education programme seems most promising, as does elite mobilization.

The central findings

This book outlines the broad contours of young people's political engagement in an attempt to better capture the way young people engage with politics in the twenty-first century. In completing a 'stock-take' of young people's political engagement the central findings of this book are:

- Voter turnout among young people is not in secular decline but rather is much more volatile than some of the literature would lead us to believe. This volatility seems to be driven by low levels of civic duty. This volatility also means that young people are markedly absent from some elections.
- Political trust is quite volatile across the Anglo-American democracies and young people broadly follow the general population in terms of patterns of political trust.
- Political interest is not in secular decline among the young although age gaps between the young and old have opened up over time.

- What I term electoral engagement is declining among the young (this is especially true of party identification and party membership).
- Young people are more likely than older people to be engaged in non-electoral forms of political participation such as signing a petition and attending a demonstration.
- Young people are much more engaged than older people in politics on the Internet.

Part I

Voter turnout

This first part of this book constitutes one chapter examining voter turnout. I begin with voter turnout because, for most citizens, voting is the single most important aspect of their engagement with the political world. This section also frames later discussion. In Part III I will return to some of the themes raised in Chapter 1 by considering the broader dimensions of young people's political participation beyond voting.

1 Is turnout declining among the young?

Old people vote, young people don't. This is the message coming out of much of the academic and popular literature on young people and voting. In this literature young people are depicted as ritual non-voters as compared to older regular voters who are holding up their end of the civic bargain. Book titles such as *Is Voting for Young People?* (Wattenberg, 2006) typify the tenor of much of the literature on voter turnout among the young. But does this hold true for the Anglo-American democracies? Would this chapter be more appropriately titled 'why don't young people vote'?

In this chapter I examine turnout in regards to lifecycle and generational effects on voting. Any study of turnout among the young needs to see turnout in the context of these effects. Lifecycle effects predict that young people will become more involved in electoral politics as they assume the responsibilities of adulthood and move through the lifecycle. Generational effects predict that cohorts will be affected by the circumstances that they grew up in that in turn affect their present and future voting patterns. The assumption in the literature (that finds support for generational effects) is that generational replacement will drive down turnout levels over time as non-voters come to replace regular voters. If this is confirmed this has concerning implications for democracy and suggests that the aggregating mechanism elections play may be compromised.

This chapter shows that generational effects do seem to be at work but not in the way much of the literature assumes. Rather than driving down turnout generational effects seem to be creating more volatile voting patterns by which young people turn out in relatively high numbers at some elections and abstain from others. In support of this proposition is evidence from the International Social Survey Programme (ISSP) showing that young people are much less likely than older people to see voting as a civic duty. This chapter shows that rather than characterizing young people as non-voters it would be better to characterize them as volatile voters.

Why is voting important?

Before moving to the analysis it is worth asking why voter turnout should be such a major concern. It could be argued that voting is but one of many forms of political participation (see following chapters for greater discussion). Marsh and Kaase (1979a, 86) went so far as to exclude voting from their analysis of political participation in advanced western democracies arguing that

> voting is a unique form of political behaviour in the sense that it occurs only rarely, is highly biased by strong mechanisms of social control and social desirability enhanced by the rain-dance ritual of campaigning, and does not involve the voter in informational or other costs.

Voting is one among a repertoire of political actions. However, for many, elections are 'the defining feature of the democratic process. They are the critical juncture where individuals take stock of their various political attitudes and preferences and transform them into a single vote choice' (Dalton and Weldon, 2005, 4). Voting is the most common and important political activity that citizens engage in. Milner (2010, 77) calculates that voting is about four times as common as any other electoral form of participation and much more common than any non-electoral form of activity. Thus, for the vast majority of citizens political participation constitutes voting in elections. Given that many citizens pay very little attention to politics in between elections, elections also play an important educational role. In the weeks or months surrounding a campaign 'people are educated about the issues facing the country' (Butler, 1995, 124). Clearly voting is not the only measure of political engagement and not always the best gauge of a healthy democracy. However, voter turnout remains the best, albeit imperfect 'thermometer we have to measure the health of the body politic' (Milner 2010, 78). If, as is often said, democracy is inconceivable without political parties, then democracy is impossible without voting. This is a theme that I return to in Part III.

Because elections mobilize a broad section of the population, elections also serve to iron out some of the participatory inequalities that characterize other forms of political participation. Voting serves as an equalizing device because almost everyone has the right to vote and no vote, in a basic sense, is worth more than another. As Verba et al. (1995, 12) argue: 'All democracies use elections as a great simplifying mechanism for dealing with the problem of political equality.' Accordingly, voters have been found to be relatively representative of the population, much more so than for other forms of political participation (see Verba et al., 1995, 512). This means that the people's 'voice' as expressed through elections is much less biased than is the 'voice' of the people as expressed through other more demanding forms of activity that I cover in Part III of this book. This is one of the most important reasons why we should be concerned about turnout decline.

It has also been proven empirically that it matters who votes. Burnham (1987, 99) remarked that 'the old saw remains profoundly true: if you do not vote you do not count' (cited in Lijphart, 1997, 5; see also Green and Shachar, 2000, 570). Wattenberg (2002, 98) comments that 'as long as young people have low rates of participation in the electoral process, they should expect to be getting relatively little of whatever there is to get from government' and that until young people start showing up in greater numbers in the polls 'there will be little incentive for politicians to focus on programmes that will help them.' Intuitively the above statements seem to be true: Do not vote and you will be ignored seems to reflect the conventional wisdom. But what is the empirical evidence to support this? Dalton (2011a, 9) argues that if young people participated at a higher level in the 2000 and 2004 US elections the election results would have been reversed and it would be hard to argue that that would not have changed the direction of the country. Other studies that have concentrated on young people have confirmed these findings. Wattenberg's analysis of the 2000 US election shows that had young people turned out at a higher rate they would have influenced the outcome as they would have the outcome of the 1994 mid-term election, leading Wattenberg (2002, 118) to conclude that 'who votes does make a difference.' Research in Britain on the effect of non-registrants following the introduction of the poll tax showed that those who failed to register to vote (many of whom were young) could have changed the outcome of the narrow Conservative party victory in 1992 (Dorling *et al.*, 1996, 37). All of this suggests that non-voters are different from voters and that their lack of participation has real effects on political outcomes.

Background: generational and lifecycle effects

As stated in the introduction we need to examine political engagement in light of two effects (i.e. lifecycle and generational). Lifecycle effects see little aggregate change over time whereas generational effects should be viewed much more seriously as it could mean, for example, that non-voters may eventually come to replace regular voters. Studies have found evidence of generational declines in turnout among the young. The most comprehensive study of generational effects, *The New American Voter*, concluded that 'Generational replacement has been a dominant source of change in participation in voting turnout for the electorate as a whole' (Miller and Shanks, 1996, 510). Generational effects have also been found in Britain (Clarke *et al.*, 2004, 269) and Canada (Blais *et al.*, 2004, 227; Blais and Loewen, 2011, 17).[1] Thus, the research suggests that young people are turning out at the polls in lower and lower numbers over time.

Other research supports these findings. Research shows that voting is a habit that if not acquired early on is less likely to be acquired in later years, as the lifecycle effect would predict, and attributes a large part of the generational change in turnout to voting not becoming a habit in the early years. Mark Franklin (2004, 12) argues that voting is a habit that most acquire early and 'those who find reason to vote in one of the first elections in which they are eligible generally continue to vote in subsequent elections, even less important ones' (see also Stolle and Hooghe, 2005, 158). In this sense, the past leaves a 'footprint' in subsequent elections that reflects the low turnout of an earlier period (Franklin, 2004, 43). Plutzer (2002, 43) also found that 'A citizen's voting history is a powerful predictor of future behaviour.' Green and Shachar (2000) have called this 'consuetude.' Consuetude refers to their finding that 'merely going to the polls increases one's chance of returning' even after a host of individual factors that typically predict turnout are controlled for (Green and Shachar, 2000, 562).

If confirmed, this accumulated evidence of generational effects has some troubling consequences. If young people fail to acquire the habit of voting then a new generation of non-voters will eventually come to replace older regular voters. While the effect might be marginal at first this will accumulate over time and 'will continue until the new rate of voting is reflected throughout the electorate—a development that could take as much as fifty years to run its course' (Franklin, 2004, 12–13). Franklin (2004, 12–13) predicts that this could translate into a 12.5 per cent decline over 50 years noting that 'turnout might be undergoing substantial long-term decline in many established democracies.' This could have serious consequences. In regards to the US Zukin *et al.* (2006, viii) argue: 'that sizeable portions of two successive generations have now opted out of electoral political life portends a less attentive citizenry and potentially dire consequences for the quality of our democracy.' The same could be said for all the Anglo-American democracies if the findings above are confirmed. In the sections below I examine turnout among the young which will tell us how alarmed we should be in regards to generational and lifecycle effects.

The data: voter turnout among the young

In this section I examine turnout among the young using across-time data. It is widely known that age is the best predictor of turnout (Norris, 2002, 89; Blais *et al.*, 2004, 222) and almost all studies find turnout to be lowest among the young (Adsett, 2003, 247; Phelps, 2005, 482; Rawnsley, 2005, 2; Fieldhouse *et al.*, 2007). It is therefore reasonable to expect that turnout will be lower among the young in the analysis below. But to what extent requires greater investigation. Furthermore, it is important to understand (in relation to lifecycle and generational effects) how this has changed over time and how this differs by country. Figures 1.1–1.4 show reported turnout over time using each country's respective national election study. The figures show reported turnout over time among three age groups (18–29, 30–59 and 60+).

Using the American National Election Study (ANES) data Figure 1.1 shows the percentage of Americans who voted between 1952 and 2008 by age. In Figure 1.1 we can see that turnout has remained quite high among the middle-aged and older age groups. Among the middle-aged turnout has never fallen below 75 per cent. Among the older Americans turnout has never fallen below 70 per cent. With the exception of 1968 and 1972, when turnout was lower among older people, turnout has remained consistently high for both of these age groups. The picture is very different for young people. Turnout among the young is much more volatile than it is for older people. However, turnout among the young is not in secular decline. In fact, in 2008 turnout is higher (by a small margin) among the young than it was at the beginning of the time series in 1952.

It is worth considering young people's volatile voting patterns in light of history. To begin, we can see turnout did increase among the young in the 1960 Kennedy/Nixon election which is to be expected given Kennedy's youthfulness and his 'changing of the guard' appeal, and the closeness of the election. Turnout then fell in 1964 and recovered somewhat in 1972. But after 1972 turnout is very volatile among the young. This is also the period in which the voting age was reduced to 18 which may have had the

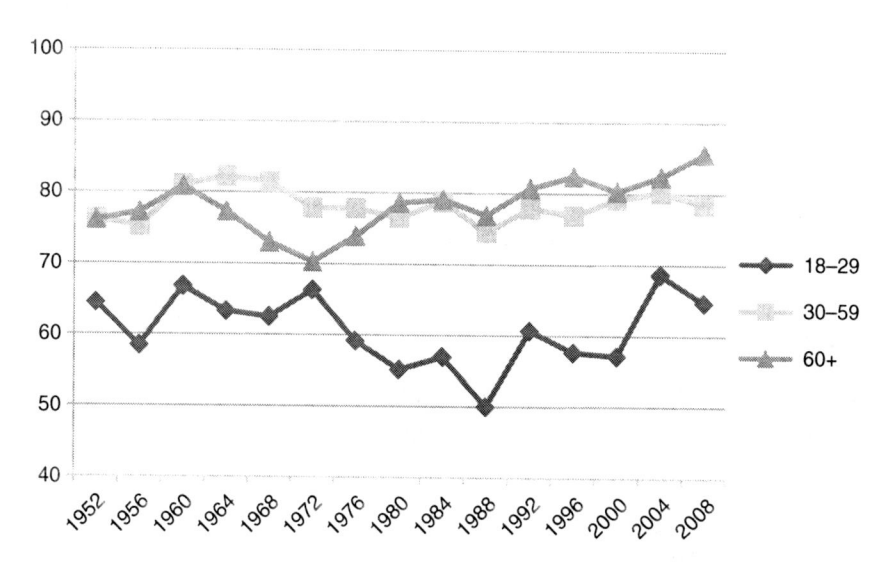

Figure 1.1 Voter turnout in the US (1952–2008) (source: American National Election Study).

Note
For question wording changes see www.electionstudies.org/nesguide/toptable/tab6a_2.htm. For the 1952–1968 period the voting age was 21 (therefore the first age category is 21–29 in this period).

effect of driving down turnout in some elections following the introduction of this law (see Franklin, 2004). Turnout falls precipitously from 1972 to 1988. It reaches a low point of 50 per cent in 1988. It then recovers in 1992 probably owing to a combination of Clinton's youthfulness, charisma and youth outreach, a long period of Republican dominance coming to an end as well as a third party candidate (although on the latter point third-party candidates do not seem to have mobilized greater numbers of young people to vote in the 1980 and 1996 elections). Turnout declines slightly in 1996 and again in 2000 and then increases sharply in 2004 (perhaps because the 'voting doesn't matter' stigma was removed following the 2000 election result).

The ANES then registers a fall in turnout among the young in 2008. This finding should be treated cautiously. The question wording for the turnout question was changed for some of the ANES sample in 2008 by which respondents were primed with different statements in an attempt to get a more honest answer from them about whether they voted or not. This could have made the young more likely to answer the question honestly whereas for older groups (who are more likely to have actually voted) it had a smaller effect. Other evidence that is more comparable across time suggests that voter turnout among the young increased in 2008, even after higher turnout among the young in 2004 (CIRCLE, 2008; Falcone, 2008; Milner, 2010, 89). Higher turnout among the young in 2008 also refutes Franklin's (2004) argument that the closeness of the election will have a large effect on turnout given that the 2008 election was not a particularly close one.

Figure 1.1 shows that turnout among the young is not in secular decline. However, over the time series we can see a larger age gap between the young and old opening up. For example, in 1952 there was an 11 percentage point difference between the young and old. This gap expands to a high point of 27 in 1988 and at the end of the time series in 2008 has closed to 21 percentage points.[2] This is much larger than the average gap in the 1950s, 1960s and 1970s. Thus, it is in the 1980s, 1990s and 2000s that larger gaps have opened up (especially in the 1980s and 1990s). Although young people have always been less likely to vote than older people this trend has become more pronounced over time. This should be concerning and suggests that young people are becoming less likely to vote over time as compared to older people, providing some support for the findings of generational effects cited above. However, what is striking about Figure 1.1 is the volatility of voting patterns among the young rather than a secular decline in voting (as I will elaborate upon below).

We now look across the border to Canada. Drawing from the Canadian Election Study (CES) Figure 1.2 shows reported turnout in Canada. We only have data going back as far as 1965 but we see here a very similar picture to that in the US. Turnout among middle-aged and older people remains high and reasonably stable over the period covered here.

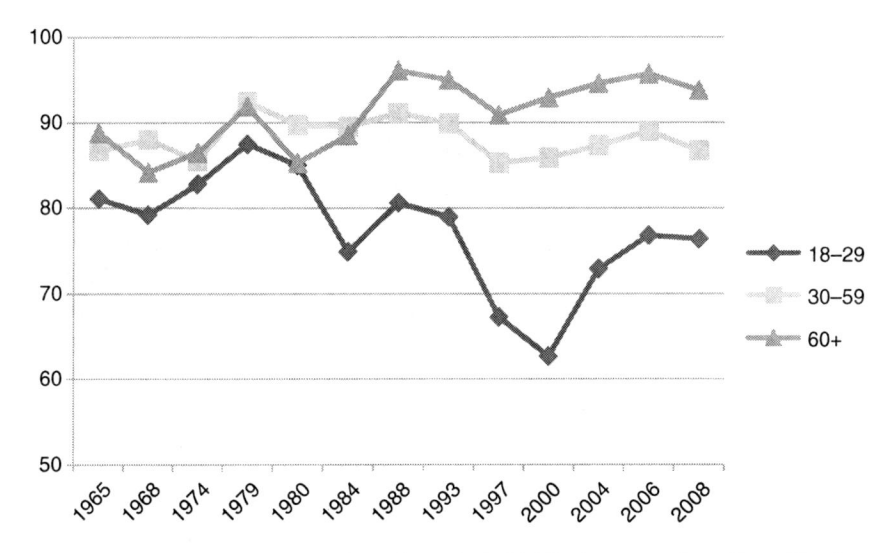

Figure 1.2 Voter turnout in Canada (1965–2008) (source: Canadian Election Study).

Note
The voting age was reduced from 21 to 18 in 1969. 1965 and 1968 figures only include those aged 21–29.
  Question wording: 'Did you vote in the election?' Question wording prompts differ in some years.

This is particularly true of older people where turnout in 1988 and beyond exceeds 90 per cent. Among young people voting is much more volatile. As was the case in the US turnout among the young does not appear to be in secular decline. At the end of the time series a young person was only five percentage points less likely to vote than a young person in 1965. As in the US young Canadians are volatile rather than absent voters and, as was also the case in the US, this volatility has increased in recent years.

At the beginning of the time series young people's turnout is high. Turnout increases among the young in 1974 (the second election at which 18-year-olds could vote) and in 1979 where it reaches a high point of 87 per cent perhaps driven by the popularity of the *Parti Québécois* and salience of politics in Quebec which reverberated around the country (see LeDuc *et al.*, 2010, 311). Turnout then decreases among the young in 1980 and 1984 (despite the latter election being regarded as one of the most important in Canadian history) (LeDuc *et al.*, 2010, 339). 1980 marks the beginning of a long period of decline in turnout among the young. Between 1980 and 2000 turnout among the young declines unbroken (with the exception of 1988).[3] This occurs despite greater competition from regional parties and the opening up of the party system. The 2000 election will be remembered for, up until that point, the lowest turnout in

Canadian history, especially owing to low turnout among the young. After 2000 turnout sharply recovers in 2004 (when the Sponsorship Scandal, an investigation into how money was used by the Liberal Party to promote federalism, reignited interest in politics among the general public), again in 2006 and holds steady in 2008 (following a close election in 2006 in which the Conservatives formed a minority government).[4]

Figure 1.2 shows that turnout does not seem to be in secular decline among the young. However, if we look at young people's turnout in comparison to older people a slightly different story emerges. As was the case in the US, an age gap between the young and old has opened up over time. In 1965 young people were only 8 percentage points less likely to vote than older people; this gap opens up to 30 percentage points in 2000 and then closes to 18 percentage points in 2008. In this regard there is some support for the generational effects argument.

While some evidence of generational effects is found in Figure 1.2 the more interesting pattern is the increasingly volatile voting patterns found among the young. Canada has long been regarded as a dealigned and volatile electorate. Voters with weaker ties to parties are more difficult to mobilize in elections. Therefore, whereas stable party identification may drive citizens in the other Anglo-American democracies to consistently vote this force is much weaker in Canada. But this seems much more apparent among the young as compared to middle-aged and older Canadians. As will be shown in Chapter 4 young people's party identification is much more volatile in Canada and this is likely to have had an effect on young people's higher voter turnout in the 2004–2008 period. This may also be tied to the lower civic duty among the young (as argued below). LeDuc *et al.* (2010, 469) argue that civic duty no longer propels people to the polls and there seems to be clear evidence of this here in regards to the volatility of young people's voting patterns (as will be elaborated upon below).

We now move across the Atlantic to Britain. The turnout data on the US and Canada is encouraging in the sense that turnout among the young has not been shown to be in secular decline but rather has been shown to be more volatile, even if larger gaps between the young and old are opening up. Figure 1.3 shows reported turnout among registered voters (1964–2010) among three age groups using data collected by the British Election Study (BES). Figure 1.3 shows that turnout remains relatively high among the young until 1992 after which time it falls precipitously. There is clear evidence of generational effects here. However, the recovery in turnout among the young in 2010 suggests that turnout may not be in a state of secular decline.

Examining young people's turnout patterns over time we can see that turnout falls in 1966 among all age groups but more sharply among the young in an election in which Labour was expected to win easily and no new issues were introduced (see Butler, 1995, 24). It rises again slightly among the young in 1970 perhaps owing to Northern Ireland becoming

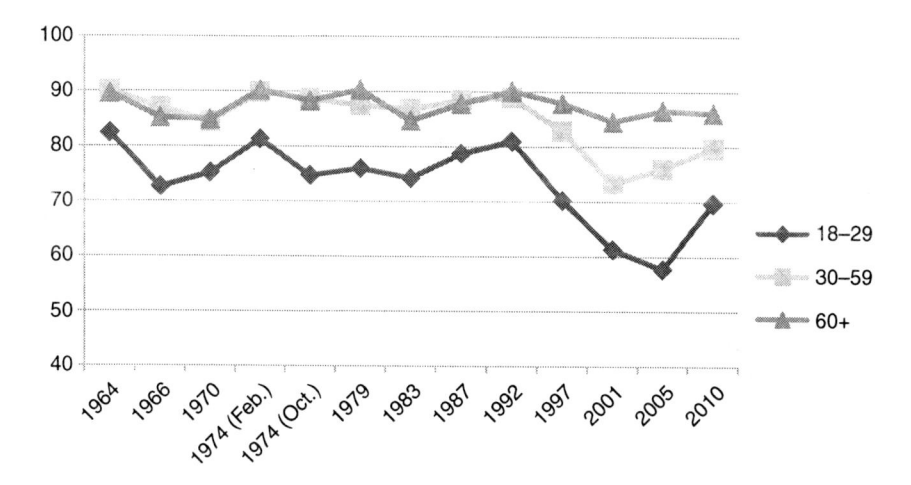

Figure 1.3 Voter turnout in Britain (1964–2010) (source: British Election Study).

Note
The voting age was changed from 21 to 18 in 1969 so the 1964 and 1966 figures for young people are for those aged 21–29.
 Question wording: 'Did you vote in the most recent General Election?' Minor question wording and prompts changed in some years.

a more important issue and protests over Vietnam (see Butler, 1995, 25). Turnout also recovers in the February 1974 election, regarded as the first 'crisis' election since 1931 and greater competition by 'third' parties (see Denver, 2005). Turnout then falls quite sharply among the young in October 1974 and remains low in the 1979 and 1983 elections. Turnout rises again among the young in 1987 and again in 1992 when the poll tax ignited interest and the Liberal Democrats fought their first election. The 1992 election was regarded as the most interesting in many years (see Birch, 1993, 103) and this may have stimulated more young people to vote as we see increased turnout again among the young in 1992.

After 1992 turnout falls steeply among the young. The period 1997–2005 marks a massive fall in turnout among the young. Turnout falls from 81 per cent in 1992 to 58 per cent in 2005—a whopping 23 percentage point drop. Explanations for low turnout among the young from 1997 to 2005 may be attributed to a lack of competition, frustration with the electoral system and the ruthless targeting of competitive seats (Denver, 2005, 151). This may have had a more marked effect on the young. Labour's courting of the middle class may also have disillusioned young people during this period. This period also sees large age gaps opening up. Whereas in 1964 the young were only 8 percentage points less likely to vote than older people by 2005 this gap had opened up to 29 percentage points.

30 *Voter turnout*

However, in 2010 we see turnout recover quite strongly among the young in what was, as in the US and Canada in 2008, a high interest election. Among the young turnout increased 12 percentage points. Thus, turnout among the young has recovered in Britain although it is too early to tell whether this pattern will hold in the next election as it has in Canada and the US. What seems more likely is that turnout in elections will be more unpredictable in the future owing to young people lacking the civic duty that seems to propel older people to the polls. Denver (2005, 91) argues that the British electorate are 'now more hesitant, volatile and unpredictable' and this is particularly true of the young, many of whom stay home at some elections but are mobilized for others. Short term factors seem to be having a larger effect on the young and this will likely remain the case in the future.

Voting is compulsory in Australia (and enforced by way of a small fine) so the data presented here is not comparable to that presented in the previous figures. However, what is interesting to look at here is how many people would vote if voting were not compulsory. Does compulsory voting compel citizens to vote and how does this differ by age? The Australian Election Study (AES) asks respondents whether they would 'definitely vote,' 'probably vote,' 'might vote' or 'might not vote': those who responded 'probably' or 'definitely' are presented in Figure 1.4 (Jackman, 1999 discusses some of the problems associated with

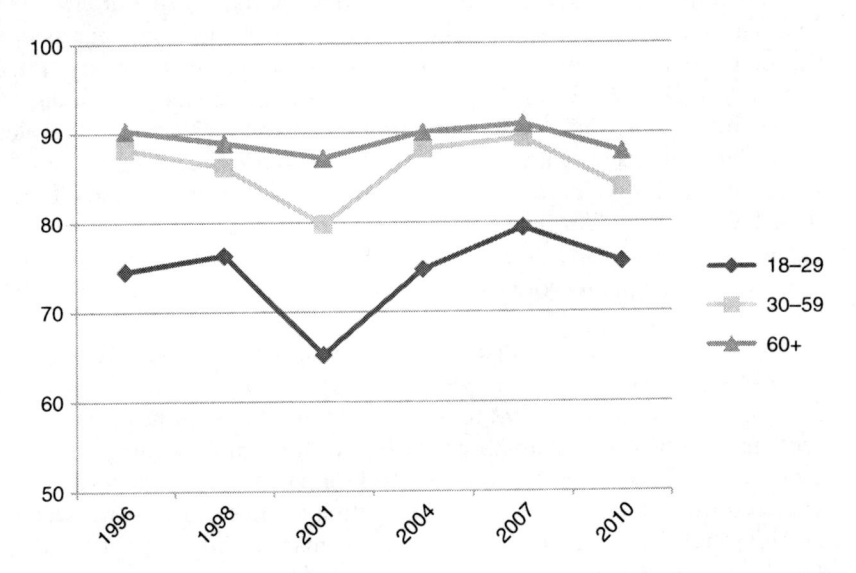

Figure 1.4 Would vote 'if not compulsory' in Australia (1996–2010) (source: Australian Election Study).

Note
Question wording: 'Would you have voted in the general election if voting had not been compulsory?' Responses combine 'definitely' and 'probably.'

responses to this question). Unfortunately, we only have data as far back as 1996 but we can track responses to this question over a 14-year period.

We can see here that young people are consistently less likely to say that they would vote if voting were not compulsory. Owing to the short time period covered there is no overall trend here. Young people were less likely to say they would vote in 2001 (much less than older people) after an election in which Labor offered little alternative to the ruling Coalition. This figure increases in 2004 and 2007 (when a change of government occurred after 11 years of conservative rule) and then decreases in 2010 (after what was widely perceived to be an uninteresting election in which the parties offered little of substance). Young people are less likely to say they would vote than older people throughout the time series with the gap between the young and old widening in 2001 and narrowing in 2010. Overall, the gap between the young and old sits around the 10–15 percentage point mark. Thus, we could infer from this that if compulsory voting ever were abolished (an unlikely scenario) young people would be less likely to turn out—consistent with the findings of Print *et al.* (2004, 2).

This inference has support in other areas. For example, the AES targets respondents from the Australian electoral roll. However, prior to the 2010 election the Australian Electoral Commission (2010) reported that there were 1.4 million people missing from the electoral roll and one-third of these people were aged 18–24 and 70 per cent were aged 18–39. Thus, that the percentage of the voting age population (as opposed to the registered population) who vote is much lower among the young and much higher among the old. In this regard the findings in Figure 1.4 are suggestive of a wider problem.

Summarising the four figures: volatile rather than absent voters

Do we find evidence of generational declines in turnout in these four figures? This was the expectation formed by much of the literature on turnout among the young (as cited above). But this chapter has so far painted a more complicated picture. Turnout among the young is lower than turnout among older people in every country and this age gap has increased over time. In this regard the generational effects found in much of the literature cited above are supported. But overall generational effects seem to play out in terms of volatility rather than secular declines in turnout among the young. For example, beginning in 1993 turnout in Canada declined precipitously among the young but then recovered in the 2000–2008 period. The pattern over the period covered by the CES is not decline but rather volatility. While older Canadians tend to turn out at high and reasonably consistent levels young people

32 *Voter turnout*

seem to be much more affected by the character of the election and thus opt to vote in certain elections and not in others. We find a similar pattern in the US. While turnout among the young was quite stable prior to 1972 after this period it fluctuates quite dramatically registering steep increases in the 1992 and 2004 elections—and other evidence suggests turnout also increased among the young in the 2008 election. Thus, the pattern is not secular decline but rather volatility from the 1970s onwards. In Britain we saw what looked like a secular generational decline in turnout among the young reversing itself in 2010. There are some signs here that turnout among the young is recovering. In Australia young people are less likely than older people to say they would vote if it were not compulsory but this has not changed a great deal over time (relative to other age groups). The US, Canada and Britain show that while turnout can decline among the young it can also recover. This data shows that future patterns are hard to predict. The predominant pattern in the US, Canada and Britain is volatility, not secular decline. Thus, we would expect turnout to fluctuate more depending on the character of the election as new volatile voters replace older more stable voters. These findings challenge the assumption that voter turnout among the young is in secular decline. Nevertheless, it should be concerning that young people vote in very low numbers at particular times such as the 1988 US election and the 2005 British election.

Some supplementary evidence: the ISSP importance of vote question

Using reported turnout from each national election study is the most consistent and reliable way to establish turnout levels across several countries over time among different age groups. Taking data from each of the national election studies also has the advantage of being roughly comparable across countries in terms of how the questions were asked and how the surveys were administered in regards to their quality. However, overreporting is a well known problem in surveys (Granberg and Holmberg, 1991; Teixeira, 1992).[5] The most common reasons for overreporting are that voting is seen as a socially desirable activity (Granberg and Holmberg, 1991), people who respond to surveys tend to be regular voters (Denver, 2003, 37) and that responding to surveys (in a pre-post-election survey, for instance) increases one's propensity to vote (Granberg and Holmberg, 1991, 1992).

Because of the problems to do with overreporting we can examine other data that is available (albeit not across time) which serves to supplement the reported turnout data. One of the ways to get around problems such as overreporting is to examine other evidence which measures civic duty such as the question featured in the International Social Survey Programme

(ISSP) 2004 Citizenship survey in which respondents were asked how important it is to vote regularly in elections on a scale of 1 to 7. This question will presumably be less biased by those saying they voted when they did not (fearing fines or other penalties). There is no penalty (real or perceived) for responding that voting is not important in a survey. Therefore, respondents should feel at liberty to answer this question honestly. Furthermore, there has been found to be a positive relationship between importance of vote and reported vote (Milner, 2010, 7). This data is useful because civic duty has been shown in the literature to be low among the young in Britain (see Topf, 1995a, 46; Pattie et al., 2004, 70), the US (see MacManus, 1996, 44; Zukin et al., 2006, 7) and Canada (Blais et al., 2004, 229). The ISSP asked 'how important is it to always vote in elections?' Respondents were asked to respond on a scale of 1 to 7, 1 being 'not at all important' and 7 being 'very important.' Figure 1.5 shows those who responded that voting is 'very important.'

We can see here that in each country young people are much less likely to say that voting regularly in elections is 'very important.' Most striking is the data on Britain where only 14 per cent of young people said it was 'very important' to vote regularly in elections—this is consistent with the findings of Clarke et al. (2004, 271) who found the young in Britain to have low levels of civic duty. This is compared to 68 per cent of older people who responded that it was 'very important' to vote regularly in

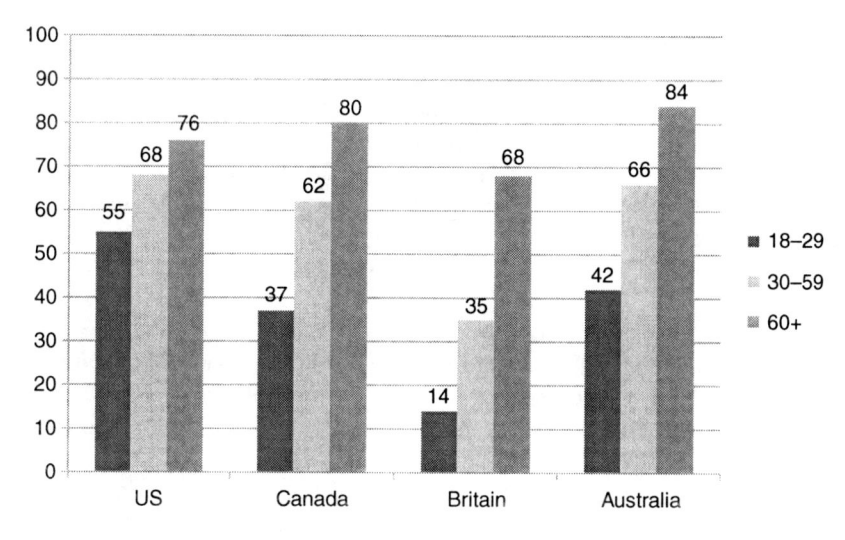

Figure 1.5 Civic duty in the Anglo-American democracies (source: International Social Survey Programme Citizenship Survey (2004)).

Note
Question wording: 'There are different opinions as to what it takes to be a good citizen. As far as you are concerned personally on a scale of 1 to 7, where 1 is not at all important and 7 is very important how important is it to always vote in elections?' Responses are 'voting is very important.'

34 *Voter turnout*

elections—in other words older people are more than four times more likely than young people to say voting is very important. In Canada only 37 per cent of young people said it was very important to vote in elections, compared to 80 per cent of older people—representing a two-to-one difference. The same pattern is true in Australia with older people being twice as likely to say voting is very important (the respective figures being 42 and 84). In the US young people are more likely to say voting is important but the age gap is much narrower (21 percentage points). This may reflect the importance of voting as relayed through the nation's education system.

Figure 1.5 suggests the volatility found in the previous figures in regards to turnout among the young is related to wider beliefs about the importance of voting—this link has been established previously in the turnout literature which stresses the importance of civic duty as a predictor of voting (Wolfinger and Rosenstone, 1980; Blais, 2000). Furthermore, the low civic duty found among the young here has been shown to be related to generational factors (see Levine, 2007, 202; Milner, 2010, 36) so it is likely that the findings above also represent generational effects. Thus, it seems, young people are not inheriting civic duty from their parents and grandparents as previous generations seem to have.

The implication of this is that young people are less likely to be regular voters. Older people have stronger feelings of civic duty and thus see voting as important regardless of the character of the election. This likely accounts for the stability of their voting patterns found in the data (Figures 1.1–1.4). In contrast, young people, who are more highly educated, seem to be more likely to weigh up the pros and cons of the election (whether a party appeals to them, whether their vote may or may not matter) (see Franklin, 2004) and vote based on these factors rather than out of civic duty. This is consistent with the arguments of Inglehart and Welzel (2005) who argue that young people, as a result of increased education levels, act more autonomously than older people. In this sense non-voting might be seen as a rational response by the young to voting at the individual level having no influence on election outcomes (see Downs, 1957) although this overlooks the powerful aggregating mechanism that elections play (as argued in Part III).

The consequence of all of this is that we see much more volatile voting patterns in which young people turn out at some elections and abstain from others. (A clear example of this is the 2004 US election that captured young people's imagination and thus mobilized young people to vote.) This inference is supported by the ISSP findings and the respective national election study findings in which young people vote in a much more volatile manner than older people.

Conclusion

This chapter has shown that voter turnout among the young is more complicated than the picture presented in the academic literature. Turnout among the young in the Anglo-American democracies is not in secular decline but is much more volatile. There is clear evidence of this in the three cases for which we have comparable data (the US, Canada and Britain). In these three cases turnout has declined over certain periods but also recovered over the last decade (albeit in a more consistent way in the US and Canada). Suggestions that young people are becoming less and less likely to vote over time may have seemed true ten years ago but today look less valid. As at 2008 in the US and Canada young people were not particularly less likely to vote than were young people 40 or 50 years ago. In Britain, young people are much less likely to vote than young people 40 years ago but there are some signs there that turnout is increasing among the young. Furthermore, this volatility has become more pronounced in recent decades. Thus, generational effects seem to be playing out in terms of volatility rather than secular declines in turnout.

This is not to suggest that we should not be worried about turnout levels over time among the young. The data shows that there are age gaps opening up between the young and old. Furthermore, young people are markedly absent from some elections and this lack of representation at particular times should be concerning (for example, young people turned out at very low rates in the 2000 US election and the 2005 British election). This seems to be linked to low levels of civic duty among the young which no longer propels young people to consistently vote. It seems then that young people have not inherited the civic duty of their parents and grandparents. In this regard the socialization process seems to have broken down. The volatile voting patterns suggest many young people will opt out of elections that do not engage them in the future. In the US, Canada and Britain young people today are distinctly different from their predecessors in regards to their voting patterns and attitudes. Young people today are not consistent voters and have very low levels of civic duty. Voting, it seems, is attractive to young people at times and at other times it is not. Thus, at this stage it would be better to characterize young people as being volatile voters rather than ritual non-voters.

Part II
Political attitudes

Part II of this book examines political attitudes. Political attitudes have been regarded as an important part of political engagement beginning with the early literature on voter behaviour. *The Civic Culture* was concerned with subjective orientations to politics and the political culture of a country 'essentially derives from the attitudes of its citizens' (Fuchs, 2007, 163). Political attitudes are essential to democratic theory and practice (Kornberg and Clarke, 1992, 61). Furthermore, 'How citizens view politics tells us much about the health of a political system' (McAllister, 2011, 85). This is particularly relevant to the young because 'at the core of anxieties about the political disaffection of young people are concerns about young people's attitudes towards the political system itself' (Fahmy, 2006, 71). Attitudes are also important because they have been shown to have behavioural consequences. Accordingly, the following two chapters examine political trust and political interest drawing again from the national election studies which have asked roughly comparable questions over a long period of time.

2 Political trust
The not particularly less trusting young

> Contemporary democracies are facing a challenge today. This challenge does not come from enemies within or outside the nation. Instead, the challenge comes from democracy's own citizens, who have grown distrustful of politicians, skeptical about democratic institutions, and disillusioned about how the democratic process functions.
>
> (Dalton, 2004, 1)

> 'Politics' is a dirty word, a term that has come to acquire a whole array of almost entirely negative associations and connotations in contemporary discourse.
>
> (Hay, 2008, 153)

The concerns expressed in the quotes above are not new. In fact, 'trust among citizens in those who govern them has been a consistent theme in political philosophy, going back as far as antiquity' (McAllister, 2011, 71). In regards to the social sciences political trust has been a prominent theme beginning with the early literature on voter behaviour (Stokes, 1962; Almond and Verba, 1963). Political trust has become an even more important topic of late with the perceived decline in trust in many advanced democracies capturing more and more attention among scholars and policy makers alike. Present concerns regarding political trust have, in some quarters, reached fever pitch levels. For example, in relation to the US Crewe (1995) has argued that 'There is no doubt that distrust and alienation has risen to a higher level than ever before. It was always fairly prevalent; it is now in many regards almost universal' (cited in Dalton, 2006, 246). Crewe's statement reflects much of the conventional wisdom which suggests that 'political disaffection has worsened in recent decades, with significant consequences for democratic government' (Norris, 2011, 4).

Because political trust is thought to have such significant consequences it has caught the attention of elites. For example, President Carter in 1979 warned that declining trust in government 'was a fundamental

40 Political attitudes

threat to American democracy' (cited in Dalton, 2004, 1). In 1997, departing US Senator Bill Bradley commented that 'Voters distrust government so deeply and so consistently that they are not willing to accept the results of virtually any decision made by this political process' (cited in Dalton, 2004, 2). Chief Justice Breyer also expressed his concern 'about the indifference and cynicism because indifference means nonparticipation and cynicism means the withdrawal of trust ... without trust and participation, the constitution cannot work' (cited in Dalton, 2004, 202). Concern regarding political trust is not confined to the US. The Blair government's constitutional renewal programme was aimed at increasing political trust in Britain. In 1998 Lord Chancellor Derry Irvine said: 'We are determined to clean up politics and rebuild the bond between Government and citizens ... The radical program of constitutional renewal is a powerful weapon in our battle against citizen disillusionment' (cited in Fahmy, 2006, 158).

More specifically, the decline in trust among the young has also been the focus of attention at the highest levels. For example, the American President's Commission for a National Agenda for the Eighties expressed particular concern about 'distrust of young adult voters' (Abramson, 1983, 193). Yet, while the downward trend in trust in advanced democracies has been well documented (Nye *et al.*, 1997; Pharr and Putnam, 2000; Dalton, 2004), our understanding about political trust among young people is incomplete. Even though young people are often singled out as being the least trustful, levels of trust among the young, and how these differ from those of older people, are not very well established in the literature.

This chapter will rigorously examine how trust varies among different age groups and whether young people are less trusting than older people. I do this by analysing levels of trust over time. I will also examine support for democracy to establish levels of support at the regime level. Stokes (1962, 65) writes that the composition of trust across social groups and its role in prompting other forms of participation 'holds a key to understanding a political system in which public opinion is a principal force.' I will examine to what extent this vital aspect of public opinion differs among the young and old which will thereby inform us as to how worried we should be about political trust.

Defining political trust

Before proceeding to the empirical analysis it is important to clarify exactly what we mean when speaking of political trust. There are certain vagaries surrounding the use of the term trust. 'Political trust is an ambivalent concept. Because of its inherent relationship to the performance of political institutions, it is difficult to separate it from evaluations of government' (Catterberg and Moreno, 2005, 45).[1] In this book I refer to trust as it relates to the political culture literature. Political culture deals with the effects of individual attitudes and subjective orientations towards the political world. Dalton (2006, 247) explains that:

> Political culture encompasses everything from beliefs about the legitimacy of the system itself to beliefs about the adequacy and appropriateness of political input structures, government policies, and the role of the individual in the political process. The most important of these attitudes is a generalized feeling toward the political system, or system effect.

It is these more generalized feelings toward the political system that the respective national election studies tap and are of greatest interest to this chapter.

There is some debate about whether a term like trust is the most suitable for capturing these generalized feelings towards the political system. Norris (1999a, 1) writes that 'rather than just talking about "political trust," in every case we need to specify its object.' Norris (1999a, 1) prefers the term 'political support.' Norris distinguishes between five levels of political support, from support for political authorities to support for the political community. If we had data which better tapped the dimensions that Norris specifies this would be an appropriate classification to use. Unfortunately, the across-time data used in this book is not well specified enough for us to do this. Therefore, a term like trust which refers to 'more broadly-based values about how government acts within the society as a whole' (McAllister, 1992, 47) is preferred. However, this chapter also examines political trust at the regime level in terms of support for democracy.

Background: the literature on political trust

Political trust

Research shows that 'there is clear evidence of a general erosion in support for politicians and government in most advanced industrial democracies' (Dalton, 2004, 30).[2] The Anglo-American democracies are no exception to this trend. In the US, where the most research has been done, declines have been dramatic. In the 1950s and 1960s when the public was asked 'how much of the time can you trust the government in Washington to do what is right?' three-quarters of respondents said 'most of the time' or 'just about always.' By 1998, just over a third of people felt this way. In the 1960s, two-thirds of Americans disagreed with the statement 'most elected officials do not care what people like me think.' By 1998, nearly two-thirds agreed (Putnam et al., 2000, 9; see also Rosenstone and Hansen, 1993, 148; Dalton, 2006, 251).

42 *Political attitudes*

The evidence in Canada conforms to this general picture (Putnam *et al.*, 2000, 10; Catterberg and Moreno, 2005, 36; Tanguay, 2009, 228). In Australia political trust has also been found to be very low—for example, in 2003 the Australian Survey of Social Attitudes found that 60 per cent of respondents expressed an untrusting attitude towards the government (Bean, 2005, 127)—and Papadakis (1999, 76), Dalton (2004) and Leigh (2010) all argue that political trust has declined over time (for a counter view see Goot, 2002; McAllister, 2011). In Britain early surveys showed a public who were generally more trustful of politicians than citizens in other countries (Birch, 1993, 18; Pattie *et al.*, 2004). However, as in the other Anglo-American democracies political trust has also been found to be in decline in Britain (Norris, 2011, 72; see also Catterberg and Moreno, 2005, 36). A MORI poll in 2002 found that politicians were ranked the lowest out of 16 professions with only 19 per cent of respondents expecting politicians to tell the truth (Rawnsley, 2005, 7).

In regards to young people the findings are more mixed. Early research in the US showed young people to be more positive about the political system than their elders and found that trust declined as adults accumulated experience with the political system over the lifespan (Easton and Dennis, 1969). However, since this time very little research has been done. Where it has, much of the evidence points to generational declines in trust. Dalton examined generational changes in trust in his book *Democratic Challenges, Democratic Choices*. Dalton (2004, 94) shows that whereas the young were once more trusting than older cohorts in the US 'the young are now more likely to display lower levels of political trust and greater cynicism towards politicians and political institutions' (see also Abramson, 1983, 237; MacManus, 1996, 44; Rahn and Transue, 1998, 546). Dalton (2004, 93) also found that 'this same pattern of generational change occurs in most of the other nations for which we have data ... all told, the long-term decrease in political support has been disproportionately greater among the young' so that members of younger generations now begin their political experience as cynics, whereas before they were more supportive and became less trustful. Inglehart and Welzel (2005) also argue that the more educated and less deferential young are more critical of government.

Some research paints a similar picture in regards to the other Anglo-American democracies. The young have been found to be less trustful in Britain (White *et al.*, 2000; Pattie *et al.*, 2004, 65; Henn and Weinstein, 2006). Wilkinson and Mulgan (1995, 10) argue: 'For many young people in Britain today politics has become a dirty word ... The overwhelming story emerging from our research, both qualitative and quantitative, is of an historic disconnection' (cited in Fahmy, 2006, 10). Fahmy's (2006, 143) and Marsh *et al.*'s (2007) qualitative work also found very low levels of trust among the young. There have been similar findings in studies in Australia (Print *et al.*, 2004).

However, other studies dispute these findings. Galston (2007, 626) found that there

> is no systematic evidence that younger Americans are less likely to trust government than are older Americans. ... For example, 18 to 25 year olds are least likely to see government as inefficient and wasteful, or to believe that the federal government controls too much of Americans' daily lives.

Putnam (2000, 261) also finds the young to be no less trusting of politicians or parties than older cohorts in the US (see also Zukin *et al.*, 2006, 120). In Canada, young people were actually found to be less dissatisfied than older cohorts (Gidengil *et al.*, 2003, 3; see also Blais *et al.*, 2002; O'Neill, 2007, 17; Howe, 2010). These findings are consistent with early studies that found trust to be higher among the young than among older cohorts (Jennings and Niemi, 1974, 142). This may be because young people have not accumulated negative experiences with the political system which have the effect of depleting trust over the lifespan.

Other studies also suggest that the decline in trust has occurred across the electorate and is not confined to any particular group. Orren (1997, 86) found that the decline in political trust cuts across age, party, gender, occupation, family income and race lines and is not specific to any particular demographic. Therefore, we can summarize these findings by saying that while the picture is bleak with precipitous declines in trust in politicians and political parties across time, the extent to which this is occurring among young people is not entirely clear.

Support for democracy

But what about support for democracy? Is support for democracy much higher than trust in government? Support for democracy relates not to trust in authorities (government) or institutions (such as the public service) but support for the regime of democracy. This is the highest level of support, or what Easton (1975) referred to as diffuse support. Support for democracy is important because as the subject of dissatisfaction broadens (from authorities to institutions to the regime) so too do the implications. Easton (1975, 437) observed that 'not all expressions of unfavorable orientations have the same degree of gravity for a political system. Some may be consistent with its maintenance; others may lead to fundamental change.' Support for democracy is thought to be very important as it shows how supportive people are of the regime itself. The democracy as the best form of government question (which I draw from below) measures a higher level of generalized support as 'the object of the attitude is not the functioning of a particular system of democracy but the very idea of democracy' (Fuchs *et al.*, 1995, 348).

44 Political attitudes

The research on support for democracy paints a much brighter picture. There is a lot of evidence to suggest that although citizens are increasingly distrustful of politicians and parties, citizens continue to be supportive of democracy. Democracy enjoys overwhelming support as the best form of government. In general about 90 per cent of publics in advanced democracies say that democracy is better than any other form of government (Dalton, 2006, 257; see also Holmberg, 1999, 114; Norris, 1999a, 17; Dalton, 2004, 41; Inglehart and Welzel, 2005; Norris, 2011, 93).

The support for democracy question measures general support for the notion of democracy itself while trust in the authorities and institutions represents a more evaluative dimension that is likely related to the performance, not the legitimacy, of the democratic regime. A public that is supportive of democracy but dissatisfied with the way it works have been labeled 'dissatisfied democrats.' Klingemann (1999, 32) notes that 'A significant number of people around the world can be labeled as "dissatisfied democrats." They clearly approve of democracy as a mode of governance, but they are discontented with the way their own system is currently operating.'

Where research has been done in relation to young people Fuchs *et al.* (1995, 336) found that support for democracy had actually increased slightly over time among young people. Haerpfer *et al.*'s (2002, 7) study of young Europeans found that 87 per cent of respondents still agree that 'democracy may have problems but it's better than any other form of government.' This suggests that young 'dissatisfied democrats' will be supportive of democracy even if they are distrustful of government. The research suggests that young people's lack of trust in political authorities and institutions has not generalized to feelings towards democracy itself.

This evidence has undermined earlier 'crisis of democracy' theories (Crozier *et al.*, 1975; Huntington, 1981) and tempers fears that declining trust in political authorities and institutions poses a threat to democracy. By distinguishing between different levels of trust and support the picture seems more benign than earlier theorists suggested. For example, Norris (1999a, 3) finds evidence of 'critical citizens' who support democratic values but see existing avenues for participation as insufficient and call for greater use of referendums, devolution and grass roots mobilization. Nye (1997, 3) argues that at the constitutional government regime level, the current situation is 'not like France in 1968, much less 1789' and Putnam *et al.* (2000, 28) report that changes in levels of trust 'have not included any serious threat to fundamental democratic principles and institutions. In this sense we see no significant evidence of a crisis of democracy.' Thus, in the empirical analysis political trust among young people needs to be seen in this context. Hence, we may distinguish between soft and hard antipathy towards government and examine to what extent there has (or hasn't) been an erosion of support at the regime level.

The data: trust in government

'Public concerns about the democratic process normally begin with questions about the holders of power' (Dalton, 1999, 61). Trust in government is an essential component of this. Figures 2.1–2.4 show levels of trust in the Anglo–American democracies using each country's national election study which include roughly comparable data. To begin with the US Figure 2.1 shows the results from the American National Election Study. The ANES asked respondents: 'How much of the time do you think you can trust the government in Washington to do what is right?' Figure 2.1 shows those who responded 'just about always' and 'most of the time.'

Figure 2.1 shows an astounding drop in political trust across the period (1964–2008) covered by the ANES. This decline is particularly pronounced between 1964 and 1980 when trust falls from around 70 per cent to about 30 per cent—which could be attributed in particular to the Watergate scandal, the Vietnam War and the protests surrounding this. There was a recovery in trust in 1984—which could be attributed to the optimism of the Reagan presidency—before falling again between 1984 and 1992—which could be related to the Iran-Contra scandal and Bush breaking his 'no new taxes' policy. It recovered again in the 2000s (the exception being older Americans in 2004) perhaps owing to Clinton's optimism and youthfulness, and plummeted again in 2008 in the midst of a financial crisis and what was widely regarded as

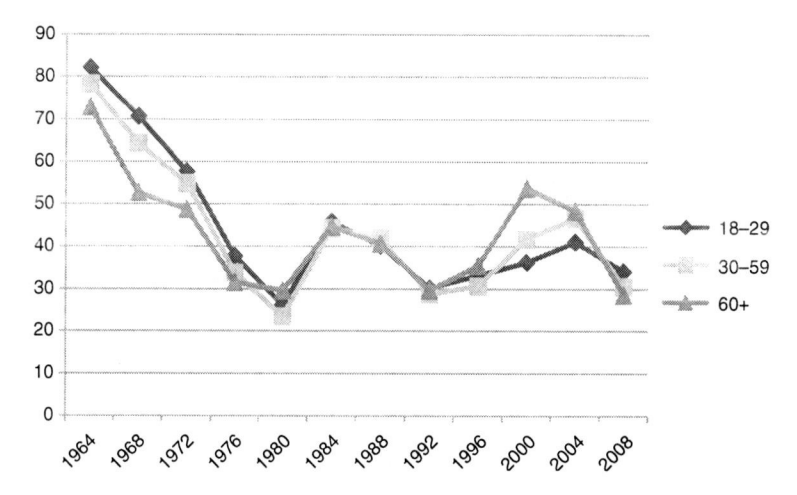

Figure 2.1 Trust in government in the US (1964–2008) (source: American National Election Study).

Note
Question wording: 'How much of the time do you think you can trust the government in Washington to do what is right?' Responses combine 'just about always' and 'most of the time.'

a 'lame duck' Bush presidency. Despite the variation from 1984 onwards, political trust never approaches its post-war highs. This evidence confirms the fears of many who are concerned that the public has moved from being supportive of political authorities to increasingly sceptical (Abramson, 1983; Nye *et al.*, 1997; Pharr and Putnam, 2000; Dalton, 2004).

Consistent with Easton and Dennis (1969) young people are found to be more trusting than older people in 1964. Young people's political trust remains higher than the political trust of older people but then converges in the mid 1970s and early 1980s. From that period on the young have about the same or lower levels of trust than older people until 2008. In other words, the age pattern has reversed over time. However, this pattern should not be overstated. The more striking pattern here is the similarity in levels of trust between the three age groups. It seems that young people have been affected by the decline in trust among the general population and reflecting this they enter the electorate with low levels of trust. Whereas young people started their adult lives being more positive about politics than older people in the 1950s and 1960s (supporting Easton and Dennis, 1969) they now start their adult lives as political cynics (supporting Dalton, 2004).

This evidence has two important implications. It supports Abramson's (1983, 237) finding that that generational replacement has seen trusting cohorts being replaced by less trusting cohorts. Young people now enter the electorate with very low levels of trust as compared to their predecessors (i.e. a young person entering the electorate today is much less likely to be trusting than a young person entering the electorate in the 1960s). But it does not appear that generational replacement is a significant factor in driving down trust as trust has declined almost uniformly among all age groups. This suggests political events and other factors have an effect on all age groups. Galston (2007, 626) found that there 'is no systematic evidence that younger Americans are less likely to trust government than are older Americans' (see also Putnam, 2000, 261). The findings here are consistent with those of Galston and Putnam. Young people are very untrusting of government (and much more than they were 50 years ago) but so are older people.

We now turn to Canada. Unfortunately, the data for Canada is not as reliable and consistent as the American data. This is because different questions have been asked in different survey years. In 1965, 1968, 1988 and 1993 respondents were asked if the government can be trusted to do the right thing 'always,' 'most of the time' or 'some of the time' (denoted by v1). Shown below are responses for 'always' and 'most of the time.' However, in 1979 and 1984 respondents were asked if they 'strongly agree,' 'agree,' 'neither agree nor disagree,' 'disagree' or 'strongly disagree' that the federal government can be trusted (denoted by v2). The responses shown are 'strongly agree' and 'agree.' Then between 1993 and

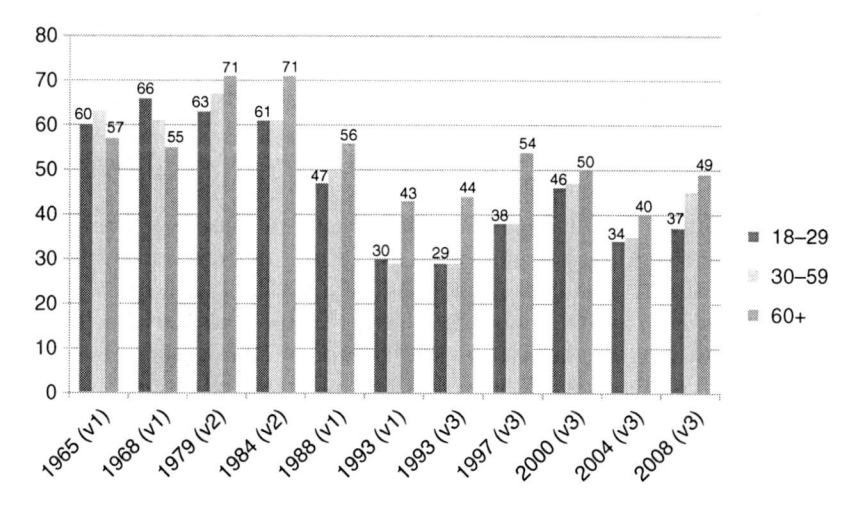

Figure 2.2 Trust/confidence in government in Canada (1965–2008) (source: Canadian Election Study).

Note
Question wording changes noted in text.

2008 respondents were asked if they had confidence in the federal government; respondents were then given the option to respond 'a great deal,' 'quite a lot,' 'not very much' or 'not at all' (denoted by v3). The responses shown are those who answered 'a great deal' and 'quite a lot.' To further complicate matters the 1993–2008 questions were only asked in the mail-back survey not in the usual immediate post-election surveys that this book relies on predominantly. Figure 2.2 shows the response to these questions.

Acknowledging the problems of comparability a few remarks can be made: overall, we can see that overall levels of trust seem to have declined over the time series and gaps have opened up between the young and old. Young people were more trusting than older people in 1965 and 1968 (supporting Easton and Dennis, 1969) but then (similar to the US) this pattern is reversed and young people become less trusting than older people for the rest of the time series. For example, if we compare data from 1965, 1968, 1988 and 1993 where comparable question have been asked trust is much lower in the later years and age gaps between the young and old have opened up. These age gaps remain through to 2008. In 2008 young people are 12 percentage points less trusting than older people although trust among the young does increase from its 1993 lows (in particular in 2000). However, that only 37 per cent of young people have 'a great deal' or 'quite a lot' of confidence in the government should be concerning. Although the question wording changes prevent us from making any definitive conclusions it does seem that generational

48 *Political attitudes*

replacement has driven down levels of trust over time. Whereas in 1965 young people seem to be socialized into levels of trust similar to that of their parents and grandparents in recent years young people deviate from older people and seem to be forming more independent judgements of government.

We now turn to Britain for which we have more limited data again. Unfortunately, comparable political trust questions have only been asked since 1987 and these relate to trust in political parties, not the government generally as per the other trust questions included in this chapter. Furthermore, the political trust question analysed here was not included in the 2010 British Election Study.[3] Figure 2.3 shows that there is a very low level of trust in political parties in Britain with fewer than 30 per cent 'disagreeing' or 'strongly disagreeing' that parties are interested in people's votes, not in their opinions. Between 1987 and 2005 the overall trend is downwards with a large portion of that decline occurring between 1987 and 1997 (coinciding with the period in which turnout declined precipitously). But again young people are not dramatically different from older people. Young people begin by being as trusting as those aged 60 and over and end up being more trusting than older people and slightly less trusting than the middle-aged (contrary to findings by White *et al.*, 2000; Pattie *et al.*, 2004, 65; Henn and Weinstein, 2006). While gaps do appear among different age groups young people largely shadow the trend of older age groups and are not particularly distinct in this regard. Thus, young people conform to the general pattern found in the US.

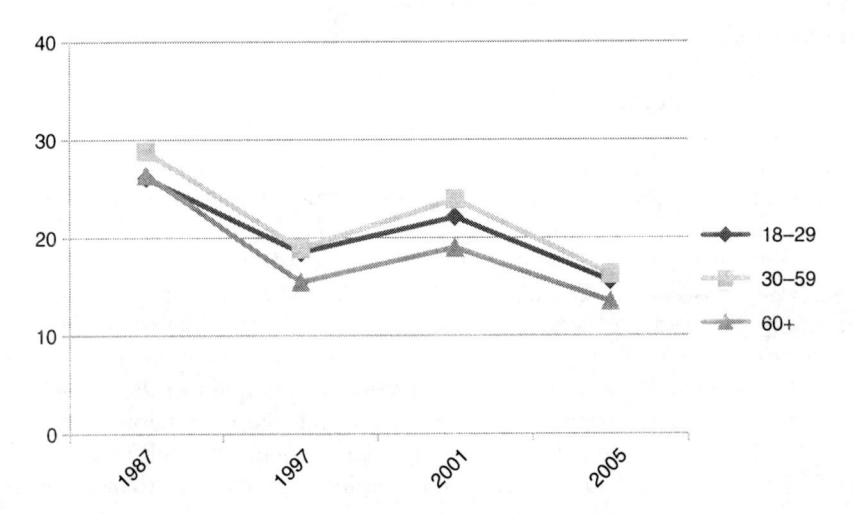

Figure 2.3 Trust in political parties in Britain (1987–2005) (source: British Election Study).

Note
Question wording: 'Parties are only interested in people's votes, not their opinions.' Responses combine 'disagree' and 'strongly disagree.'

A few remarks should be made in regards to political events. Political trust starts off at a very low point given that in Britain 'For much of the twentieth century both elite and mass opinion was confident that the political system worked well' (Pattie et al., 2004, xv). This may be because parties have served as scapegoats for Britain's post-war economic decline. Trust in parties declines steeply between 1987 and 1997 which could be attributed to the 'sleaze' allegations which led to the downfall of the Conservative government (McAllister, 2011, 72). In response to perceived declining levels of trust the Blair government introduced a series of reforms in an attempt to increase political trust. In 1998 Lord Chancellor Derry Irvine said: 'We are determined to clean up politics and rebuild the bond between Government and citizens ... The radical program of constitutional renewal is a powerful weapon in our battle against citizen disillusionment' (cited in Fahmy, 2006, 158). Blair introduced the Human Rights Act of 1998, the Freedom of Information legislation in 2000 and established an Electoral Commission and Committee on Standards in Public Life (Wright, 2003, 62). This all seems to have had little effect on political trust. Two responses could be made to this. One would be to say that the Blair government reforms did not go far enough (see Fahmy, 2006, 158; Pattie et al., 2004, xvii; Marsh et al., 2007). Another response would be to say that trust would have declined further still absent these reforms. The effect of the Blair government reforms is also confounded by the Iraq War and Blair's part in this which seems to have led to a decline in trust between 2001 and 2005. Unfortunately, we do not have comparable data to examine what effect the 'expenses scandal' in 2009 had on trust in parties but it is difficult to think of why this wouldn't have led to a further decrease in trust given how widespread coverage of this scandal was.

In Australia we have data over a longer time period than in Britain but again there are some limitations in terms of comparability. In 1969 and 1979 respondents were asked: 'In general, do you feel that the people in government are too often interested in looking after themselves, or do you feel that they can be trusted to do the right thing nearly all the time?' and were then asked to respond to those two options. From 1993 onwards respondents were asked: 'In general, do you feel that the people in government are too often interested in looking after themselves, or do you feel that they can be trusted to do the right thing nearly all the time?' and were given the options of responding 'usually look after themselves,' 'sometimes look after themselves,' 'sometimes can be trusted to do the right thing' and 'usually can be trusted to do the right thing.' Figure 2.4 shows those who responded that government can be trusted to 'do the right thing nearly all the time' in 1969 and 1979 and those who responded that that the government can 'usually' or 'sometimes' be trusted to do the right thing between 1993 and 2010.

50 *Political attitudes*

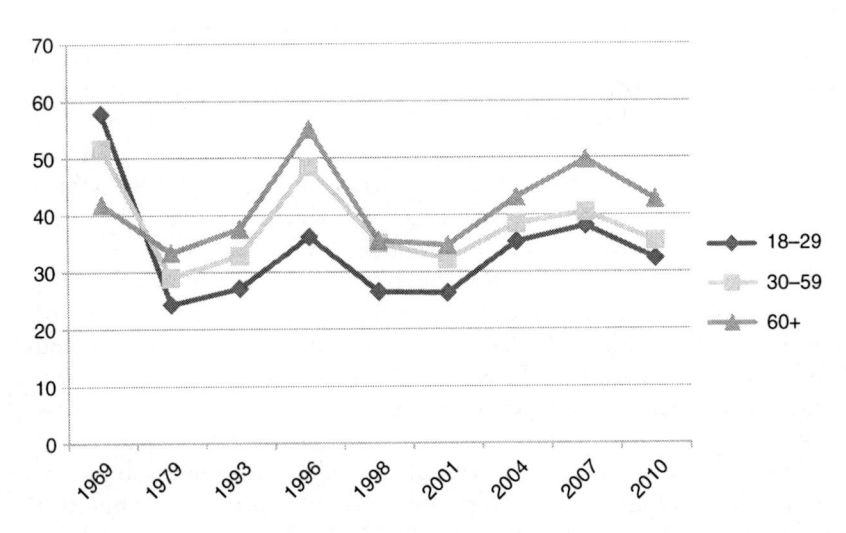

Figure 2.4 Trust in government in Australia (1969–2010) (source: Australian Election Study).

Note
Question wording: In 1969 and 1979 respondents were asked: 'In general, do you feel that the people in government are too often interested in looking after themselves, or do you feel that they can be trusted to do the right thing nearly all the time?' Responses are government can be trusted to 'do the right thing nearly all the time.' From 1993 onwards respondents were asked: 'In general, do you feel that the people in government are too often interested in looking after themselves, or do you feel that they can be trusted to do the right thing nearly all the time?' Responses combine 'usually' or 'sometimes'.

In Figure 2.4 we can see that trust is variable over the time period covered with no overall pattern. In regards to age differences the young start off as much more trusting than older people but then trust declines precipitously in 1979 (and falls less sharply among older Australians). The most plausible explanation for this decline is the sacking of Prime Minister Gough Whitlam by the Governor-General in 1975 with the co-operation of opposition leader Malcolm Fraser who became the caretaker Prime Minister and subsequently Prime Minister between 1975 and 1983. But the question remains as to why this had such a large effect on young people. The answer seems pretty straightforward. For many young people this is the first major negative political event that they witnessed. Older people most probably had a larger store of negative experiences to draw from and were thus less shocked by the events of 1975. Of course, the Whitlam dismissal had a negative effect on all age groups but much more on the young.

The data between 1993 and 2010 is more comparable in terms of question wording. Over this period trust is quite volatile and is not in general decline as suggested by Papadakis (1999), Dalton (2004) and Leigh (2010). Rather, the pattern seems to be more cyclical (consistent with Goot, 2002; McAllister, 2011, 73). Political trust is quite low in 1993 and then recovers sharply among middle-aged and older Australians in 1996 after the election of John Howard as Prime Minister of the conservative party after a long period of Labor rule (1983–1996). Furthermore, the election of John Howard in 1996 had a larger effect on older people. Trust falls quite sharply in 1998 and then recovers in 2004 and 2007 when the Labor government was returned to power and then falls again in 2010. Young people after 1969 are always less trusting (supporting Bean, 2003; Print et al., 2004) but they do not deviate from older age groups in any dramatic fashion. Generational replacement does not seem to be the driver of political trust. Rather, political events seem to affect all age groups.

Discussion: political trust

The data above presents a mixed picture. For example, in Canada whereas young people were once more trusting they are now less trusting than older people. We observe the same pattern in Australia. This provides partial support for Inglehart and Welzel's (2005) argument that respect for authority is eroding among the young. However, the more interesting point in relation to the focus of this book is that young people do not deviate wildly from the population average in terms of their political trust. In this regard there is little support for the argument that generational change has driven down levels of political trust. The more overwhelming pattern is that of young people's levels of trust shadowing those of older people. Young people seem to have been socialized into the low levels of trust that existed when they entered the electorate.

However, although young people seem to have been socialized into a low trust environment this does not mean that they hold onto those views throughout their lifetimes. Rather, political events seem to have an effect on all age groups. This finding is important in relation to cultural accounts of trust which have traditionally emphasized the durability of norms from early socialization and the limited impact of external situations (Jackman and Miller, 1995, 478). The data above shows that trust is much more variable among all age groups than would be expected if external events had little impact on political trust. In other words, political trust seems to be much more of an evaluation of the political system as opposed to an unquestioned norm received through the socialization process. This is true of all age groups, not the young in particular.

As a consequence, a young person today is less likely to be trustful of politicians and parties than a young person 50 years ago; but on the other hand an older person today is also less likely to be trusting than an older person 50 years ago. Declining levels of trust among the general population seem to have affected the young so that they now conform to the

52 *Political attitudes*

population average. Thus, generational change does not seem to be driving changes in political trust. This is consistent with the findings in *Bowling Alone* (Putnam, 2000) which show the young to be no less trusting than the old. It seems then that historical forces have had an effect on the young and old alike.

The data: support for democracy

So far this chapter has examined levels of trust in regards to attitudes towards the authorities (i.e. politicians and parties). However, in order to get a more complete picture of political trust we also need to examine trust at the regime level (i.e. support for democracy). To do this we can draw from the Comparative Study of Electoral Systems (CSES) data. The CSES (Module 2) asked respondents to agree or disagree (on a four-point scale) with the statement: 'Democracy may have problems but it's better than any other form of government.' Figure 2.5 shows those who responded 'agree' or 'strongly agree' by age.

Consistent with past research (Holmberg, 1999, 114; Norris, 1999a, 17; Dalton, 2004, 41; Inglehart and Welzel, 2005; Dalton, 2006, 257) Figure 2.5 shows that the overwhelming majority of people support democracy as the best form of government. Generally speaking over 90 per cent of people support democracy as the best form of government. Young people are the age group least likely to respond that democracy is the best form of government. However, in every country except Britain 85 per cent or more

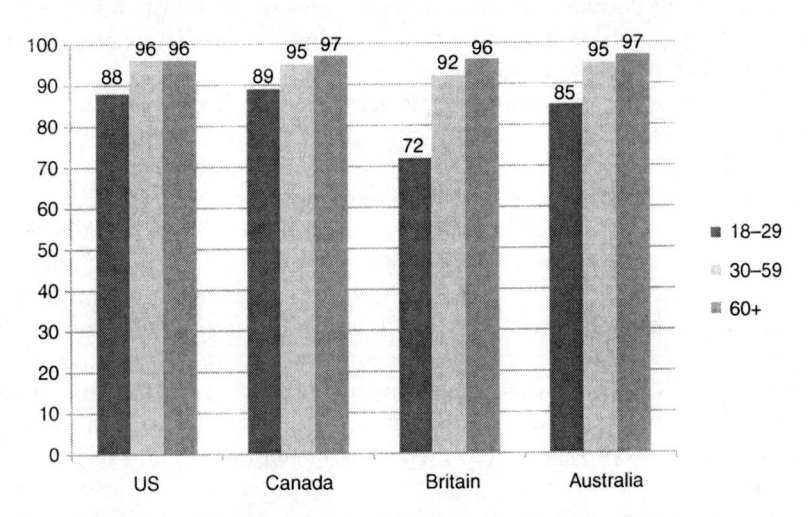

Figure 2.5 Agree democracy is best form of government (source: Comparative Study of Electoral Systems (2004–2005)).

Note
Question wording: 'Democracy may have problems but it's better than any other form of government.' Responses combine 'agree' and 'strongly agree'.

of young people say democracy is the best form of government. One obvious explanation for this age gap is young people not being politically aware during the Cold War which means that they may not hold as negative a view of other political regimes as those who lived through the Cold War and anti-communist campaigns. Therefore, older age groups who have a fresh memory of the Cold War and perhaps fought—or know someone who fought—in the Second World War are more likely to value democracy than those who have not been faced with a challenge to democracy in their lifetime. Nevertheless, young people are still overwhelmingly supportive of democracy.

From the CSES data we can say that the young are still overwhelmingly supportive of democracy (albeit slightly less supportive than older people)—this evidence supports Inglehart and Welzel (2005). In other words, there is no legitimation crisis among the young any more than there is among the old. Thus, the position of young and old alike seems to be that of 'dissatisfied democrats' who are dissatisfied with the functioning of government but very supportive of democracy as the best form of government. This does not necessarily mean we should be sanguine about these findings. Support for democracy may be because citizens perceive 'no alternative, and are simply resigned to a form of government they no longer associate with the satisfaction of their most basic political desires' (Hay, 2008, 33). Furthermore, citizens may have become 'less concerned with democracy as better than some alternative system and more concerned with the reality of democracy measured against normative expectation' (Fuchs *et al.*, 1995, 352). That said, the data above, at the very least, tempers concerns that the regime of democracy is under threat.

Political trust and its implications

The findings above relate to a long-running debate between Arthur Miller and Jack Citrin who debated the interpretation of the trust items in the ANES. Miller (1974a, 951) argued that the lack of trust in authorities is 'very likely to be accompanied by hostility toward political and social leaders, the institutions of government, and the regime as a whole.' Citrin (1974, 978) responded by arguing that the meaning of recent decreases in political trust 'remains ambiguous, and to decisively conclude that there exists widespread support for radical political change or pervasive alienation from the political system is premature, if not misleading.' Citrin (1974, 975) showed that even the least trusting are still supportive of the American form of government and only 25 per cent favour a 'big change' in their form of government from which he concludes 'many political cynics focus their disaffection on incumbent authorities rather than systemic values or processes.' To summarize, Citrin saw political trust as a largely ritualistic attitude with no substantive attitudinal or behavioural implications whereas Miller viewed the implications of low levels of trust as much more serious.

Following on from this debate, there have been various arguments made as to how concerned we should be about the overall lack of political trust that has been found in this chapter. The lack of trust in authorities is of great concern to some and of little concern to others. 'Most scholars argue that the survival of democracies rests on a broad and deep foundation of support among the citizenry' (Klingemann, 1999, 32). In this view, democracy functions with little coercive power because the system is seen as legitimate. However, some argue that 'declining feelings of political trust and political support can undermine this relationship and thus the workings of democracy' (Dalton, 2004, 159: see also Hetherington, 1998).

The findings above suggest that negative feelings towards authorities are not accompanied by feelings of hostility towards the regime. These separate evaluations seem to be distinct and unrelated to one another. Almond and Verba (1963) were concerned that 'if people become disillusioned with the perceived performance of democratic governments, over successive administrations, then in time this might erode their belief in democracy itself' leading to democratic values being undermined (cited in Norris, 1999a, 2). If this process is occurring over time it has not shown up in the data. The analysis here has shown that the lack of trust in government seems not to have affected support for democracy. In this sense there is no support for the crisis of democracy theories (Crozier *et al.*, 1975; Huntington, 1981).

Conclusion

While this chapter did find very low levels of trust overall, young people are not particularly distinct in this regard. For the most part young people's level of trust shadows that of older people. At least at this stage, the fears of the American President's Commission for a National Agenda for the Eighties that expressed particular concern about 'distrust of young adult voters' (Abramson, 1983, 193) do not seem well founded in the US or elsewhere. Perhaps then the direction of future research should be to understand why the entire population is lacking trust, and research need not be directed at young people in particular who are often singled out as being less trustful. This chapter also showed that support at the regime level remains very high among young and old alike. In this sense, 'dissatisfied democrats' is a good characterization of both the young and old.

3 Political interest among the young

Political interest is a vital aspect of political engagement. Because of its importance political interest has been among the most important themes in the voter behaviour literature. Dalton and Klingemann (2007, 4) write that 'One of the enduring debates of political behaviour research involves basic questions about the public's political abilities—the public's level of knowledge, understanding, and interest in political matters.' Beginning with the early political culture literature (Almond and Verba, 1963) political interest and attention to public affairs was seen to be an integral part of a successful and healthy political culture (Jackman, 1987, 417). However, publics across the advanced democracies have generally been depicted as uninterested in politics. Erikson *et al.* (2002, 78) summarize this situation well when they write that 'Five decades of research on political behaviour have painted a portrait of voters who know next to nothing and prefer to think about issues other than politics.' Outside of the academy the public's perceived lack of interest in politics has also caught the attention of elites such as Paul Martin (then Minister of Finance in Canada) who expressed concern about low levels of political interest in 2002 (Tanguay, 2009, 221).

But how does all of this apply to the young? Where research (much of it cross-sectional) has been done, young people have been shown to have very low levels of political interest in the US (Lyons and Alexander, 2000; Zukin *et al.*, 2006, 7), Canada (Gidengil *et al.*, 2003; Blais *et al.*, 2004) and Britain (Pattie *et al.*, 2004, 92). It might be assumed that this is a product of the lifecycle and once young people are freed from the distraction of youth they will become more politically interested. However, research (largely based on the US case) suggests that low levels of political interest among the young is a generational phenomenon, not a lifecycle one (Putnam, 2000; Milner, 2002; Patterson, 2002; Wattenberg, 2006). For example, Galston (2007, 629) reports that in the US between the 1960s and 2000 all measures of political interest declined by one-half among young people. Outside of the US the dynamics of political interest over time are less clear. Furthermore, many of the Anglo-American democracies have had high interest elections in recent years so we may expect an increase in political interest in recent years.

56 *Political attitudes*

This chapter will examine levels of political interest over time among the young thereby building on the existing literature. I do this first by outlining how political interest should be understood. Second, I review the literature which will inform our expectations in terms of the empirical analysis and in the third section I look at levels of political interest in the Anglo-American democracies. Lastly, I discuss the implications of the findings in this chapter.

The concept of political interest

What exactly political interest refers to requires some elaboration before we move on to the data analysis. It could be said that political interest refers to a general interest in political issues and events. However, the means by which political interest is conceptualized is debated in the literature. For this reason some scholars prefer to use terms other than political interest. Robert Zaller (1992, 21) uses the term 'political awareness' to refer to 'the extent to which an individual pays attention to politics *and* understands what he or she has encountered' … it denotes an 'intellectual or cognitive engagement with public affairs as against emotional or affective engagement or no engagement at all.' Zaller (1992, 21) sees this best measured through tests of neutral factual information which 'captures what has actually gotten into people's minds, which, in turn, is critical for intellectual engagement with politics.' Other terms are also used such as 'political literacy' which is defined by Milner (2010, 12) as 'a minimal familiarity with the relevant institutions of decision making, combined with a basic knowledge of the key positions on relevant issues and the political actors holding them.' While these are all reasonable arguments political interest is the preferred term in this book because the national election study questions that have been asked over time measure political interest more generally and do not directly measure 'political awareness' or 'political literacy.'[1]

It could be argued that hard measures of political interest such as knowledge are superior to more subjective measures such as self-evaluations of political interest (see Zaller, 1992; Milner, 2010). This is no doubt true. However, we simply lack good cross-national measures of political knowledge over time. Measuring political knowledge cross-nationally has been proven to be extremely problematic as seen in the Comparative Study of Electoral Systems' (CSES) decision to drop the political knowledge questions from their third module (see also Milner, 2002). Given this, it is very difficult to make any claims about generational differences in political knowledge over time and/or cross-nationally.

Is then political interest a variable worth studying? McAllister (2011, 62) argues that 'The public's interest in politics represents a convenient indicator of their general view of the political world, and in the view of many is the pre-requisite for accumulating political knowledge.' Verba *et al.* (1995, 345) also argue that political interest is important because it is hard to imagine that at least some psychological engagement with politics is not required for almost all forms of political participation. ... Those who choose to devote scarce resources to political activity rather than to other pursuits would, presumably, differ in their orientations to politics.

Verba *et al.* (1995, 358, 367) show that political interest is linked to many types of political participation. Furthermore, political interest is particularly relevant to young people because 'attention to politics and public affairs may be a valuable indicator of likely future participation' (Zukin *et al.*, 2006, 54). Obviously, the data utilized here is not perfect. Ideally, the respective national election studies would contain a broader set of questions which allow us to tap the dimensions of political interest discussed above. However, the national election studies do allow us to measure what is a vital aspect of political engagement in a meaningful, if limited, way.

The literature: young people and political interest

At the aggregate level the research on political interest reveals a mixed picture. Inglehart (1997, 231) found that political interest and political discussion has increased over time across a range of advanced democracies (see also Dalton, 2000a, 929; Dalton, 2006). In contrast, Putnam (2000, 36) in *Bowling Alone* finds that political interest has declined over time in the US (see also Galston, 2007, 629). This has also been confirmed in regards to the young among whom political interest has been found to be in decline. Galston (2007, 629) reports that in the US between the 1960s and 2000 all measures of political interest declined by one-half among young people. For example, in the 1960s 60 per cent of young people thought it was important to keep up-to-date with politics. By 2000 this had declined to less than 30 per cent (Galston, 2007, 629). Putnam (2000) also finds that young Americans are becoming less interested in politics (see also Patterson, 2002; Wattenberg, 2002; Zukin *et al.*, 2006, 81; Levine, 2007, 202). In Britain, Jowell and Park (1998, 14) argue that young people's lack of political interest 'appears to signal a generational change rather than just an effect of the lifecycle at work' (cited in Henn *et al.*, 2002, 170; see also Pattie *et al.*, 2004, 92). Similarly, Blais *et al.* (2002, 6) found that young Canadians are much less interested in politics than older generations (see also Blais *et al.*, 2004; Gidengil *et al.*, 2004).

Much of the research cited above points to generational declines in political interest. This is counter to the belief that young people will become more interested in politics as they are freed from the distractions of youth and have more time to engage in politics. As people grow older, the thinking goes, they will learn more about politics, become more familiar with parties, grow more attached to parties and acquire political skills and knowledge as well as social contacts that enhance political interest

58 Political attitudes

(Rosenstone and Hansen, 1993, 137). However, the research suggests that declines in political interest owe more to generational than lifecycle factors. This is summarized well by Milner (2010, 6) who argues that 'young people in North America and most comparable countries are less attentive to political life ... than previous generations.'

In the analysis below I analyse political interest over time to examine whether generational or lifecycle effects are at work. While the US and some British evidence points to generational declines in political interest this needs to be explored in more detail across the Anglo-American democracies. Support for lifecycle effects would temper the negative findings of much of the literature above by showing that young people become more politically interested as they age. However, if generational effects are found this has worrying consequences as through the process of generational replacement young less interested cohorts will come to replace more interested cohorts, thus driving down overall levels of interest over time.

The data: are the young really less interested in politics?

In the analysis below I test the expectations informed by the literature. The analysis below tests the conventional wisdom that 'suggests that young people are becoming increasingly disengaged from politics' (Henn et al., 2002, 167). Using the national election studies we can examine levels of political interest over time among different age groups. The national election studies have all asked comparable questions over time. The following four figures show the percentage of people who are interested in politics over time broken up by age. To begin, Figure 3.1 shows the American data.

In Figure 3.1 we can see that political interest in the US has been variable over time but has been much more variable among the young. Political interest increases among the young in 1964 which was likely associated with the Civil Rights Act which saw a much greater mobilization of black voters (see Miller and Shanks, 1996, 25) and again in 1972. Political interest then declines steeply among young people between 1972 and 1980 (which may be attributed to disgust following the Watergate crisis). Political interest increases in 1992, steeply falls in 1996 and 2000 and recovers in 2004 and a high level of interest is maintained in 2008. We can see here that political interest among the young seems to respond to political events such as the rise of a youthful and optimistic nominee in Bill Clinton (1992). It declines steeply for the low interest election of 2000 and then rises steeply for the high interest 2004 election. This trend is much less pronounced for older people whose level of political interest is much more stable. Again (like turnout among the young) we can see here that political interest among the young is affected much more by political events, as compared to older people. This is not to suggest that young people are paying close attention to politics and government policies but at a broad

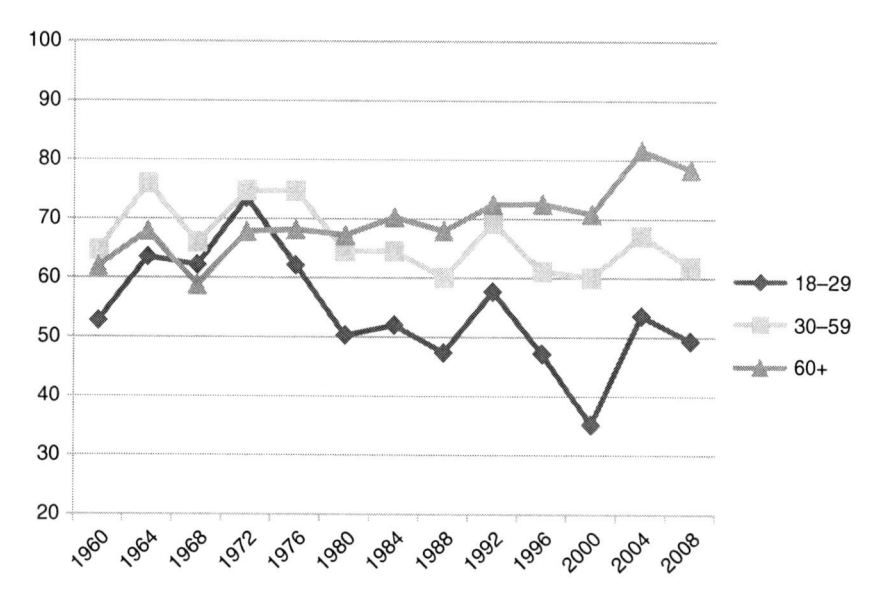

Figure 3.1 Interest in government and public affairs in the US (1960–2008) (source: American National Election Study).

Note
Questions wording: 1964 and later: 'Would you say you follow what's going on in government and public affairs most of the time, some of the time, only now and then, or hardly at all?' Responses combine 'most of the time' and 'some of the time.' 1960 question wording: 'Would you say you follow politics very closely, fairly closely, or not much at all?' Responses combine 'very closely' and 'fairly closely.'

level they seem to be affected by large events in the political system such as presidential nominees who capture the attention of the young (Clinton and Obama) and the low interest election of 2000. These events seem to affect the young much more than they do the old. The overall trend in relation to young people's political interest is not decline but rather volatility. A young person today is not particularly less interested than a young person at the beginning of the time series in 1960.

However, a wider age gap has opened up in regards to levels of interest among the young and the old over time. At the beginning of the time series (in 1960) 53 per cent of young people expressed interest in politics whereas 62 per cent of older people were interested (representing a 9 percentage point difference). By 1988 the gap in political interest between the young and old widens to 21 percentage points, 36 percentage points in 2000 and 29 percentage points at the end of the time series in 2008. Therefore, the analysis shows some support for generational effects in terms of young people becoming less interested in politics as compared to older people. But generational effects are not supported in terms of young people becoming less interested in politics over time. Young people today are not

60 *Political attitudes*

particularly less interested in politics than were young people at the beginning of the time series. In this regard much of the literature cited above is not supported.

We now turn to Canada where the data are less reliable than the American data. The CES asked about level of interest in politics (those answering 'some' or 'a good deal' are shown here) from 1965 to 1980 (denoted by v1), in 1984 and 1988 respondents were asked about their attention to politics generally (those who answered 'very closely' or 'fairly closely' are shown here) (denoted by v2) and from 1997 onwards respondents were asked to rate their level in interest in politics on a scale of 0 to 10. Those who rated their level of political interest as 7 or above were deemed to be interested in politics (this cut-off was chosen in a somewhat arbitrary way because using this cut-off point meant levels of political interest corresponded roughly with levels of interest in 1988) (denoted by v3).

While the data over time is not strictly comparable it does allow us to examine age related differences over time. In examining age related differences we can see larger gaps opening up between the young and old over time. In 1965 the gap between the young and the old is hardly noticeable and in 1984 this gap opens up to 30 percentage points (the largest age gap in the time series). The age gap then remains above 15 percentage points for the rest of the times series. Although the questions are not strictly comparable political interest among the young seems to reach a low point in 2000 when young people turned out to vote in very low numbers. 2000 also represents a low point of political interest among older people as well

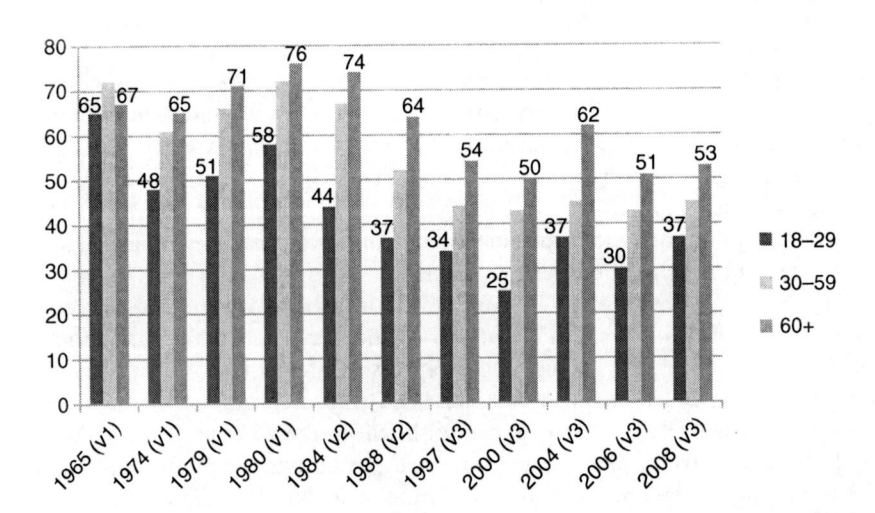

Figure 3.2 Interest in politics in Canada (1965–2008) (source: Canadian Election Study).

Note
Question wording changes noted in text.

but they still turned out to vote in quite high numbers in the 2000 election suggesting political interest has a larger effect on the young.

We now turn our attention to Britain. Figure 3.3 shows those who had a 'good deal' or 'some' interest in politics (1974–1979), and those who had a 'great deal', 'quite a lot' or 'some' interest in politics between 1997 and 2010. We can see here that the young are less interested in politics than the old but overall the age gaps are not as large as in the US and Canada. Overall, the picture is more of gradually increasing interest among the young as compared to the volatility seen in the American and Canadian data (although this may be partly owing to the more limited time period covered and the nature of the election years featured). A few comments can be made. Despite the tumultuous events surrounding the 1979 election, the first 'crisis election' since 1931, political interest is actually lower in this period than it is in 2010. Wright (2003, 100) argues that by the 2000s 'There was a sense that politics had become much less central to the life of people in Britain than in the 1950s.' While we do not have data going back to the 1950s this is not borne out over the period covered here. We can see across the time series that political interest is trending upwards, not downwards. This is true of the young and the old. There is no support here for generational declines in political interest. Also, whereas political trust declined over the period covered here (see Figure 2.3) this has not been accompanied by a decline in political interest.

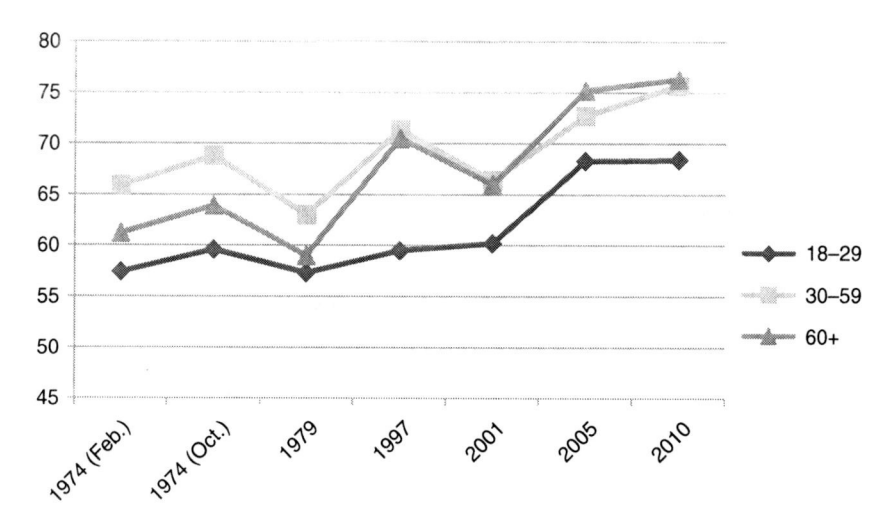

Figure 3.3 Interest in politics in Britain (1974–2010) (source: British Election Study).

Note
Question wording: 'How much interest do you generally have in what is going on in politics?' Minor question wording changes have occurred. 1974–1979 responses combine 'a good deal' and 'some' and 1997–2010 responses combine 'a great deal,' 'quite a lot' and 'some.'

62 Political attitudes

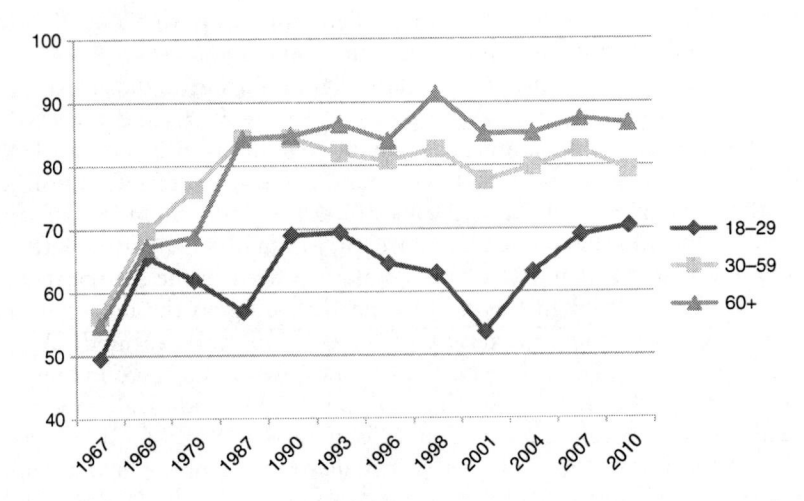

Figure 3.4 Interest in politics in Australia (1967–2010) (source: Australian Election Study).

Note
Question wording: 'Generally speaking, how much interest do you usually have in what's going on in politics?' Question wording differs slightly before 1987. Responses combine 'a good deal' and 'some.'

We now turn to Australia. Figure 3.4 shows those who have 'a good deal' or 'some' interest in politics between 1967 and 2010. We see here that political interest is not in secular decline among the young in Australia but is rather much more volatile. For example, political interest was particularly low among the young in 2001 (probably owing to an election in which the major parties were perceived to have converged on some important issues). It then increased substantially between 2001 and 2010 (perhaps owing to the environment becoming a more hotly debated topic). However, age gaps between the young and old have opened up over time. Whereas in 1967 and 1969 there was a very small age gap, a large age gap opened up in 1987 that has never really closed. At the end of the time series young people are 16 percentage points less likely to be interested in politics than older people despite political interest increasing among the young in 2004, 2007 and 2010. Again we see mixed evidence of generational effects. Young people have become less interested in politics as compared to older people but young people today are actually more interested than were their counterparts 40 years ago.

Discussion

Are young people less interested in politics today than they were 40 or 50 years ago? The literature cited above suggested that they would be.

But the findings contradict this evidence. In fact, in Britain and Australia political interest among the young has actually increased. In the US young people today are not particularly less interested than were young people at the beginning of the time series. However, in regards to whether young people have become less interested in politics as compared to older people over time the answer is yes. We see an increased age gap between the young and old in the US, Canada and Australia. That is, a young person 40 or 50 years ago was more likely to share their parents' or grandparents' level of political interest than a young person today. Therefore, there is mixed support for the generational effects argument. While there is little support for the argument that political interest is in secular decline among the young (as suggested by the likes of Putnam) the young have become less interested in politics as compared to their elders over time.

The data here shows a good deal of volatility in young people's political interest over time. As compared to older people who have quite stable levels of political interest over time young people's level of political interest seems to be more affected by political events. For example, political interest among the young increased dramatically in the US in 1992 when Clinton ran for the presidency and again in the 2004 election when terrorism and the Iraq War emerged as important issues. The importance of political events helps explain the high level of variability in the findings as they relate to the young. Clearly, interest is not in secular decline among the young. Young people are still interested in politics but this varies from year to year. Thus, it seems that political events have the ability to increase political interest in particular periods and this seems especially true of the young. Therefore, socialization effects (by which, for example, young people inherit their political interest from their parents) seem less important than the power of political events to increase political interest.

These findings are consistent with Schudson's (1998) argument in regards to what he calls 'monitorial citizens.' Schudson (1998, 310) argues that

> Citizens can be monitorial rather than informed. Monitorial citizens scan (rather than read) the informational environment in a way so that they may be alerted on a wide variety of issues for a very wide variety of ends and may be mobilized around those issues in a large variety of ways.

Therefore, some citizens may appear to be apathetic (as was the case in regards to young people in 2000 in the US or 2001 in Australia) when really they are waiting for an issue or candidate to engage them. 'The monitorial citizen,' argues Schudson (1998, 311), is 'engaged in environmental surveillance more than information gathering.... They look inactive, but they are poised for action if action is required.' There is some evidence for this view here. Take, for example, the 2004 US data in which issues (such as terrorism and the Iraq war) seem to have engaged the young. Thus, rather than increased education levels translating into incrementally higher levels of political interest over time among the young (as the resource model would predict) increased levels of education may play out in terms of education allowing young people to be 'monitorial' rather than 'engaged' citizens.

That political interest is so volatile among the young suggests that motivation is a more important factor than ability. Older people—who have lower levels of education and therefore less of an ability to become interested and informed about politics—maintain quite high levels of political interest. However, young people today who have a much greater ability to become more politically interested and informed (owing to higher levels of education) do not appear to be motivated enough to do so during certain periods. When political events stimulate the young to become more interested in politics they do but they seem to switch off during what they perceive as 'boring' periods of political activity, such as in 2000 in the US. This is all in line with Schudson's argument.

This may be owing to a multitude of reasons: young people may not see it as an important civic duty to be politically interested; young people may be distracted by new technologies that weren't available to former generations of young people; young people may not see much of a connection between politics and their own lives. The question that follows from this is how to get young people more motivated, a question I will address in Chapter 7.

Underpinning these findings is the question of whether political interest is more important to the young today than it was 40 years ago. In regards to non-electoral forms of political activity (that I will explore in Chapter 5) I would argue that it is. Non-electoral forms of participation require high levels of political interest. In the past those with low levels of political interest have been mobilized to participate in politics through class and other cleavages and the political parties representing these cleavages. For example, nineteenth century class, religion, rural/urban divides mobilized citizens by heightening people's interest in politics. These divides 'informed people and helped them to understand the logical connection between the issues of the day and the casting of their ballots' (Rosenstone and Hansen, 1993, 232). Absent these traditional forces of mobilization political activity becomes even more reliant on the motivation of the individual. This is particularly true of non-electoral forms of political activity that are heavily reliant on resources and motivation. In this regard political interest may come to carry a heavier load than it has in the past.

Conclusion

This chapter has shown that patterns of political interest among the young are more complicated than much of the literature suggests. Young people today are *not* less interested in politics than young people 40 or 50 years ago. In the cases of Britain and Australia young people are actually more interested. In the US young people are not particularly less interested than were young people at the beginning of the time series. This is counter to many of the expectations informed by the literature. However, young people have become less interested in politics as compared to older people. In this regard there is some support for generational effects. Overall, young people's level of political interest is very volatile and this seems to be owing to political events which seem to engage young people at some times and leave them disinterested at other times. In this regard motivation seems to be a more important factor than ability. Thus, young people may be described as being 'monitorial citizens' who are interested in politics at some times and not at other times. More broadly this chapter has suggested that the conventional wisdom that young people are becoming less interested in politics is wrong.

Part III
Political participation beyond voting

Part III returns to and builds on some of the themes raised in Chapter 1 on voter turnout. Chapter 4 examines electoral engagement more broadly in terms of party identification, party membership, contact and mobilization. In Chapter 5 I examine non-electoral forms of participation such as attending a demonstration and signing a petition. Chapter 6 takes this a step further by examining young people's political engagement on the Internet. In Part III I break from relying predominantly on the national election studies and draw from a wider range of data in order to better capture the changing nature of young people's political participation.

4 Electoral engagement
A disengaged youth

In Chapter 1 I examined voter turnout and found that voting was more volatile among the young than would be expected based on the literature. In this way, voting seems to be an attractive way for young people to have their voices heard at some times and less attractive at other times. However, voting is but one of many forms of political participation related to the electoral world. In fact, Marsh and Kaase (1979b, 86) excluded voting from their analysis of political participation arguing that 'voting is a unique form of political behaviour in the sense that it occurs only rarely, is highly biased by strong mechanisms of social control and social desirability enhanced by the rain-dance ritual of campaigning, and does not involve the voter in informational or other costs.' While I take a very different position to Marsh and Kaase (as per arguments made in Chapter 1) Marsh and Kaase's comment attunes us to the fact that voting is one among many forms of participation.

It is important then that we examine young people's engagement with the electoral world more broadly. This chapter examines what I term electoral engagement (beyond voting). Electoral engagement refers both to psychological engagement with electoral politics (identifying with a party) and behavioural forms of electoral engagement (such as joining a political party and contacting a politician). In this way, this chapter examines how electorally engaged young people are as compared to older people. This is important because missing from much of the analyses cited in this chapter is a thorough investigation of electoral engagement in the Anglo-American democracies among different age groups using across-time data sources.

Defining political participation

In the literature political participation has been defined in a number of ways. For Verba and Nie (1972, 2) 'political participation refers to those activities by private citizens that are more or less directly aimed at influencing the selection of governmental personnel and/or the actions they take.' They confined themselves to 'activities "within the system"—ways of influencing politics that are generally recognized as legal and legitimate'

(Verba and Nie, 1972, 3). Verba and Nie (1972, 47) classified four modes of political activity: voting, campaign activities, individual citizen-initiated contacting and group or organizational activity. These acts were also the focus of the work of Verba et al. (1978). This chapter focuses on these more conventional types of political activity that are largely centred around the electoral world and political parties.

However, as protest and other sorts of political activity increased throughout the 1960s and 1970s research gradually came to reflect this. Barnes and Kaase (1979) took a broader approach and examined protest which was conceptualized as citizens' willingness to engage in strikes, boycotts, signing petitions and attending demonstrations. This work broadened the meaning of political participation by considering non-electoral forms of political activity. The authors examined to what extent activity 'within the system' has been offset by increases in participation 'outside the system.' This book takes a broad view of political participation by considering political participation 'within the system' and 'outside the system' (i.e. electoral and non-electoral forms of political participation). While this chapter concentrates on activity 'within the system' (i.e. electoral engagement) the next chapter considers political participation which could be considered as occurring 'outside the system' (i.e. non-electoral forms of political participation). In this way the following two chapters consider various forms of political engagement which allow us to test arguments made by Putnam and Inglehart and Welzel.

The literature: electoral engagement

Early research on political participation focused on electoral forms of political activity and showed that very low numbers of people participated in politics beyond voting. Campbell et al. (1960, 91) found that no more than 10 per cent of the American electorate in 1952 and 1956 were actively involved in a political organization, a political campaign or a political party. Similarly, Verba and Nie's (1972, 31) research showed that most acts of political participation are only ever performed by a small number of people. Furthermore, research that has tracked electoral forms of participation over time has generally found these forms of political activity to be in decline. For example, Putnam's (2000) research finds steeply declining levels of participation in the US, as does Stoker (2006) in Britain.

This is particularly the case in regards to political parties. Dalton et al. (2004, 124) show that party membership has declined in many advanced democracies over the last few decades (see also Inglehart, 1997, 230). Research has also shown that party membership has declined in the US (Verba et al., 1995, 73), Australia (Leigh, 2010, 59) and Britain (Norris, 1997, 103; Stoker, 2006, 34). It is widely remarked in Britain that 'the Royal Society for the Protection of Birds now has more members than all the political parties put together' (Wright, 2003, 77) This evidence points to the declining role political parties play in mobilizing citizens into political participation.

What about young people? The research shows these trends to be particularly pronounced among the young. Putnam (2000) finds generational declines in electoral forms of political activity in the US. In relation to parties, it is the young in particular who are less likely to become party members. Youth sections of political parties, once very important, are now on the brink of disappearing (Hooghe, 2004, 332) and other evidence suggests that young people are opting out of party membership in Canada (Blais *et al.*, 2002, 8). The research on young people and electoral engagement is not abundant however and this chapter will help establish what percentage of young people are electorally engaged. Furthermore, there is little research on whether young people's low levels of political participation are owing to generational or lifecycle effects.

In this chapter I also pay particular attention to partisan identification which mobilizes people to vote and participate in politics. According to Dalton and Wattenberg (2002) partisanship has declined over the past two decades in 17 of the 19 advanced democracies they examined (see also Norris, 2011, 34). Again, the young have contributed disproportionately to this decline. Miller and Shanks (1996, 99), Clarke *et al.* (2004, 195), Henn and Weinstein (2006, 525) and Zukin *et al.* (2006, 158) find very low levels of party identification among young people.[1] This means that young people are not only not joining political parties but are also failing to develop an attachment to a party. This is important 'because party identification has been central to theories of mass political behaviour for more than four decades' and 'its decline should have fundamental implications for the nature of citizen politics' (Dalton *et al.*, 2002, 37). This chapter examines how young people have contributed (or not) to this decline in party identification.

In this chapter I also look at the percentage of young people who have contacted a politician as well as looking at the 'supply side' efforts of parties to mobilize young people. While individuals need to go to politics, politics also needs to come to them so it is important to examine the mobilization efforts of parties (see Rosenstone and Hansen, 1993).

The data: levels of electoral engagement

Party identification

Figure 4.1 shows that between 1952 and 2008 young people became less likely to identify with a party over time. In 1952 29 per cent of young people did not identify with a party. By 2008 this had increased to 52 per cent. We can see that there is a general pattern of decreasing partisanship across the time series but again patterns among the young are much more

72 Political participation beyond voting

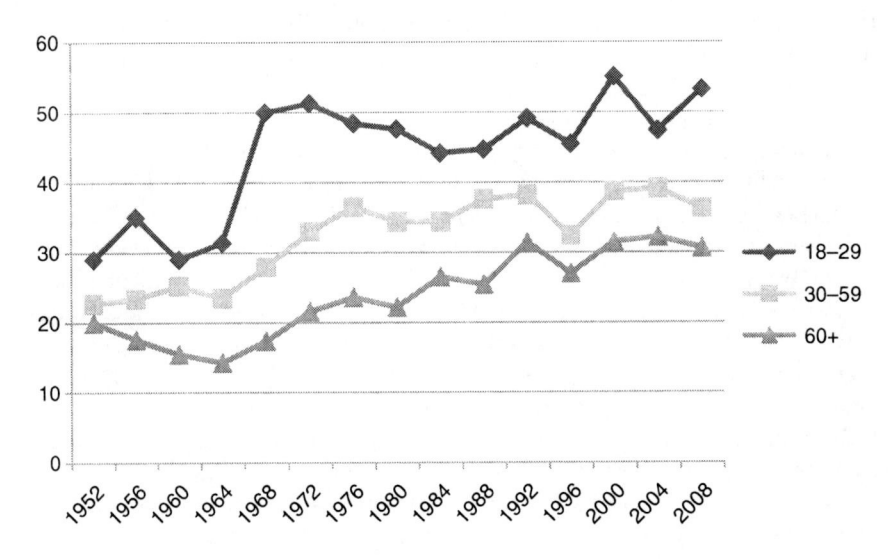

Figure 4.1 Non-party identifiers in the US (1952–2008) (source: American National Election Study).

Note
Following Miller and Shanks (1996, 127) I classify leaners as non-identifiers who lack a *permanent* or *enduring* sense of party identification as well as in the next figure. I also excluded the vague 'apolitical' category from the analysis as advised by a 2009 ANES memo.
Question wording: 'Generally speaking, do you usually think of yourself as a Republican, a Democrat, an Independent, or what?'

volatile in this regard. There is a sharp increase in non-identifiers among the young in 1956. In 1960 there is a sharp decrease in non-identifiers among the young (and old). Partisanship then steadily decreases between 1964 and 1972 among all age groups. However, 1968 stands out as a landmark year in regards to the young. Between 1964 and 1968 the percentage of young people who do not identify with a party increases from 32 to 51, representing a 19 percentage point increase from which it has never since recovered.

So, what was it about 1968? There are numerous plausible explanations for this decrease in partisan identification among the young. There was the Vietnam War and race riots between 1965 and 1968. There were the youth protests at the 1968 Democratic Convention in Chicago following what some saw as the disappointing presidency of Lyndon Baines Johnson (LBJ) which included LBJ escalating the war in Vietnam. It seems likely that these political events had a marked impact on the young in terms of whether or not they identified with a party. Furthermore, this period was one of declining deference to authority (as expressed through the counterculture movement). The effect of this change may have made young people more immune from inheriting their parent's party identification. In other words, the decline in deference means that the socialization process by

Electoral engagement 73

which young people inherit a party identification from their parents is much less powerful than it once was. This would account for the number of young people who have continued to not identify with a political party since 1968.

Overall, we can see that since the 1960s the number of citizens who do not identify with a party has been trending upwards for all age groups. However, largely due to the massive surge in non-identifiers in 1968, young people are much less likely to identify with a party in 2008 than older people. Whereas about one in three young people didn't identify with a party in 1952 today more than half of all young people do not identify with a party. Accompanying this is an age gap that has opened up between the young and old over time. At the beginning of the time series the gap between the young and old is 9 percentage points. By 2008, this age gap more than doubles to 22 percentage points. Therefore, it is not just the lifecycle effect at work here (by which young people develop a partisan identity as they age). Rather, generational effects are much stronger. While the Democrats and Republicans were doing a reasonably good job at representing young people in the 1950s today young people are much more estranged from the two major parties.

The Canadian data tells a different story from the US data. Between 1965 and 1984 there was a decrease in those who did not identify with a

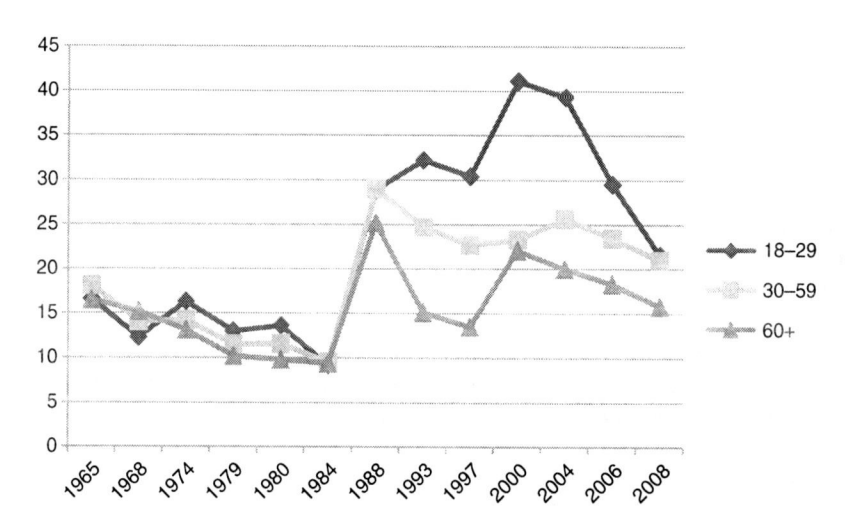

Figure 4.2 Non-party identifiers in Canada (1965–2008) (source: Canadian Election Study).

Note
A major change in categories available to respondents came in 1988 when respondents were no longer required to volunteer the option 'none of these.' Other minor question wording changes have occurred over time.
Question wording: 'In federal politics, do you usually think of yourself as a (parties differ by year)?'

74 *Political participation beyond voting*

party with all age groups showing the same pattern here. There is then a spike among all age groups in those who do not identify with a party in 1988 which could be attributed in large part to CES respondents being given the option of not identifying with a party whereas in previous surveys respondents had to volunteer this without prompting. In 1993 young people begin to show different patterns of party identification to older people. In particular, the percentage of non-identifiers reaches a high point among the young in 2000 with over 40 per cent of young people not identifying with a party—this coincides with very low turnout among the young in 2000. Young people are almost twice as likely to not identify with a party as compared to older people in 2000. After 2000 there is a sharp decrease in those who do not identify with a party among the young. Between 2000 and 2008 the percentage of young people who do not identify with a party decreases from 41 per cent to 22 per cent. Thus, we can see here that the 2000–2008 period is an important one during which politics seems to have become more salient for the young which has affected party identification. The overall trend here is one of volatility, especially among the young. This is what would be predicted given the 'brokerage' model of Canadian politics which works against citizens developing a long-lasting party identification. These findings confirm that no party can rely on party identification for support as party identification is very fickle. Canada has long been said to be a dealigned and volatile electorate and this is especially true of the young, a trend which has increased in recent years.

We now turn across the Atlantic to look at the percentage of people who do not identify with a party in Britain. Here the trend lines look a lot more like those we saw in the US with the number of non-identifiers increasing over time. We can see here that in 1964 the percentage of citizens who did not identify with a party was always under 10 per cent among all age groups. The percentage of non-identifiers then trends upward after 1970 among all age groups but particularly so among the young. This coincides with the period in which citizens in Britain were increasingly described as a dealigned electorate (see Norris, 1997, 18; Denver, 2005, 67). This increase in non-identifiers among the young continues unabated until 1992 but then shoots up again among the young in 1997. 1997 has been called a classic dealignment election (Denver, 2005, 93). This is less true for older age groups but especially true of the young. And following 1997 there was a sharp rise over time in young people who lacked a party identification. The Blair government then seems to have had a particularly large effect on party identification. Wright (2003, 100) argues that 'The clash of ideologies had become much more muted, as party differences narrowed.' This seems to have had an effect on young people's party identification in particular. Thus, as in the US, we find clear evidence of generational effects here. In 2010 a young person was more than two and a half times as

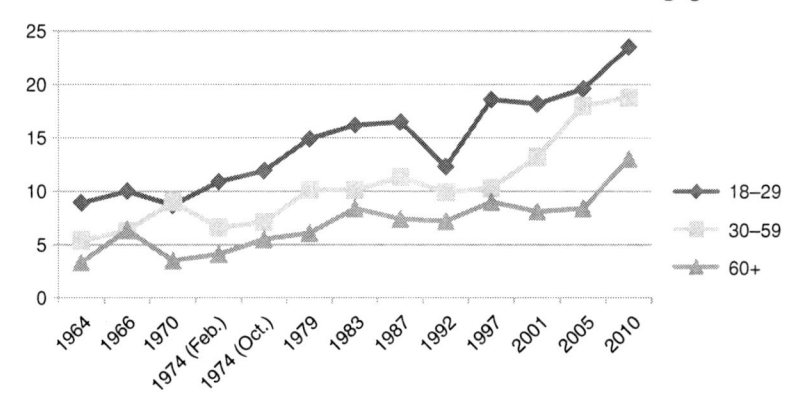

Figure 4.3 Non-party identifiers in Britain (1964–2010) (source: British Election Study).

Note
Question wording: 'Generally speaking, do you think of yourself as a (parties differ by survey year), or what?'

likely to not identify with a party as compared to a young person in 1964.

This overall pattern of young people becoming less likely to identify with a party is similar to the pattern we saw in the US in relation to age differences as well. As in the US, an age gap between the young and old opens up over time. In 1964 the age gap between the young and old was just 6 percentage points but by 2010 this had increased to 11 percentage points. Political parties have become a lot less attractive to the young. This is in stark contrast to older people who have remained largely stable in their party identification over time (although 2010 represented a big shift for older people). Therefore, it is clear that the increase in those who do not identify with a party is driven by generational replacement. As in the US the socialization process by which young people inherit a party identification from their parents seems to be breaking down.

We now turn to party identification in Australia. In early studies Australians were found to have a high level of party identification (Aitkin, 1982). However, in recent years there has been found to be an increase in those who do not identify with a party (McAllister, 2011, 40). Of interest here is to what extent young people have contributed to this. As was the case in the US and Britain young people in Australia have become less likely to identify with a party over time. Figure 4.4 shows that in 1967 only 13 per cent of young people did not identify with a party. By 2010 this figure doubled to 24 per cent. Furthermore, as was also the case in the US and Britain, young people have become less likely to identify with a party as compared to older people. In 1967 the gap between the young and the old was just 5 percentage points which by

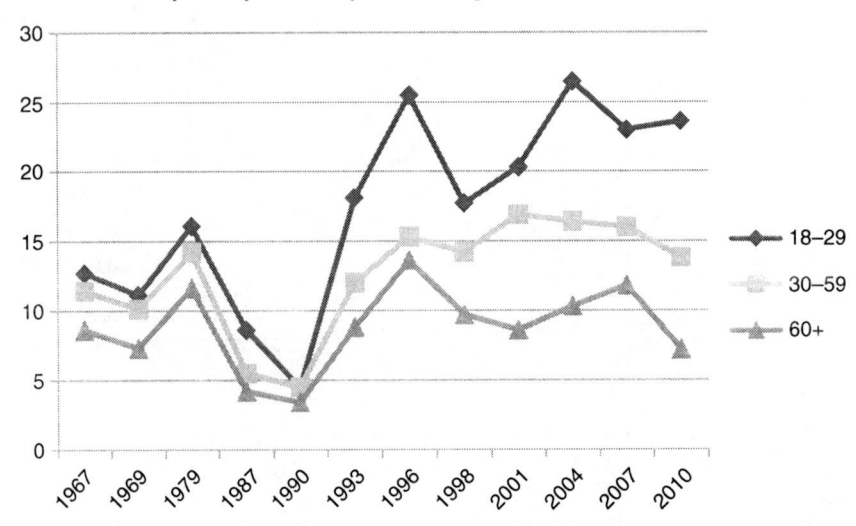

Figure 4.4 Non-party identifiers in Australia (1967–2010) (source: Australian Election Study).

Note
Question wording: 'Generally speaking, do you usually think of yourself as Liberal, Labor, National, or what?' Question wordings differ slightly before 1993.

2010 had increased to 17 percentage points. Therefore, we find evidence of generational effects and the declining influence of the socialization process.

Party identification is quite volatile over the period covered here. In terms of volatility particularly notable is the sharp decrease in those who do not identify with a party among all age groups between 1979 and 1990. This could be owing to the enormously popular and charismatic Prime Minister Bob Hawke (1983–1991). The percentage of non-identifiers then increased dramatically between 1990 and 1996, particularly among the young when it increased from 5 per cent to 26 per cent, a more than five fold increase! This increase is much more slight among older people. This increase looks similar to that in 1968 for the young in the US. Therefore, we must ask again, what was it about the 1990–1996 period that caused such a massive increase in non-identifiers? A few explanations could be offered. The trend could reflect the disillusionment with the Labor Party which instituted a number of pro-market reforms (unprecedented for the Labor Party) of which people were increasingly becoming aware by 1993. It may also be that the leadership tussle between PM Bob Hawke and Treasurer Paul Keating had an effect on partisanship. Furthermore, the Liberal Party had a number of leadership disputes of its own in this period. The rise of John Howard who became Prime Minister in 1996 (and was thought to have moved the conservative party to the right) may also have had an effect on those identifying with the party. It is not easy to account for why these events had such a large effect on the young except to say that young people were particularly affected by these events as new entrants to the electorate. Nevertheless, despite the volatility young people have become much less likely to identify with a party over time and generational replacement is playing a role here as was the case in the US and Britain.

Political party membership

This section moves the analysis from psychological to behavioural forms of electoral engagement in terms of political party membership. Research suggests political party membership is in decline and that this trend is particularly pronounced among the young (Milner, 2010, 77). I explore this below. Unfortunately, the survey data on party membership is not as detailed as that on party identification. However, we do have across-time data on Canada and Britain and can draw from cross-sectional data on the US and Australia.

Figure 4.5 shows the percentage of people who belong to a political party by age in the US drawing from data from the 2004 International Social Survey Programme (ISSP) Citizenship Survey. The overall percentage of people who are party members is higher here than in the other Anglo-American democracies because of the procedure by which citizens

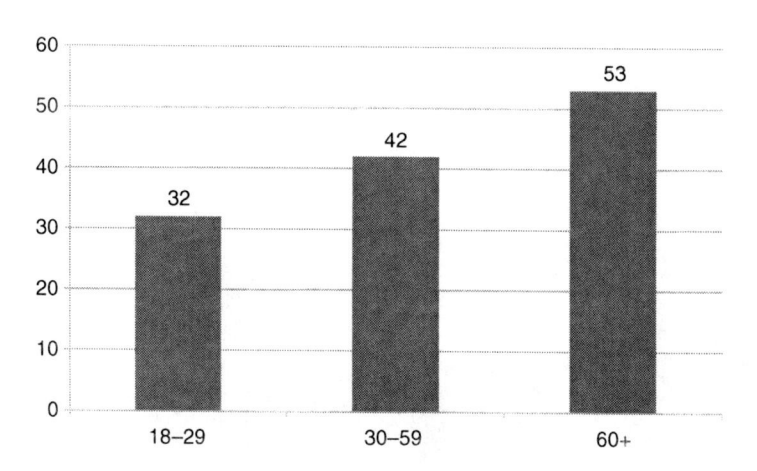

Figure 4.5 Party membership in the US (source: International Social Survey Programme Citizenship Survey 2004).

Note
Question wording: 'People sometimes belong to different kinds of groups or associations. For each type of group, please indicate whether you—"belong and actively participate," "belong and don't actively participate," "used to belong but do not any more," "have never belonged to it": A political party.' Responses combine 'belong and don't actively participate' and 'belong and actively participate.'

78 *Political participation beyond voting*

become party members/affiliates in the US through registering to vote. In the US there is no real analogue to party membership in the other Anglo-American democracies. Party membership in the US indicates much less commitment than being a party member in the other Anglo-American democracies and party membership is understood in a different way in the US from the other Anglo-American democracies which has likely contaminated the responses. That said, here we can see that young people are much less likely to be a member of a political party. While only 32 per cent of young people are party members 53 per cent of older people are party members.

We have slightly better data from Canada where we can chart party membership over a 20-year period from 1988 to 2008. What we can see here is that there has been a generational decline in party membership among the young over time. For example, 5 per cent of young people were party members in 1988 and this figure more than halved to 2 per cent in 2006 and 2008. This decline in party membership affects other age groups as well. All citizens have become less likely to be members of a party but this is particularly true of the young. That young people in particular have such low levels of party membership should be concerning in regards to the representativeness of party members. The generational decline in party membership also suggests that membership levels will reach even lower levels in the future.

We have better data again from Britain with the across-time time data

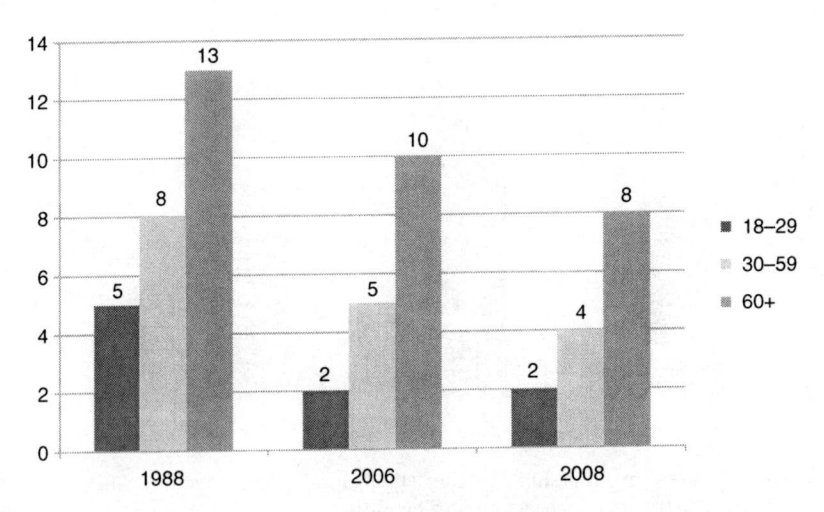

Figure 4.6 Party membership in Canada (1988–2008) (source: Canadian Election Study).

Note
Question wording: 1988: 'Are you a member of a federal political party?' 2006–2008: 'Have you ever been a member of a federal political party? Are you still a member?' Responses 2006–2008 show per cent who are still members.

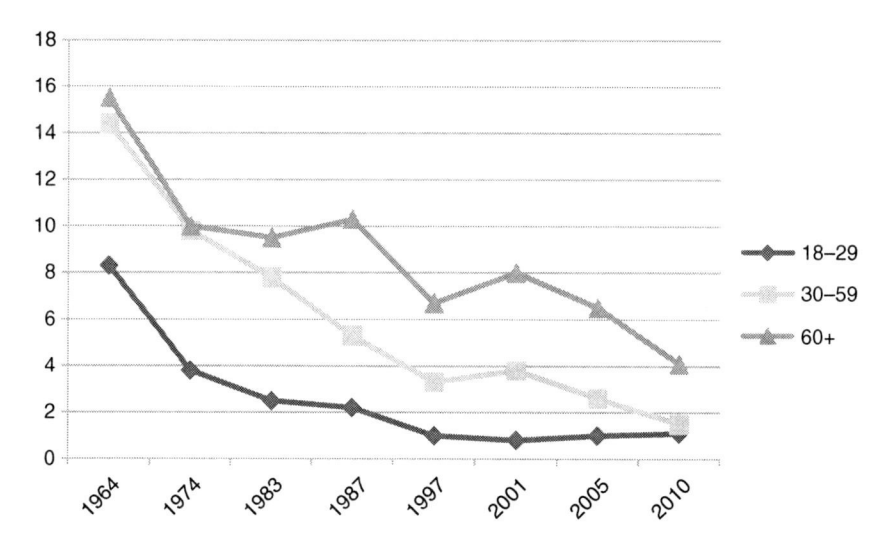

Figure 4.7 Party membership in Britain (1964–2010) (source: British Election Study).

Note
The 1974 figure is from the October 1974 election study.
Question wording: 1964: 'Have you paid a subscription to any political party in the past year?' 1974: 'Are you a paying member of any political party or some other political organisation?' 1983–2005: 'Are you a member of a political party?' 2010: 'Are you a member of a political party, that is, do you pay an annual subscription to be a member of a political party?'

stretching back to 1964. We can see here that there is a clear trend of declining party membership among all age groups. Party membership has always been lower among the young but is declining and shows no sign of recovering. Among young people party membership has declined from 8 per cent in 1964 to 1 per cent in 2010. That only 1 per cent of young people in Britain are party members is very worrying. Political party membership has also declined steadily among the other age groups (particularly the 30–59 age group) suggesting that the process of generational replacement will drive down overall levels of party membership in Britain over time.

Figure 4.8 shows the percentage of people who are party members in Australia, again using cross-sectional data from the ISSP. Figure 4.8 shows that young people in Australia are much less likely than older people to be a member of a political party. Just 3 per cent of young people are a member of a political party. This is compared to 10 per cent of those aged 60 and over who are party members. Therefore, young people in Australia are no more engaged than young people in the other Anglo-American democracies. As in the other Anglo-American democracies young people

80 *Political participation beyond voting*

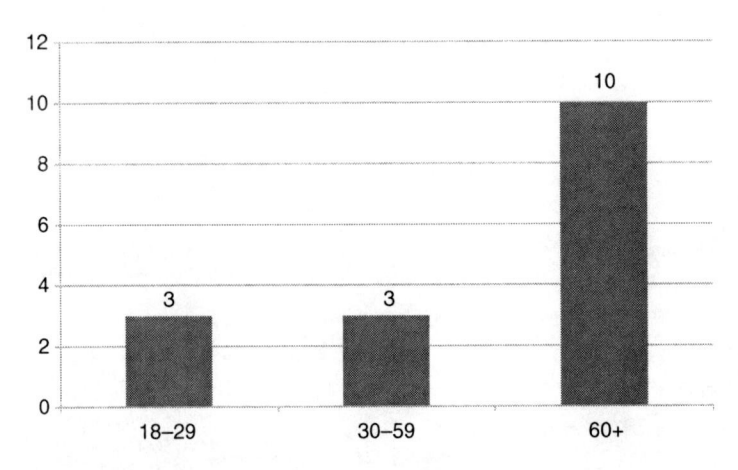

Figure 4.8 Party membership in Australia (source: International Social Survey Programme Citizenship Survey 2004).

Note
Question wording: 'People sometimes belong to different kinds of groups or associations. For each type of group, please indicate whether you—"belong and actively participate," "belong and don't actively participate," "used to belong but do not any more," "have never belonged to it": A political party.' Responses combine 'belong and don't actively participate' and 'belong and actively participate.'

seem to be driving what has been found to be a more general decline in party membership over time (Leigh, 2010, 59).

Contacting a politician or civil servant

Another form of electoral participation is contacting a politician or civil servant. We have limited data in regards to this form of electoral engagement. However, we can draw again from cross-sectional data from the ISSP. Figure 4.9 shows the number of people who contacted, or attempted to contact, a politician or civil servant in the past year. Here we can see that young people are less likely than middle-aged and older people to have contacted, or attempted to have contacted, a politician or civil servant in the past year in every country. For example, in the US 25 per cent of older people contacted a politician or civil servant in the past year whereas just 11 per cent of young people did this. In Canada 20 per cent of older people contacted a politician or civil servant in the past year while just 10 per cent of young people did. The numbers for Britain and Australia are 5 and 7 and 7 and 13 respectively. Therefore, we can again see that very low numbers of people are involved in this activity. We can't make too much of these findings because they only represent one time period and it is likely that young people will become increasingly likely to contact politicians as they age and have concerns (such as schooling or road safety) which they may contact politicians about.

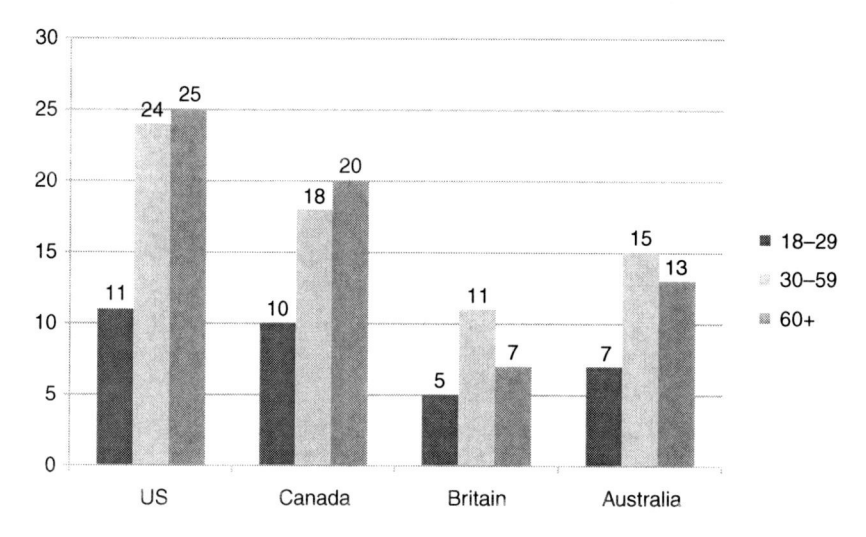

Figure 4.9 Contacted a politician or civil servant in past year (source: International Social Survey Programme Citizenship Survey 2004).

Note
Question wording: 'Here are some different forms of political and social action that people can take. Please indicate, for each one "whether you have done any of these things in the past year," "whether you have done it in the more distant past," "whether you have not done it but might do it," "have not done it and would never, under any circumstances, do it": Contacted, or attempted to contact, a politician or a civil servant to express your views.' Responses are done 'in past year'.

However, if we see these findings in light of the previous findings that show young people to be very disengaged from electoral politics it is likely that at least some of the data here captures generational effects.

Being contacted

As mentioned in the introduction citizens go to politics (i.e. they develop a party identification or become a member of a party) but politics also comes to them by way of mobilization by parties and politicians. According to Rosenstone and Hansen (1993, 23) mobilization subsidizes the cost of obtaining political information and underwrites the cost of political participation. Absent this mobilization, it is argued, rational ignorance and the paradox of participation 'would defeat much citizen involvement in politics' (Rosenstone and Hansen, 1993, 37). Therefore, mobilization by parties and politicians may be an important part of understanding why young people are not engaged in electoral politics. Accordingly, Figures 4.10–4.12 show the percentage of people who have been contacted by a party or politicians in the US, Canada and Britain (we have no data for Australia). This will provide us with some indication of party mobilization.

82 *Political participation beyond voting*

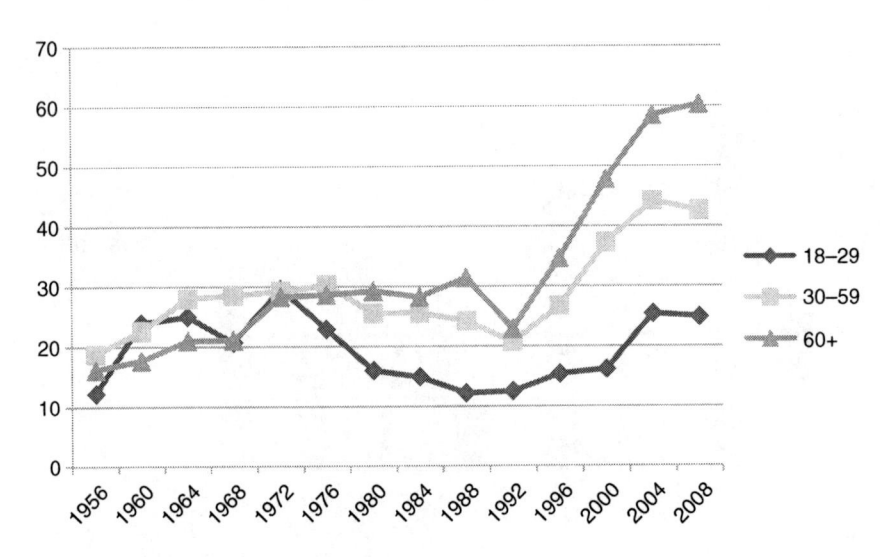

Figure 4.10 Contacted by a political party in the US (1956–2008) (source: American National Election Study).

Note
Question wording: 'Did anyone from one of the political parties call you up or come around and talk to you about the campaign this year?' Minor question wording changes occurred in some years.

Figure 4.10 shows the percentage of people who were contacted by a political party between 1956 and 2008. Young people today have not become less likely to be contacted as compared to young people 40 or 50 years ago. However, young people have become less likely to be contacted by a party relative to older people over time. In 1956 12 per cent of young people were contacted by a party, as compared to 16 per cent of those aged 60 and over. In 2008 these figures were 25 and 60. It has been in the last few decades that this age gap has opened up. Since 1996 the parties have become much more likely to contact older people but only marginally more likely to contact young people. That said, young people were more likely to be contacted in 2004 and 2008 and this seems to have had an effect on turnout rates among the young (see Figure 1.1).

In Canada we have less consistent data as there have been significant question wording changes in regards to being contacted by a party. For example, in 1965 respondents were asked whether they were canvassed by a party at home. Between 1974 and 1993 respondents were asked if they were contacted by a local candidate or party worker in their riding ('in person or by telephone' was added to the question wording in 1988 and 1993). In 2000 respondents were asked if they were contacted by a party during the campaign. In 2004 respondents were asked if anyone from a party contacted them (although this was only asked in the mail-back

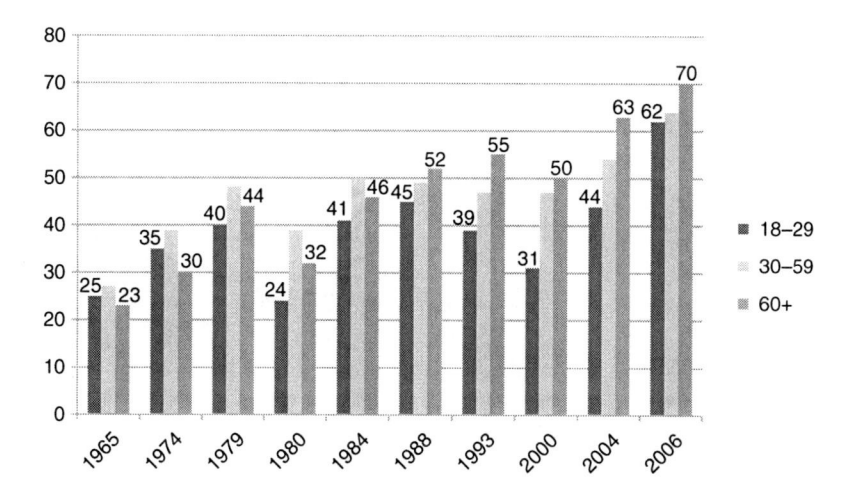

Figure 4.11 Contacted by candidates or a party in Canada (1965–2006) (source: Canadian Election Study).

Note
See in text for question wording changes.

survey) and in 2006 respondents were asked if they were contacted by a political party by phone, in person or some other way.

These question wording changes mean that across-time trends are hard to detect. However, Figure 4.11 does allow us to observe age differences over time. In regards to age related differences we can see a similar pattern to that in the US. That is, relative to older people young people have become less likely to be contacted by a politician or party than older people over time. For example, in 1965 and 1974 young people were *more* likely to have been contacted than older people. This pattern reverses in 1979 and the gap between the young and old has widened in the last few decades. In 2004 young people were almost 20 percentage points less likely to be contacted although this age gap closes in 2006 in what was a very close election. However, with the exception of 2006 political parties since 1993 seem to be paying less attention to contacting young people.

Figure 4.12 shows the percentage of people who were contacted by a party at home during the campaign between 1964 and 2005 in Britain. This figure shows party contact has been variable since 1964 with party contact declining steeply in 1997 (coinciding with the period that turnout declined) and then declining further among the young in 2005. In 2010 just 16 per cent of young people were contacted by a party at home as compared to 23 per cent of those aged 60 and over.[2] However, the age gaps are much smaller in Britain than in the US and Canada.

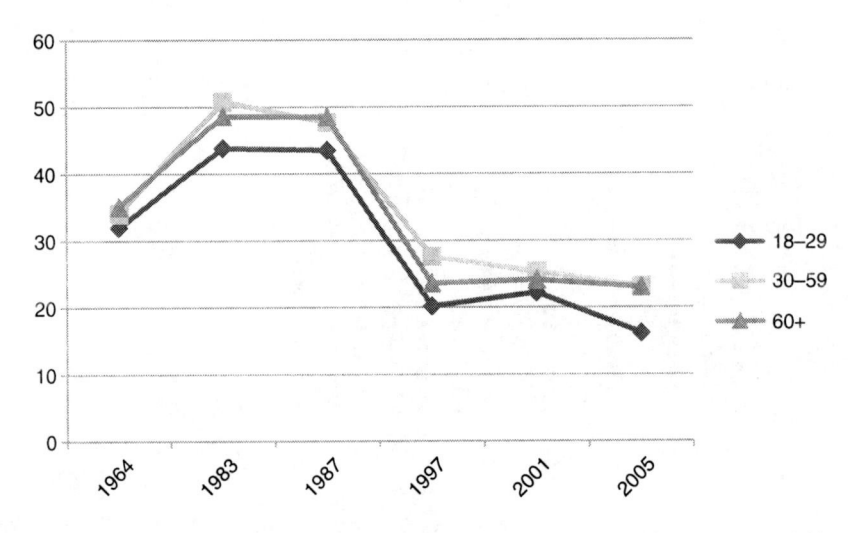

Figure 4.12 Contacted by a party at home in Britain (1964–2005) (source: British Election Study).

Note
Question wording: 'Did a canvasser from any party call at home to talk with you during the election campaign?'

Discussion

This chapter has concentrated on the role of political parties. Political parties are the most important of any mobilizing agency and the key linkage institution between the citizen and the state. Norris (2011, 35) has argued:

> Parties in the electorate, as organizations, and in parliament play an essential role in representative democracy. Parties serve multiple functions: simplifying and structuring electoral choices; organizing and mobilizing campaigns; articulating and aggregating disparate interests; channeling communication, consultation, and debate; training, recruiting, and selecting candidates; structuring parliamentary divisions; acting as policy think tanks; and organizing government.

Similarly, McAllister (2011, x) argues that 'In effect, political parties shape the whole political process.' This chapter has shown that young people are becoming less and less attracted by electoral politics over time. There are a number of different patterns here and the data, in some cases, prevents us from making any definitive statements. However, it is clear that young people in the US, Britain and Australia have become less likely to identify with a party over time. This should be concerning because 'partisan loyalties are a central element in an individual's belief system, serving as a source of political cues for other attitudes and behaviours' (Dalton, 2006, 179). Without this heuristic young people in particular are less likely to have their political behaviours and attitudes shaped by parties. This means that young people's attitudes and behaviour may become more erratic over time.

This data suggests the decline in party identification among the young is owing to generational effects. These findings support Abramson's (1983, 119) argument that 'the ongoing processes of generational replacement are the major dynamic that contributes to the erosion of party loyalties.' This is true not only of the US but of Britain and Australia as well. It also seems that pre-adult partisanship which was found to be transmitted from parent to child in the early socialization research (see Jennings and Niemi, 1974, 37) has broken down. Young people do not seem to be inheriting their parents' party identification and this could have a corrosive effect on electoral engagement in the future. These findings bring into question the future role of partisanship that was seen as so essential in early models of voter behaviour (Campbell *et al.*, 1960).

There is also other data which suggests that young people are becoming less and less enamoured with the electoral world. The UK Electoral Commission has written that parties seem to repel young people (Milner, 2010, 127). And this seems equally true of the other Anglo-American democracies. In regards to being a member of a political party the data shows that young people are not joining parties. We have clear evidence of generational declines in party membership in Britain and Canada. This is further evidence of the waning influence of political parties in shaping political participation. In line with this the data shows that young people are not contacting politicians. The blame cannot be put at the feet of young people alone, however. In regards to parties contacting citizens we saw that young people in the US, Canada and Britain are much less likely to be contacted by a party than young people 40 or 50 years ago, relative to their older counterparts.

Putnam and Inglehart and Welzel both argue that electoral engagement has decreased through the process of generational change. Putnam sees this as a symptom of a broader disengagement from public life among younger people. This is seen as a very negative development. Inglehart and Welzel see this change in very different terms. Inglehart and Welzel (2005) see a waning attachment to political parties as a product of young people's increased cognitive capacities which means they no longer have to be mobilized by hierarchical organizations (see Inglehart and Welzel, 2005). Therefore, Inglehart and Welzel (2005, 44, 116) are much more sanguine about the findings above. They argue:

> One the one hand, bureaucratized and elite-driven forms of participation such as voting and party membership have declined; but intrinsically motivated, expressive, and elite-challenging forms of

participation have risen dramatically.... Elite-led forms of participation are dwindling. Mass loyalties to long-established hierarchical political parties are weakening. No longer content to be disciplined troops, the public has become increasingly autonomous and elite challenging.

While Putnam sees this as a threat to democracy Inglehart and Welzel (2005, 253) interpret these trends, that young people are at the forefront of, 'as conducive to democracy.' I will return to the implications of these findings in terms of these theories in the next chapter.

Conclusion

This chapter has pointed to the waning importance of electoral politics for young people. This reflects generational effects. The importance of electoral politics that seems in the past to have been transmitted from parent to child seems to have broken down. On a number of different fronts young people are less electorally engaged than were young people 40 or 50 years ago. This is in line with Zukin *et al.*'s (2006, viii) argument in relation to the US that 'the generational chain has been broken, at least in the electoral realm.' The same could be said of the other Anglo-American democracies. However, it is important not to view these findings in isolation. In the next chapter I will analyse non-electoral forms of political participation so that we can compare levels of electoral engagement with levels of non-electoral political participation. At the end of the next chapter I will draw out the larger implications of this disenchantment with electoral politics among the young as it stands next to engagement in non-electoral forms of political participation.

5 Non-electoral forms of participation
A brighter picture?

As foreshadowed in the previous chapter, political participation can be defined in a number of ways. The previous chapter concentrated on electoral engagement and showed electoral engagement to be very low among the young. Yet, while there has been a steady secular erosion in electoral engagement the late twentieth century saw an expanding array of political activity that citizens are engaged in such as attending a demonstration and boycotting consumer products for political reasons. I have classified such activities as non-electoral forms of political participation. Hay (2008, 26) argues that 'A mounting body of recent research suggests that, far from being apathetic politically, a significant proportion of those who regard themselves as having disengaged entirely from formal politics are actively engaged in modes of informal yet collective political conduct.' Therefore, this chapter takes into account non-electoral forms of political participation in order to put the erosion in electoral engagement documented in the previous chapter in broader perspective.

This chapter evaluates the debate between those who argue that political participation is in decline (Putnam, 2000; Stoker, 2006) and those who argue that political participation is evolving with non-electoral forms of participation such as signing a petition or attending a demonstration becoming more common (Inglehart, 1997; Norris, 2002; Inglehart and Welzel, 2005; Dalton, 2008). What is important about these debates in relation to the young is that many scholars (Inglehart, 1997; Norris, 2003; Inglehart and Welzel, 2005; Zukin *et al.*, 2006; Dalton, 2011a) argue that it is the young who are driving the increase in non-electoral forms of participation whereas Putnam and others are much less sanguine. In light of these debates, this chapter will examine how engaged young people are in non-electoral forms of political participation. The data cited in this chapter also gives us entrée into a wider debate in regards to participatory inequalities that arise from non-electoral forms of activity which then allows us to explore one of the central concerns of this book: the future of electoral politics. I argue below that there is a dark side of modernization theory that many have overlooked in terms of underestimating the power of electoral politics.

The literature: non-electoral political participation

The previous chapter showed that young people have become less engaged in the electoral world in regards to identifying with a party and being party members. In Chapter 1 I showed that while turnout is not in secular decline among the young the volatility in voting patterns means that young people are markedly absent from some elections. Furthermore, young people have a very low level of civic duty. However, research that narrowly focuses on electoral forms of engagement may overlook non-electoral forms of political activity which are an important part of the overall story of political participation. In *Democratic Phoenix* Norris (2002) criticizes much of the comparative research for being excessively narrow in its conception of what constitutes political participation (see also Gauthier, 2003; Hooghe, 2004, 333; Dalton, 2008). Following on from the early work of Barnes and Kaase (1979), Norris (2002) argues that non-electoral forms of participation such as protesting, signing a petition and boycotting are often overlooked giving an unduly pessimistic picture of political participation. In line with this, Inglehart (1997, 231) also finds that petition signing has risen cross-nationally. For example, in the US those who reported having signed a petition rose from 58 per cent in 1974 to 71 per cent in 1990; in Britain the percentages rose from 22 per cent in 1974 to 75 per cent in 1990. These findings have been supported by a wealth of other research (see Dalton *et al.*, 2004, 124; Inglehart and Welzel, 2005, 122; Listhaug and Gronflaten, 2007, 294; Rucht, 2007; Blais, 2010, 175). Inglehart (1997, 231) goes so far as to argue that all of this amounts to 'dramatic evidence of rising mass political activism.'

Other research disputes this. Putnam (2000, 41) argues that Americans have become less likely to attend a demonstration over time. Rosenstone and Hansen's (1993, 63) study of the US found that signing of petitions decreased between 1973 and 1990. Stoker (2006, 35) also argues that very small numbers of people participate in politics beyond voting in Britain. Therefore, broadly speaking, we have Inglehart *et al.* on one side arguing participation is evolving and Putnam *et al.* on the other side arguing that political participation is declining.

All of this is particularly relevant to the young. In *Political Action* Marsh and Kaase (1979a, 59) argued that non-electoral forms of activity such as attending a demonstration may be particularly attractive to the young as they offer 'the kinds of satisfactions ... beyond those attainable through electoral pathways of political action.' Research has supported this proposition and the young have been found to be much more engaged in non-electoral activity in the Anglo-American democracies (see Norris, 2003; Vromen, 2003; Pattie *et al.*, 2004; Inglehart and Welzel, 2005; Zukin *et al.*, 2006; O'Neill, 2007, iii; Dalton, 2011a). Despite some evidence to the contrary (Putnam, 2000; Blais *et al.*, 2002; Gidengil *et al.*, 2003) the literature above suggests that non-electoral participation is becoming more widespread among the young. Norris (2002, 222) sums this literature up well when she writes that 'In postindustrial societies, the younger generations, in particular, have become less willing than their parents and grandparents to channel activities of their political energies through traditional agencies exemplified by parties and churches, and more likely to express themselves through' non-electoral participation. Therefore the literature suggests that young people will be more engaged in non-electoral participation across the Anglo-American democracies.

Measurement and definitional problems

In examining non-electoral forms of participation we are faced with two problems, one methodological and one definitional (although these two problems are not strictly separate). The main methodological problem is that unlike electoral engagement the national election studies that I have relied on predominantly up until now have only included non-electoral forms of participation in recent years and even then the question wording is not well suited to analysing young people. Where national election studies (such as the ANES in 2008) have asked about non-electoral participation they have not asked *when* respondents participated in a non-electoral activity or they have asked if the respondents have done these activities in the last five years. Questions worded in this way are heavily biased against young people. Older people may have participated in a demonstration in the 1960s and therefore respond that they 'have done' an activity whereas young people have had no opportunity to do so. The same applies to a lesser extent for questions that ask whether the respondent has done an activity in the last five years. Young people who may have recently turned 18 may not have had any opportunity to engage in non-electoral forms of activity. Unfortunately, the other survey that has asked about non-electoral forms of activity over time (the World Values Survey) has the same problem. The World Values Survey has in the past asked if respondents 'have done' an activity and in the more recent waves asked if respondents have done an activity 'in the past five years.' Therefore, any consistent time series data that we have is not well suited to analysing the young, a point that is rarely unacknowledged in much of the literature cited in this book (see especially Inglehart and Welzel, 2005).

There is however one data set which is better suited to analysing non-electoral political participation among the young. This is the 2004 ISSP Citizenship Survey which was used in Chapter 1 and the previous chapter. The ISSP has several advantages. The ISSP has asked about a wider range of activities than have other surveys. But more importantly it asked whether respondents had done these activities 'in the past year' so that responses are not biased against young people (especially those in early adulthood), some of whom have not yet had the opportunity to engage in non-electoral forms of participation.

90 *Political participation beyond voting*

In terms of non-electoral forms of participation that may be replacing electoral forms of participation the ISSP asked:

> Here are some different forms of political and social action that people can take. Please indicate for each one—'have not done it and never would do it,' 'have not done but might do it,' 'have done it in the more distant past,' 'have done it in the past year'
>
> Took part in a demonstration
> Signed a petition
> Boycotted or deliberately bought certain products for political, ethical or environmental reasons

The ISSP data allows us to take into account non-electoral forms of participation that have been said to be overlooked by scholars who have concentrated on electoral forms of participation. However, the ISSP data does not completely resolve this problem. In trying to measure and analyse non-electoral forms of participation we run into definitional problems. While the variables in the ISSP cover a wider range of activities than many other studies the boundary between political and civic engagement is not always clear (see Zukin *et al*., 2006, 52). Norris (2003, 5) points out that for many types of non-electoral participation the division between 'social' and 'political' breaks down. We can see this in terms of the question wording in the ISSP by which respondents are asked whether they 'Boycotted or deliberately bought certain products for political, ethical or environmental reasons.' This is a good example of the breakdown between the 'social' and the 'political.' Hay (2008, 75) argues that 'Consumer politics takes place outside of the governmental arena, yet responds to concerns which are formally recognized politically and on which there may well be active legislative and diplomatic agendas.'

Furthermore, many types of non-electoral participation are situational rather than generic (Norris, 2002, 194). As such, some important forms of engagement may be missed. 'Jane Junn notes that if Rosa Parks had been asked standard survey questions about her civic engagement, she would not have been able to mention her most famous political act: sitting in the front of a segregated bus' (Levine, 2007, 55).[1] Schudson (1998) also argues because politics infiltrates so many parts of life measuring 'political' participation is extremely difficult (see also Marsh *et al*., 2007).

How exactly we resolve these problems is not clear. One way is to follow the approach taken by Marsh *et al*. (2007) who conducted qualitative research examining young people's engagement with politics, broadly understood. But there remains a risk that we stretch the definition of politics so far as to empty 'the political/non-political distinction of any meaning, subsuming everything within the former category' (Hay, 2008,

77). At any rate, today there seems to be less agreement about where 'politics' begins and ends. It seems clear that what is defined as 'political' has broadened (as I argue below) and this poses particular problems for academics who write surveys (as I will elaborate on in the next chapter). While acknowledging these problems this chapter tries to take into account the variety of young people's political engagement first by examining a wide array of activity and second by using a data source that better captures young people's participation.

The data: non-electoral forms of participation

Protesting: taking part in a demonstration

Taking part in a demonstration is a non-electoral form of political participation that received attention in the early literature on non-electoral participation (Marsh and Kaase, 1979a; 1979b). Figure 5.1 shows the percentage of people who took part in a demonstration 'in the past year' by age. We can see here that young people were more likely than older people to have attended a demonstration in every country with significant age differences in each country. In Australia young people were three times more likely to have attended a demonstration 'in the past year' with 6 per cent of young people having attended a demonstration and just 2

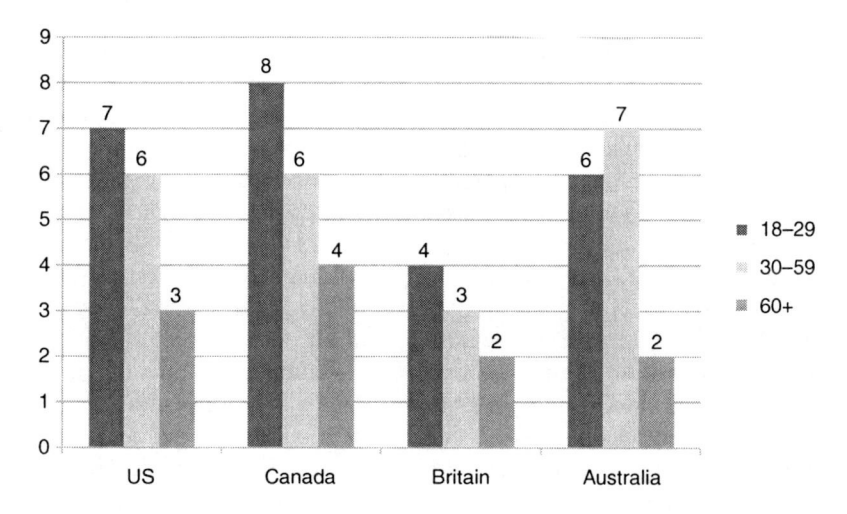

Figure 5.1 Attended a demonstration in past year (source: International Social Survey Programme Citizenship Survey 2004).

Note
Question wording: 'Here are some different forms of political and social action that people can take. Please indicate for each one—"have not done it and never would do it," "have not done but might do it," "have done it in the more distant past," "have done it in the past year": Took part in a demonstration.' Responses are 'done in past year.'

per cent of older people attending a demonstration. In the US young people were more than twice as likely than old people to have attended a demonstration. In the US 7 per cent of young people engaged in this form of activity as compared to just 3 per cent of older people. In Britain and Canada young people were twice as likely as older people to have attended a demonstration.

We can also see here that middle-aged people were also likely to have attended a demonstration and in the case of Australia were actually more likely to have attended a demonstration than young people, suggesting that protest has become more 'mainstream' (see Norris, 2011, 224). But protest has only become more mainstream in the sense that both middle-aged and younger people are engaged in this activity. In regards to the actual numbers of people engaged in protesting it is far from 'mainstream.' The results show that the overall numbers of people who took part in a demonstration are much lower than for other non-electoral forms of activity (as will be seen below). This may reflect the more demanding nature of attending a demonstration as opposed to signing a petition or boycotting a product which takes up much less time and effort. Overall, however, young people were at least twice as likely to have attended a demonstration as compared to older people.

Signing a petition

The second non-electoral form of political participation that I will analyse is signing a petition. Figure 5.2 shows the percentage of people who signed a petition 'in the past year' by age. We can see here that this is a popular form of non-electoral participation with in excess of one-quarter of respondents participating in this activity. This is in contrast to attending a demonstration where far fewer people participated in this activity overall. In regards to age related differences young people were more likely to have signed a petition than older people in every country except the US. The age gap is the largest in Canada where 53 per cent of young people signed a petition in the past year compared to 31 per cent of older people (representing a 22 percentage point difference). In Australia almost half of all young people (47 per cent) had signed a petition in the past year. This is compared to just over a third (35 per cent) of older people. In Britain the age difference is smaller with 35 per cent of young people having signed a petition and 28 per cent of older people signing a petition. It should also be added that while Figure 5.2 shows that signing a petition is more popular among the young than old in every country except the US young people are not particularly different in their behaviour from middle-aged people. Petition signing is also popular among this age group and, in the cases of the US and Britain, more popular among the middle-aged than young people. So it is clear that this form of activity has spread quite widely among the population (see also Pattie *et al.*, 2004, 77) in terms of its popularity.

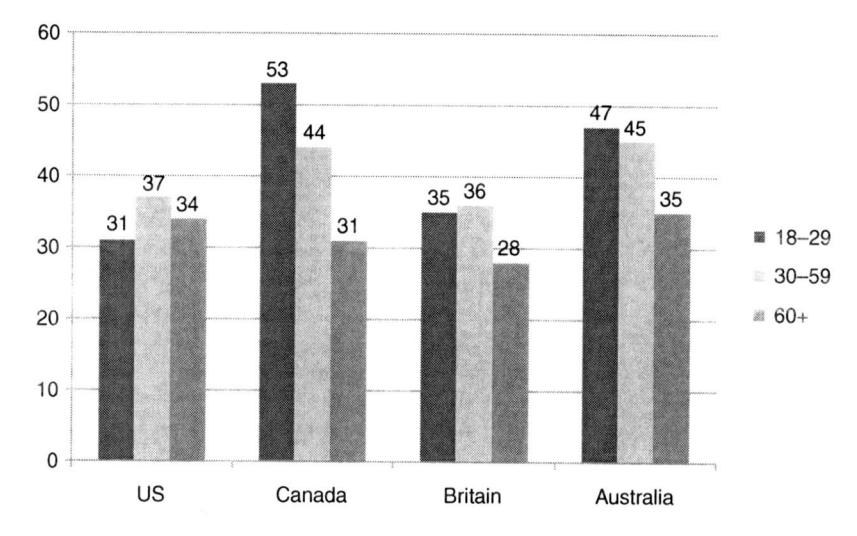

Figure 5.2 Signed a petition in past year (source: International Social Survey Programme Citizenship Survey 2004).

Note
Question wording: 'Here are some different forms of political and social action that people can take. Please indicate for each one—"have not done it and never would do it," "have not done but might do it," "have done it in the more distant past," "have done it in the past year": Signed a petition.' Responses are 'done in past year.'

Boycotting consumer products

Boycotting consumer products is another non-electoral form of activity that differs a great deal from electoral forms of participation. Zukin *et al.* (2006, 62) argued that 'The political use of consumer power attracts little scholarly attention but our surveys suggest that it is quite widespread.' Figure 5.3 shows the percentage that boycotted certain products for political, ethical or environmental reasons in the past year. Again the pattern here is similar to that in Figure 5.1 and Figure 5.2 with young people being more likely than older people to boycott a product in the past year in every country. In Canada young people were more than twice as likely to have boycotted a product than older people. In Australia the age gap is also very large with 40 per cent of young people boycotting a product but just 24 per cent of older people doing this. In the US and Britain the age gaps are much smaller. However, the young are less likely to boycott products than the middle-aged in every country expect Canada. This may reflect the differential opportunities young people have to boycott certain products whereas those in older age groups are more likely to have a more expendable income and shop at supermarkets more often than those aged 18–29. Figure 5.3 shows a similar pattern to that seen in the two previous figures. Young people were more likely to have boycotted a product in the past

94 *Political participation beyond voting*

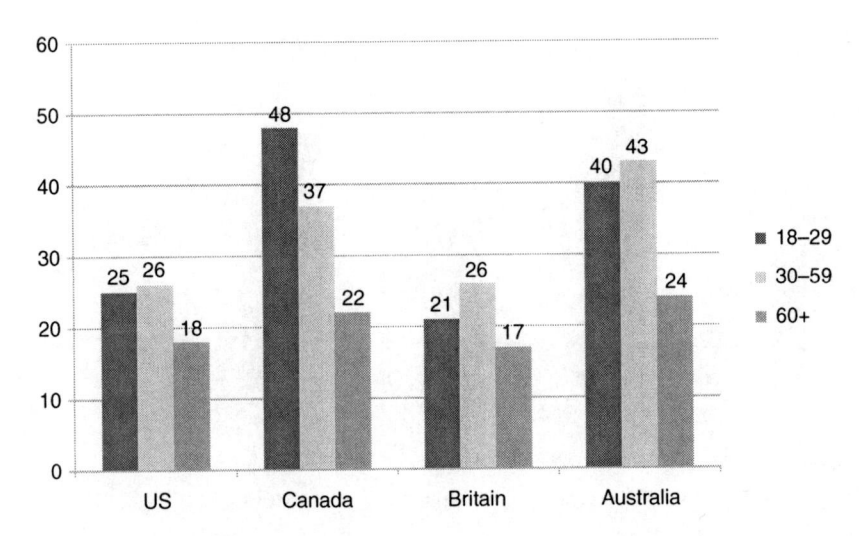

Figure 5.3 Boycotted consumer products in past year (source: International Social Survey Programme Citizenship Survey 2004).

Note
Question wording: 'Here are some different forms of political and social action that people can take. Please indicate for each one—"have not done it and never would do it," "have not done but might do it," "have done it in the more distant past," "have done it in the past year": Boycotted or deliberately bought certain products for political, ethical or environmental reasons.' Responses are 'done in past year.'

year than older people but this form of activity is clearly popular among the middle-aged as well which suggests that this form of activity is quite widespread (as found by Zukin *et al.*, 2006, 62). The data suggests that people 'in their day-to-day consumption behaviour are acting politically' (Pattie *et al.*, 2004, 77).

Discussion

Changing styles of political participation

If we take the findings of this chapter and Chapter 4 together we can see that while electoral engagement is becoming *less* popular among the young non-electoral forms of activity seem to be becoming *more* popular. Inglehart (1997, 233) writes: 'on the one hand the bureaucratized and elite-directed forms of participation ... have declined, and on the other ... individually motivated and elite-challenging forms of participation have risen.' The findings here support this view in regards to young people in the Anglo-American democracies. Young people's political participation seems very different from that of older people. While the available evidence precludes us from making any definitive statements the evidence from this chapter (seen in the context of other research) suggests that young people are at the vanguard of what is a change in styles of political participation. The findings also suggest that generational effects are at work by which young people are becoming more attracted to non-electoral participation and less attracted to electoral forms of engagement The process of generational replacement—as cohorts who are more likely to practice electoral forms of participation are replaced by those who are more likely to participate in non-electoral forms of political participation—could see non-electoral participation increase over time.

The non-electoral forms of participation that have been found to be much more popular among the young in this chapter take on a very different character from electoral engagement that is centred around political parties and social cleavages. These non-electoral forms of activity imply 'a culture characterized by the waning of broad socio-political movements for system change and an increase in limited, issue-based, and frequently regional ad hoc group actions that may well dissolve after the issue has receded' (Kaase and Marsh, 1979a, 49). Whereas political participation used to center around well institutionalized channels such as political parties and trade unions political activity among the young now seems to occur in a much more fluid way than before through groups that appear and disappear.

As to why young people are engaging in these non-electoral activities more than older people, non-electoral forms of participation seem to offer 'new possibilities for attaining political goals' (Fuchs and Klingemann, 1995b, 432) that have been taken up by the young. MacManus (1996, 119) found that young people were more likely to think of protest as a way of influencing government. This suggests that young people are engaged in activities like protest for instrumental rather than expressive reasons (supporting Fuchs and Klingemann, 1995b, 423). How effective protests are is, of course, another question. For every example of protest being effective (such as the 1992 public demonstrations in London which forced the government to back down on its plan to close down half the country's coal mines (see Birch, 1993, 260)) there is a counterexample of protest being ineffective (such as the anti-war protests in 2003).

Young people's involvement in non-electoral politics (and the broadening definition of political participation that has accompanied this) is also, arguably, a rational response to the perceived 'shrinkage of the state.' Globalization, through deregulation and privatization, is said to have shifted power away from the state and towards private and non-profit actors by which the state is said to have become 'less of a provider and more of a regulator' (Pattie et al., 2004, 11; see also Norris, 2002, 194; Zukin et al., 2006, 4). Accordingly, the salience of electoral politics may have been reduced in young people's minds. In this context it makes sense for young people to target multinational corporations and international organizations like the International Monetary Fund and World

Bank through non-electoral forms of participation. Young people's greater level of non-electoral participation is arguably 'consistent with an honest appraisal regarding where power increasingly lies in the contemporary world' (Zukin et al., 2006, 189). This is cognizant with young people's views. A survey in the US found that younger people see business as more powerful than government and thought business has more influence on their lives than government, as compared to older people who view things the other way around (Zukin et al., 2006, 115–17). Therefore, it should not be surprising that young people have changed how they participate politically. However, this view overlooks how important the state remains. It is hard to dispute the ongoing (although slightly diminished) importance of national governments (see Garrett, 1998; Bell and Hindmoor, 2009).

As argued above this shift in the nature of political participation creates measurement problems because as the line between public and private becomes increasingly porous it becomes even more difficult to disentangle public from private activity (see Schudson, 1998). This chapter, while attempting to capture as many types of political engagement as possible, has undoubtedly missed some forms of engagement as they relate to the arguments above—the next chapter, by looking at the Internet, attempts to further overcome this problem. However, what we can see is that young people's political participation does seem to be changing and this is occurring across the Anglo-American democracies.

Modernization theory: the positive

One very plausible explanation for young people's attraction to non-electoral politics concerns the transforming effect of education, as modernization theory as outlined by Inglehart and Welzel (2005) predicts. Young people today have much higher levels of education than did young people 50 years ago and this is likely linked to young people's increased propensity to engage in non-electoral forms of activity. It seems that resources such as education are making young people turn away from top down elite driven modes of participation such as joining a party and making young people more inclined to engage in activities that they have (or think they have) more control over such as attending a demonstration and signing a petition (see Inglehart and Welzel, 2005). Dalton (2006, 59) argues that 'an increasingly sophisticated and cognitively mobilized electorate is not likely to depend on voting and campaign activity as the primary means of expanding its involvement in politics.' Young people's cognitive resources mean they can act more autonomously vis-à-vis political participation. Young people don't have to rely on elite mobilization and have the ability to organize their own political activities (see Inglehart, 1997, 208). As more educated cohorts come of age and replace less educated cohorts it is likely that these non-electoral forms of participation will become more common, as modernization theory predicts.

The findings in this chapter are much more optimistic than those found in the previous chapter as this chapter has shown that young people are not tuned out of politics altogether and are more likely to be engaged in non-electoral forms of participation than older people. These findings support Inglehart's (1997, 23) rather optimistic conclusion that publics in advanced democracies are:

> less heavily influenced by the old-line oligarchical political organizations that mobilized them in the modernization era, but, far from being apathetic, these same publics are becoming more active in a wide range of elite challenging forms of political participation.

These findings could also be considered to be consistent with what Schudson (1998) has called the 'monitorial citizen.' Citizens who monitor (rather than read) the political environment could be mobilized into non-electoral participation when an issue stimulates them but remain passive at other times. Schudson (1998, 311) argues that the monitorial citizen is 'engaged in environmental surveillance more than information gathering. ... They look inactive, but they are poised for action if action is required.' In this regard, young citizens may look inactive at some times but active at others. This tendency may be more common among the young.

But I believe the optimism ends there. For two reasons: if modernization theory plays out in the way expected then participatory inequalities could become quite severe in the future and Inglehart *et al.* are more silent about this than they should be; and, second, modernization theory, in celebrating new forms of participation as an expansion of democracy, underplays the importance of electoral politics, and voting in particular. I deal with these two issues below.

The dark side of modernization theory: participatory inequalities

In the introduction of this book I outlined modernization theory as it features in the work of Inglehart and Welzel. Inglehart and Welzel (2005) argue that socioeconomic modernization, and increases in education in particular, allow citizens to act more autonomously in the political realm. However, these effects are unlikely to benefit all citizens and the role education plays in prompting different styles of participation raises questions about participatory inequalities. Activities such as signing a petition and boycotting products require a certain level of political knowledge and awareness. Furthermore, labour intensive forms of activity (such as attending a demonstration) require high levels of education and political interest. Therefore, the non-electoral forms of participation that have been shown to be more common among the young in this chapter are very likely to be attractive to the 'resource rich' (i.e. those with a higher level of education and stronger feelings of political interest and efficacy).

This has been confirmed by earlier research which shows that those who participate in non-electoral forms of participation tend to be drawn from more advantaged groups (Barnes and Kaase, 1979, 526; Norris, 1999b, 263; Dalton et al., 2004, 134; Pattie et al., 2004, 109; Verba et al., 1995, 2). The implication of this is that the voice of the 'people as expressed through participation comes from a limited and unrepresentative set of citizens ... the voices of citizens may be loud and clear, but they are decidedly not equal' (Verba et al., 1995, 2, 511). Therefore, while many types of political participation seem to be increasing (a point which Inglehart et al. celebrate) 'ironically, overall increases in political involvement may mask a growing social-status bias in citizen participation and influence, which runs counter to democratic ideals' (Dalton, 2006, 74). Given that non-electoral forms of participation are more common among the young this should be troubling.

This, historically, is a big shift from when electoral politics—largely centred around class based differences in which social background was a large determinant of party identification, vote choice and, to a lesser extent, other forms of electoral engagement—was more dominant. Whereas in the past parties have mobilized those with fewer resources of whom many, if the resource model dominated, would not get involved in politics, non-electoral forms of participation are much more attractive to the resource rich. Accordingly, if electoral forms of participation (that are the more equal) are declining and non-electoral forms (that are the most unequal) are increasing then resource inequalities could be exacerbated in the future. 'In other words, political voice may be in the center of a virtuous circle of capabilities for those advantaged in a society, but a vicious circle of capabilities for the disadvantaged' (Verba, 2003, 666). This applies particularly to the young. This is a real concern as political inequalities could be exacerbated through the process of generational replacement. Yet, modernization theory as espoused by Inglehart and Welzel has very little to say about this.

This would not matter so much if the 'resource rich' have the same preferences as the 'resource poor.' The question here is: what is the voice of the people as expressed through new forms of activity? In regards to non-electoral forms of activity there have been found to be vast differences between those who are active and those who are not (Verba, 1999, 23). Verba (1999, 23) argues that

> Those less active are groups with distinctive needs and preferences in relation to government policy. They are the more disadvantaged members of society: the poor, the less well-educated, racial and ethnic minorities. It is consequential that they are less active.

Therefore, there is a danger that the invisible will get less attention paid to them by policy makers. If more young people are completely inactive (as suggested below) then more young people may be ignored by policy makers.

With the expansion of activity there is also likely a gap opening up between those who are active and those who are not.

> Several studies have shown that there is a generalized propensity to be active or inactive, that all forms of participation are positively correlated with each other, that is, someone who votes is also more likely to be engaged in groups, to contact public officials, and even to march in the streets.
>
> (Blais, 2010, 178; see also Howe, 2010; Milner, 2010, 19)

If true, this means that non-electoral participation is not serving as a replacement to voting (as Inglehart and Welzel and others seem to imply) but rather as a supplement to voting. Therefore, the active get more active and the inactive remain inactive. Hay (2008, 27) argues that 'Many, especially young, citizens who have chosen either to engage or disengage, or never to engage in the first place, in formal politics are active in informal politics.... Whatever they are, they are not apathetic politically.' But this group is likely a very small one and this group hardly justifies the sanguine tone of Inglehart and Welzel's work. Research suggests that the number of inactives is actually increasing and that this subsection of citizens is comprised of the most poorly educated (see Zukin *et al.*, 2006; Milner, 2010, 41). Furthermore, Zukin *et al.* (2006) have pointed out that inactives are much more likely to be young. Given that the educated are more likely to be engaged in non-electoral participation 'This enduring inequality is troubling and should be cause for concern' (Blais, 2010, 182). Political participation may be expanding but the participatory inequalities that underlie this expansion should be concerning. This is what I call the dark side of modernization theory.

Political equality is a laudable goal seldom achieved. While the registering of preferences through the ballot box has proved hugely successful in equalising participation the same cannot be said for non-electoral forms of political participation that exacerbate resource inequalities. If, as argued in the previous chapter, electoral engagement among the young is decreasing and the use of non-electoral forms of participation are increasing, what we may see in the future is a landscape in which political inequality deepens and more and more of the resource poor are shut out of the political process altogether.

Voting matters

In Chapter 1 I argued that voting matters. Voting is still no doubt the most important activity that citizens engage in. Yet, the importance of voting is often underplayed by those celebrating the expansion of political participation beyond electoral channels. Inglehart (1997, 230) argues that 'voting turnout largely reflects the parties' ability to mobilize their supporters, and it is a misleading indicator of real interest and involvement.' This statement belies the importance of voting as an aggregating mechanism. As I argued in Chapter 1, voting alone matters more than any other single activity. It has a greater influence on the lives of more individuals than any other political activity. Elections, and the parties that take part in them, serve an unparalleled good. Citizens project an

> extraordinary (and often conflicting) range of demands and interests upon politicians and the parties are required to broker all of this into some kind of politically manageable and coherent form. This is an absolutely vital function. It is also why some of the attacks on party are badly misplaced.
>
> (Wright, 2003, 77)

Given the centrality of parties to political society it is concerning that so 'many analysts downplay the role of political parties and other traditional types of political organizations' (Milner, 2010, 5). For this reason Inglehart and Welzel and others should pay more attention to the potentially damaging effects that could follow from electoral politics becoming less important to the young in terms of young people's volatile voting patterns, low levels of civic duty, declining levels of party identification and declining levels of party membership.

That electoral politics is becoming less important to the young raises questions in regards to the future of electoral politics. Ralf Dahrendorf has stated that 'representative government is no longer as compelling a proposition as it once was. Instead, a search for new institutional forms to express conflicts has begun' (cited in Dalton *et al.*, 2004, 125). Young people seem to be driving this change and research by Zukin *et al.* (2006, 122), taken together with the findings in this book, suggests that many young people see electoral politics as irrelevant. As Zukin *et al.* (2006, 87) write, we 'may be witnessing a subtle but important shift in citizenship, away from a focus on government and elections as the mechanism for determining the public good and towards alternative avenues such as the private sector and the nongovernmental sector.'

Conclusion

Taken together, the findings of Chapter 4 and this chapter show clear differences between the young and old in regards to political participation.

Young people are turning away from electoral politics. As well as young people's low level of civic duty (as found in Chapter 1) young people are also less likely to identify with and join political parties. There is a very clear picture here that points to the waning attraction of electoral politics for the young. However, young people are much more likely to engage in non-electoral forms of activity. The process of modernization seems to have led, among the young in particular, to a 'more fundamental and long-lasting process of political change [that] is altering the style and content of mass politics' (Dalton, 1984, 281). Whereas the process of generation replacement will likely see electoral forms of engagement become less popular it is likely that non-electoral forms of political participation will increase in the future. This is all consistent with predictions made by Inglehart and Welzel.

However, this more optimistic picture should be seen in a broader context of worrying gaps opening up in regards to political equality. This is what I have called the dark side of modernization theory which has been overlooked in much of the literature. Furthermore, while the expansion of political activity should be celebrated the single most important political activity, voting—and the parties that contest elections—should not be overlooked. Liberal democracies require citizens who are active in both electoral and non-electoral politics and that some citizens have opted out of participation altogether (see Milner, 2010) should be concerning. Non-electoral participation cannot serve as a substitute for electoral participation. Voting and parties matter. Given this, in Chapter 7 I make some recommendations for how young people may be better engaged into electoral politics.

6 The Internet
Emerging new forms of participation

The evidence in Chapter 4 and Chapter 5 suggests that political participation among the young is changing with some forms of political participation declining and others increasing. The arrival of the Internet has added another channel through which citizens can participate in politics and the Internet 'has been viewed as both saviour and executioner of the current political system and its organizational infrastructure' (Ward and Gibson, 2009, 28). To optimists the Internet has the potential to revitalize political participation whereas others believe that 'Internet politics will disproportionately benefit the elite' (Norris, 2001, 13). These debates are particularly relevant to the young. The Internet could potentially be an important tool for political participation as communication technologies have been powerful in shaping political mobilization in the past (Chadwick, 2006, 114). Accordingly, it is important that new mass communications technologies such as the Internet are looked at in regards to the young. 'New forms of mass communication traditionally have had a great appeal for younger people' and young people 'are more willing to experiment with new technologies and formats' (Owen, 2006, 20). The way young people are using the Internet presently may give important clues as to young people's future political engagement.

This chapter examines to what extent the Internet is engaging young people in politics and examines the participatory distortions that may come as a result of this. This chapter explores Internet use from three perspectives. First, I examine whether young people are more likely to have engaged in political participation over the Internet. Second, I examine whether young people are more likely to use the Internet to communicate with others and find out about political matters in terms of joining a political forum or discussion group, forwarding messages with political content and visiting a political organization or candidate's website. I will then explore the Internet's potential to be used as a tool for mobilizing political activity around new social movements that often cross borders and defy conventional categorizations of political participation. In taking such an approach I am putting aside many other aspects of Internet politics. Furthermore, due to the newness and rapidly changing nature of the Internet this chapter is highly speculative, as is much of the literature. This is owing to the lack of data we have in regards to the Internet. However we can, at the very least, examine how young people are engaging in politics through the Internet and thus get a more complete picture of the diverse forms of young people's political participation.

The data used in this chapter

In examining young people's political engagement on the Internet we are confronted with severe limitations in terms of the data available. This book so far has examined various behavioural and attitudinal indicators of young people's political engagement. In doing so I have, for the most part, followed the traditional approach in the political behaviour literature. I have (with the exception of Chapter 5) been able to draw from survey questions that have been asked over a long period of time. This chapter turns to what is a much more novel instrument for political engagement: the Internet. Accordingly, the evidence is more patchy and the literature impressionistic. Because of how new the Internet is as a tool for political engagement we have to use various data sources outside of the national election studies that I have relied on most heavily up until this point. Unfortunately, 'Relatively few data account for the political uses of online sources by young people' (Owen, 2006, 25). Because of this lack of data, analysis in this chapter is confined to Australia and the US as comparable questions have been asked in these countries (in the 2011 ANUpoll in Australia and the 2006 Citizenship, Involvement, Democracy (CID) survey in the US).[1] Because the same questions were asked in these countries we can compare the data in regards to age related differences.[2] This chapter draws from these two surveys (the one exception to this is a question included in the ISSP Citizenship survey which asked citizens in Australia, Britain, Canada and the US whether they have joined a political forum or discussion group on the Internet). This chapter therefore draws on a more limited range of data in relation to the Anglo-American democracies in order to understand how young people are engaging with politics on the Internet.

The Internet as a tool for political participation

The following section examines whether the Internet is being used by young people as a tool for political participation. There is some evidence that young people are much more likely to participate in politics on the Internet in the US and Britain (Gibson et al., 2004, 5). Owen (2006, 20) also argues that 'there are indications that the Internet may be facilitating, if not invigorating youth civic engagement' (see also Zukin et al., 2006, 4). Young people were socialized at a time when political participation on the Internet was not considered all that novel. Therefore, we would expect the young to be more engaged in political participation on the Internet. In

104 *Political participation beyond voting*

the analysis below I examine how many young people in the US and Australia are engaged in political participation on the Internet.

In the 2006 CID survey and 2011 ANUpoll respondents were asked:

> And during the past year have you done any of the following: Participated in political activities over the Internet.[3]

Figure 6.1 shows the percentage of people who answered 'yes' in Australia and the US. Here we can see that in both Australia and the US young people were more likely than older people to have engaged in political activities over the Internet. In Australia young people were more likely than other age groups to have participated in political activities with 16 per cent of young people having done this as compared to 14 per cent of the middle-aged and 6 per cent of older people. In the US the pattern is a little different with 9 per cent of young people having done this, which is matched by middle-aged participation and 2 per cent of older people engaging in political activities over the Internet. Therefore, while we can say that young people are more engaged than older people in political activity on the Internet their activity rates are close to those of middle-aged respondents.

While Figure 6.1 shows that young people are much more likely than older people to participate in political activity over the Internet a major question is whether the Internet has actually engaged those that wouldn't otherwise be engaged? In other words, does the Internet have a mobilization or a reinforcement effect in regards to political participation? We

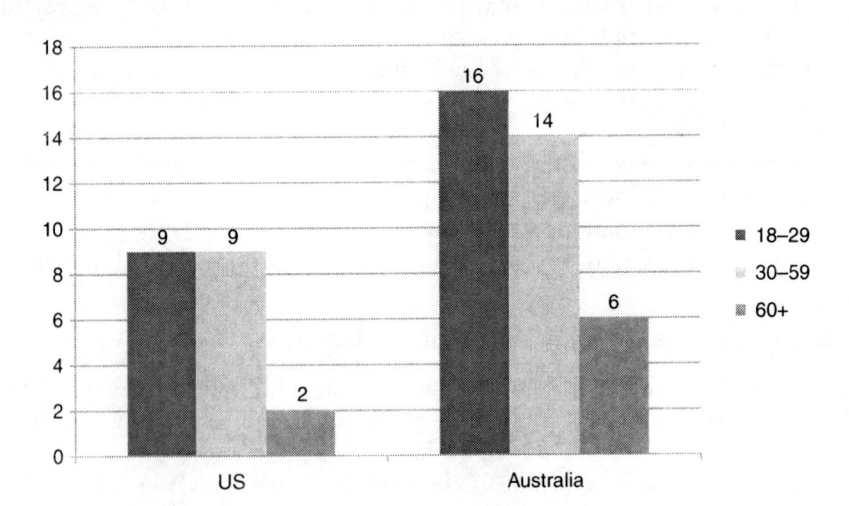

Figure 6.1 Participated in political activities over the Internet (sources: CID Survey and ANUpoll).

Note
Question wording: 'And during the past year have you done any of the following: Participated in political activities over the Internet.'

cannot answer this question with the available data. However, research suggests that the reinforcement effect is much more prevalent. Norris (2001, 238) argues that 'the Internet will largely serve to reinforce activism of the activists, facilitating participation for those who are already interested in politics.' In line with this argument research by Bimber (2003, 228) has shown that the Internet has not had an effect on overall levels of political participation (see also Ward and Gibson, 2009, 29). While some research has found that online activity stimulates non-electoral forms of political participation (Chadwick, 2006, 104) the Internet seems to be engaging the already engaged. If this interpretation is correct 'and if this situation persists as Internet use spreads and normalizes, it suggests that there will be a growing "democratic divide" in civic involvement ... the Internet may thereby function to increase divisions between actives and apathetics within societies' (Norris, 2001, 231; see also Gibson et al., 2004, 3). While this may change in the future at present it seems that the Internet is having a negligible effect on young people's overall level of political participation.

The Internet as a tool for political communication and political information

This section analyses how young people use the Internet as a means of political communication and informing themselves about political matters in terms of joining a political forum or discussion group on the Internet, forwarding messages with political content and visiting a political organization or candidate's website. These three types of activity are all low cost in terms of what is expected of the participant. However, the data will tell us something about the extent to which young people are using the Internet to contact and communicate with others and find out more about politics which may in turn have an effect on young people's political participation.

The way young people become informed and communicate with others on the Internet is very different than for generations past. Whereas with traditional media the individual is a passive recipient of news the Internet 'cedes information control to the individual consumer, who can actively search out the desired information and can edit and collate the relevant news sources' (Ward et al., 2003, 4). This seems particularly attractive to the young. 'Evidence suggests that young people are more likely than older citizens to use web-based platforms to carry out research and gain political information' (Pew Research Center, 2003 cited in Owen, 2006, 21). Vromen (2008, 94) also argues that the Internet has created a new deliberative space for young people.

In order to test these ideas the analysis below examines three different types of communication and information seeking on the Internet (joining a political forum or discussion group on the Internet, forwarding messages

106 *Political participation beyond voting*

with political content and visiting a political organization or candidate's website). It is reasonable to expect that the young will be more likely to be engaged in these activities. The important question, however, is how many young people are engaged in these activities.

I begin with joining a political forum or discussion group on the Internet. In the ISSP Citizenship survey respondents were asked:

> Here are some different forms of political and social action that people can take. Please indicate for each one—'have not done it and never would do it,' 'have not done but might do it,' 'have done it in the more distant past,' 'have done it in past year': Joined an Internet political forum or discussion group.

Figure 6.2 shows those who have participated in this form of activity in the past year. Here we can see that young people in Canada were most likely to have joined a political forum or discussion group with 9 per cent of young people having done this in the past year, in the US 7 per cent of young people had done this in the past year and in Australia and Britain 6 per cent of young people had done this. Compared to older people the age gaps are very large with young people being at least twice as likely to have done this as compared to older people. There are also quite large age gaps between the young and middle-aged in Australia, Britain and, to a lesser

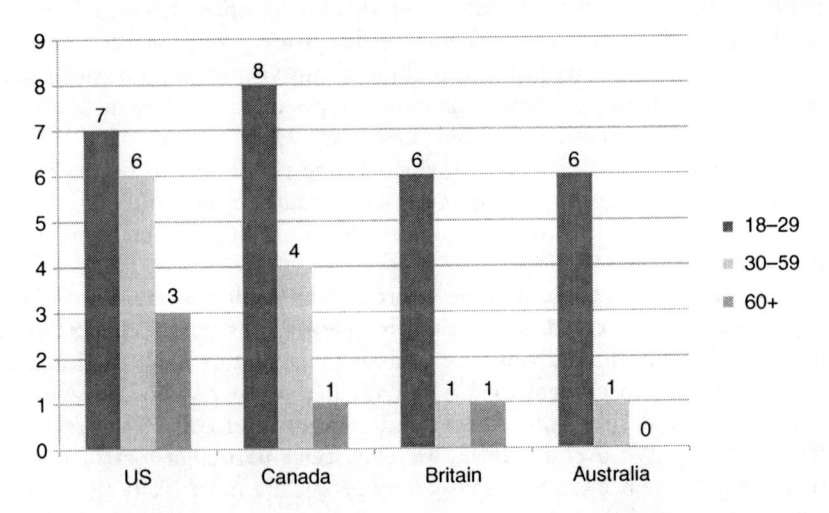

Figure 6.2 Joined a political forum or discussion group on the Internet in past year (source: International Social Survey Programme Citizenship Survey 2004).

Note
Question wording: Here are some different forms of political and social action that people can take. Please indicate for each one—"have not done it and never would do it," "have not done but might do it," "have done it in the more distant past," and "have done it in the past year": Joined an Internet political forum or discussion group.' Responses are done 'in past year.'

Political engagement on the Internet 107

extent, in Canada. Therefore, it is clear that young people are more likely to join a political forum or discussion group. This question does indicate some commitment to political communication on the Internet as opposed to, for example, just seeking political news on the Internet or being an online member showing less commitment. However, it is impossible to say anything about the quality of political discussion on political forums or discussion groups. Regardless of this the low number of people overall who are engaged in this activity creates no impression of the Internet as a common deliberative space with percentages among any group never exceeding 10 per cent.

Another form of communication is forwarding a political message on the Internet. The 2006 CID survey and the 2011 ANUpoll asked respondents in the US and Australia:

> And during the past year have you done any of the following: Forwarded electronic messages with political content.

Figure 6.3 shows that greater numbers of people have participated in this activity (probably owing to the low cost of this form of communication). However, despite the greater numbers of people overall who are engaged in this form of activity young people are actually *less* likely to be engaged in this activity than middle-aged people. In the US, 12 per cent of young

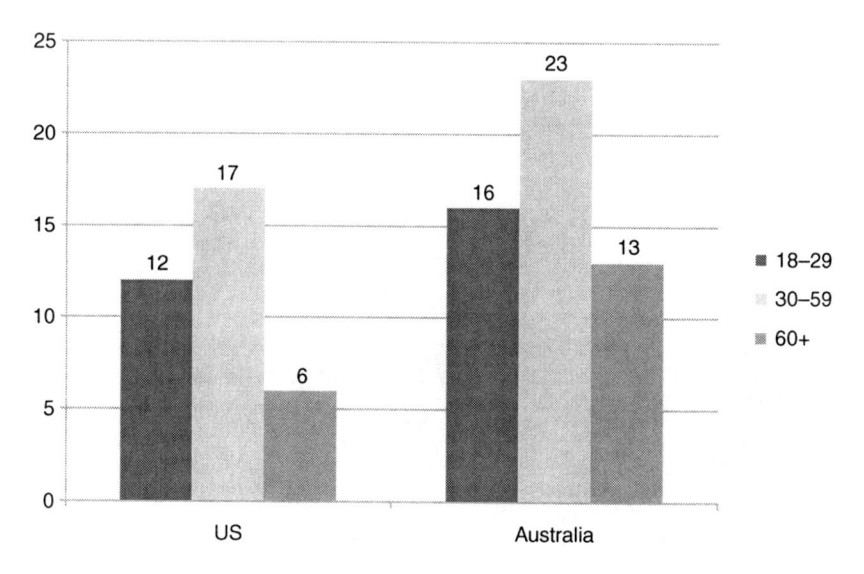

Figure 6.3 Forwarded political messages on the Internet (sources: CID Survey and ANUpoll).

Note
'And during the past year have you done any of the following: Forwarded electronic messages with political content.'

108 *Political participation beyond voting*

people had forwarded a message whereas 17 per cent of middle-aged people had engaged in this form of activity. In Australia the respective numbers are 16 and 23. Young people are however more likely to be engaged in this activity than older people. However, the relatively small numbers of people overall who are engaged in this activity (which is almost cost free) does not bode well for the Internet becoming a deliberative space in which those who were not previously engaged become engaged.

The final question in this section concerns whether or not young people seek political information on the Internet by visiting a political organization or candidate's website. The 2006 CID survey and the 2011 ANUpoll asked respondents in the US and Australia:

> And, during the last 12 months, have you done any of the following?: Visited websites of political organizations or candidates

The Internet shows potential for improving political knowledge among the young through this type of activity with young people being much more likely to have visited a political organization or candidate's website. In Australia 40 per cent of young people have done this in the past year—the largest percentage of any activity analysed in this chapter. Young people in Australia are much more likely to have done this than middle-aged people (27 per cent) and older people (13 per cent). The age

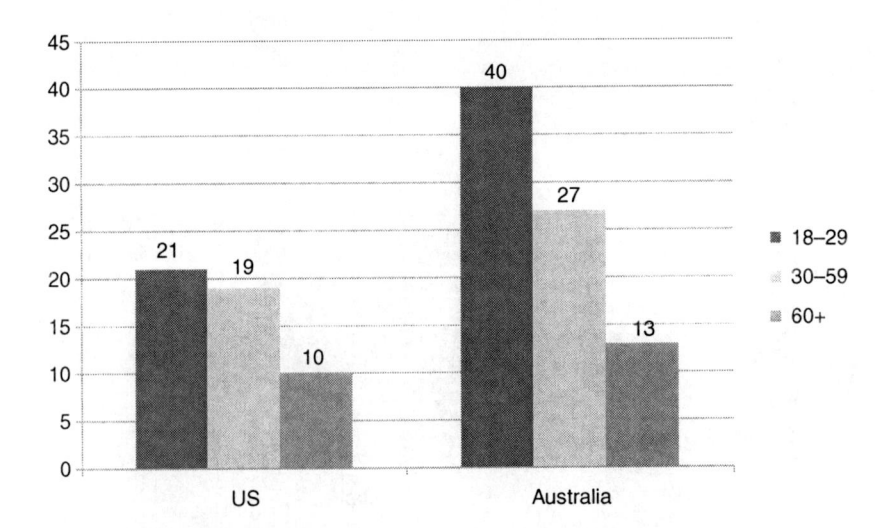

Figure 6.4 Visited website of political organization or candidate (sources: CID Survey and ANUpoll).

Note
Question wording: 'And, during the last 12 months, have you done any of the following?: Visited websites of political organizations or candidates.'

pattern is similar in the US: 21 per cent of young people have visited a political organization or candidate's website whereas 19 per cent of middle-aged people and 10 per cent of older people have done this. It is impossible to say anything about the nature of these website visits nor whether this serves as a substitute or supplement for engagement with traditional media. However, the findings here do suggest that the Internet clearly is playing some role in improving young people's political knowledge.

What are the consequences of this communication and information seeking taken as a whole? While the data above cannot answer this question we can draw from other literature to gain a better understanding of the consequences of the Internet as a political communication and information seeking medium. Chadwick (2006, 26) argues that 'it seems clear that a new form of online campaigning based on more interactive forms of communication, particularly blogs, creates a different sort of environment—one which appears to have lowered levels of apathy and increased citizen participation.' Further, a Spanish study found that Internet use (controlling for education) increased political knowledge (Milner, 2010, 66).

However, others are sceptical about electronic peer groups as a means for revitalizing political participation. Milner (2010, 50) argues:

> There is good reason to be cautious in our expectations of electronic peer groups. Changes in information technology make it possible for young persons with the necessary skills and resources to create virtual peer groups. But these are detached from a community framed by geographical and political boundaries, and thus unsuited for supplying the community-based information and skills relevant to becoming an effective citizen.

This concern relates to Putnam's (2000) argument that what matters most is face-to-face contact. But could the Internet create social capital through electronic networks? Nie and Erbring (2000, 26) found that 'Netizens' were 'home alone and anonymous' (cited in Chadwick, 2006, 103). The research suggests then that there is a gulf between those who are participating in online discussion groups or forwarding political messages and those engaged in dealing with local and national politics through traditional means. This has been said to be one of the disappointments with electronic democracy. Chadwick (2006, 91) argues that

> this dislocation between the social or community building aspects of virtual communities and the larger context of political life, which involves real-world institutions such as parties, interest groups, and legislatures, has arguably been proved the fatal weakness in most e-democracy experiments to date.

Similarly, Ward and Gibson (2009, 30) argue that 'One may join organizations online but without the real-world connections to other supporters or local connections to other supporters of local networks the net is more likely to encourage a passive chequebook membership with limited long-term ties.' According to these views Internet forums hinder rather than help political engagement. However, as I will argue in the next section, the Internet does show some potential as an instrument to engage the young in transnational political networks.

The Internet as a tool for mobilization

In this section I analyse the extent to which the Internet may be used as a mobilization device by NGOs, protest organizations and other groups. While we lack data on the extent to which young people are being mobilized into social movements via the Internet the section below examines how the Internet may mobilize young people in particular into social movements by piecing together various strands of research.

In the previous chapter I argued that non-electoral forms of political participation are particularly attractive to the young. The sorts of issues that non-electoral forms of participation (such as consumer boycotts) are aimed at are not always those centred around partisan politics or national issues which consume a lot of air time in the conventional media. Rather, young people are engaging in politics in a different way in relation to a broad range of issues. For example, non-electoral political participation is often aimed at global concerns such as free trade or sweatshop working conditions. The Internet has significant potential to mobilize young people into participation around these sorts of issues. This is because the Internet can be used as a communication and mobilization device by social movements and NGOs. The Internet as a medium allows for disparate groups of individuals to connect with one another. Chadwick (2006, 29) argues:

> It is through decentralized and flexible linkages that individuals come to form political alliances, often across national boundaries, in ways that cut across diverse campaigns and causes. The Internet allows for mobilization based upon these diverse and fragmented political identities, as individuals join many more groups and movements in the online world than they would ever consider offline.

It seems that these sorts of linkages are more attractive to the young. Owen (2006, 21) argues that young people 'have been forming issue-based organizations online as a means of expressing their concerns.'

In her book *Digital Divide* Norris (2001, 19) argues that 'digital technologies have the capacity to strengthen the institutions of civic society mediating between citizens and the state.' The Internet, according to Norris (2001), will give NGOs, protest organizations, alternative social movements and minor parties greater capacity and hence level the playing field of political competition. The innovation that the Internet affords organizations is much more common among new rather than established organizations. The Internet lessens communication costs and allows easier access to official sources (Norris, 2001, 20). New technology also makes raising money and email campaigns more efficient (Ward and Gibson, 2009, 28). Accordingly, 'Information and communication technologies have been viewed as a means of attracting additional supporters for political organizations and diversifying the social base of membership, bringing new life to traditional political organization but also sustaining new political forms' (Ward and Gibson, 2009, 28). According to these views the Internet helps new social movements and protest organizations by enhancing their communication and networking capacities. This gives these organizations the ability to disrupt politics as usual through flash campaigns like the World Trade Organization (WTO) protests in Seattle in 1999 at which young people were heavily represented.

There are many examples of the Internet being used as a tool for mobilization. Chadwick (2006) uses the Environmental Defense Fund (EDF) in the US as an example of the potential of the Internet to reorientate and reconfigure civic society organizations.[4] The EDF was set up in 1967, had a staff of 170, membership of 300,000 and an annual 24 million dollar budget. In the past it had concentrated on litigation and lobbying at the legislative level but in recent years has reinvented itself using the Internet as a tool for mobilization. In 1999 the group created a website and slimmed its core staff to 20. It used the website to find out what members were concerned about, then focused on a set of core themes like pesticides and clean air. The organization reached out in its information campaigns to beyond its members, and drew on non-paying affiliate members to send emails and faxes on particular issues. The EDF also collaborated with other groups like the Sierra Club (Chadwick, 2006, 120). Chadwick (2006, 120) argues that:

> This example illustrates how traditional, even staid groups are changing their internal organization and building new networks among previously untapped reservoirs of citizen support. It suggests the ways in which Internet technologies facilitate the bridging of organizational boundaries, often in very short periods of time, for the sake of a particular campaign. By reorganizing their efforts in this way, some groups are able to reduce costs and increase organizational flexibility.

Transnational advocacy is also an area where the Internet has significant mobilization potential. 'Transnational advocacy networks have been among the most active organizations taking advantage of the web for mobilizing, publicity, and interaction' (Norris, 2001, 171). For the reasons outlined above it is now much easier for these organizations to reach a global audience. The Internet also allows transnational advocacy networks to lobby 'elected representatives, public officials and policy elites; networking with related associations and organizations; mobilizing organizers, activists, and members using action alerts, newsletters and emails. and communicating their message via the traditional media' (Norris, 2001, 186).

It is not surprising then that transnational organizations have used this medium so effectively. A number of studies have shown the ad hoc protest groups have benefited from the organization that the Internet allows them (Gibson et al., 2004, 10). 'The Internet has facilitated the rise of new, virtual, global protest networks, such as Avaaz.org, which focuses on global justice issues, organizes around Internet tools, and targets multinational companies' as well as groups like the Jubilee 2000 campaign to end developing world debt who have 'used the web and e-mail to provide information and campaign material to activists' (Ward and Gibson, 2009, 29, 30). Other examples include the 'anti-sweatshop movement against Nike, initially coordinated by an online network, Global Exchange; the anti-genetically modified foods campaign aimed at Monsanto; and the global campaign against Microsoft, largely coordinated online by an alliance named Netaction' (Chadwick, 2006, 30). The Internet, as mentioned earlier, also played an important role in organizing the protests in Seattle in 1999 and anti-war protests in 2003 (Gibson et al., 2004, 11). Some of these campaigns may be temporary and have little success but others that have a significant online component have had more success like the International Campaign to Ban Landmines which resulted in a treaty signed by 122 nations in 1997 (Norris, 2001, 21).

Yet, while the tone of much of this literature (and the discussion above) is very positive, measuring the strength and scope of these organizations and the extent to which young people are being mobilized by these groups poses methodological difficulties. Chadwick (2006, 123) uses the example of MoveOn as a new type of hybrid organization, the type of which poses challenges in terms of our conceptual understanding of these organizations as well as related issues of measurement. MoveOn was established in 1998 and campaigned against the attempt to impeach President Clinton. MoveOn then broadened its focus. It helped organize many anti-war protests in 2003 in the US and around the world. MoveOn supported John Kerry's campaign for President and raised money from its 2.1 million email supporters including $750,000 in one day in May 2004 (Chadwick, 2006, 123). But what sort of organization should it be classified as? It is not a traditional interest group, it has a very small core staff, it avoids outright political alignment, often lobbies members of Congress as a lobby group would, has no single constituency and no fixed annual membership fee (Chadwick, 2006, 123). Chadwick (2006, 124) writes that 'It is difficult to escape the conclusion that MoveOn is a genuinely novel form of hybrid political organization.'

But how do we measure this type of organization? If MoveOn has no official members then online members may or may not identify themselves as such in surveys. And what about organizations that are more transient and/or unable to continue because they lack organizational capacity (Ward and Gibson, 2009, 37)? If participation is becoming more segmented and transient, as this chapter suggests, this poses measurement issues. If young people are disproportionately active in these new types of organizations then traditional survey questions may miss these new types of activity. If this is correct, then young people may be depicted (using standard survey data sources) as more disengaged than they actually are. It should come as no surprise then that less formalized political organizations such as MoveOn 'whilst attracting considerable media coverage have gained less coverage from academic surveys. In part, this reflects a methodological problem of how to study rather amorphous, often anonymous and rapidly changing protest campaigns' (Gibson et al., 2004, 10). If this trend continues and political parties become less important to young people and amorphous and anonymous organizations become more popular writers of surveys are going to have to come to terms with this and build in measures which may better capture more ephemeral forms of participation.

Discussion

Political participation on the Internet

This chapter has shown that young people (in the US and Australia) are more likely than older people to be engaged in political participation on the Internet. However, the numbers of citizens who are engaged in political activity on the Internet is quite small: 16 per cent of young people engaged in political activity over the Internet in Australia and just 9 per cent of young people engaged in political activity over the Internet in the US. But perhaps more important than *how many* citizens are participating is *who* is participating. Is the Internet filling in some of the participatory gaps that have been found in previous chapters? While we cannot make any definitive conclusions the answer to that question would have to be a tentative no. 'For the most part, research findings on the Internet and political participation have confirmed the rich get richer hypothesis. ... These tendencies help to explain why the Internet has exerted little effect on individual level political participation' (Brundidge and Rice, 2009, 154; see also Bimber, 2003; Margolis, 2009). There is some research which challenges this view. Mossberger (2009, 175) argues that 'Internet politics increases political participation among the young.' But this view is difficult to square with what we already know about the participatory inequalities inherent in Internet participation. Thus, the more educated and politically interested (i.e. precisely those who would participate in politics regardless of the Internet) are the group most likely to be politically engaged on the Internet.

That is not to say that participation on the Internet is not a good thing. Digital politics 'contributes toward the vitality of representative democracy' by giving those interested in politics another channel to have their voice heard on issues, for example, like global environmental concerns (Norris, 2001, 22). It also allows young people to create their own content (see Vromen, 2008, 94). But as a tool for equalizing participation it 'largely bypasses the disengaged' (Norris, 2001, 22). Overall, 'the literature suggests that the Internet has not yet lived up to its potential as an instrument of youth political involvement' (Milner, 2010, 73). The data simply does not support the view that the Internet has transformed political participation at a broad level. At present the Internet engages relatively few young people to participate politically.

This could change over time. Although the already politically interested are most likely to engage in political activity on the Internet (see Gidengil et al., 2003) there is the possibility that as parties and politicians become more adept at using new technologies more young people may be brought into this web and therefore become more politically active. Parties and politicians at present don't seem to be using the Internet as effectively as they could with web based mobilization being under-developed. However, where parties and politicians have used web based mobilization more strategically this has been shown to be effective. For example, in the 2008 US election Barack Obama was very effective in using online activities to mobilize young people. In the 2008 campaign Obama had an email list of 13 million names (Milner, 2010, 74) many of whom must have been young people. A film clip supporting Obama featuring will.i.am (of pop group Black Eyed Peas fame) became the most watched political clip on YouTube and was seen around 15 million times (Milner, 2010, 73). Presumably, a portion of the young people who were mobilized would not have been mobilized absent the effectiveness of online mobilization in the 2008 campaign. The Internet in this instance may be increasing political activity and interest among a portion of young people. To what extent this will have any long term implications is hard to say.

Political community on the Internet

While the Internet does not seem to have increased the overall level of political participation among the young has the Internet reinvented political community in terms of political forums and discussion groups? Much of the early debate surrounding the Internet and its potential to improve political literacy through online discussion and deliberation has centred on theories of direct democracy. According to this line of thinking 'The Internet forms a global network, free from centralized control with intrinsically empowering characteristics—cost-less, space-less and timeless. As the barriers to mass-communication were eroded citizens could participate more fully in decision making' (Gibson et al., 2004, 1; see also Barber, 1984).

However, such views in regards to online political forums and the like have proved too optimistic. This chapter has shown that participating in a political forum or discussion group and forwarding messages with political content is much more common among the young but is still limited to small minorities of young people in the countries for which we have data. In regards to visiting the website of a political organization or candidate the evidence is more positive. However, before citizens visit political websites they generally need 'preexisting knowledge and some degree of political interest' and many visitors to political websites are already politically active (Ward and Gibson, 2009, 29). Overall, there is little evidence here of the Internet creating a new deliberative space for young people who are not otherwise engaged in politics.

Political mobilization on the Internet

An area where there is greater cause for optimism is the Internet as a mobilization tool for social movements and other protest groups. In regards to social movements we have less data but there seem to be good reasons to be more optimistic. This chapter has shown that the Internet has made possible various types of protest such as the WTO protests in Seattle in 1999 and the anti-war protests around the world in 2003 in which young people were heavily represented. The Internet levels the playing field by giving non-elite organizations organizational capacities that they did not have in the pre-Internet age. This is significant because many of the concerns of young people centre not around political parties but rather other issues such as global environmental concerns and trade practices of multinational companies. Social movements give young people an opportunity to voice their grievances in regards to this. Furthermore, the Internet has served as a catalyst for transformation of groups like the Environmental Defense Fund which can mobilize young people through specific campaigns.

Measurement issues and defining political participation

To what extent young people are being mobilized in these sorts of activities is difficult to measure. In the previous chapter we saw that young people are more likely than older people to attend a demonstration and sign a petition. However, there are other forms of participation that are much harder to capture through standard survey questions such as young people's involvement in groups such as MoveOn. Many types of activity on the Internet are transient by nature. Therefore, standard survey research questions may overlook some types of political engagement by the young that the Internet is facilitating.

Bimber *et al.* (2009, 74) argue that 'the landscape of political organization and collective action shows change. ... These developments raise a number of theoretical questions about how organizations are conceptualized and categorized.' This point relates to a broader methodological challenge we face when studying the Internet. How exactly do we define 'political participation' on the Internet? Are political acts that academics have in mind when they write surveys the same ones respondents have in mind? And does this differ by age? For example, does forwarding a message urging others to boycott a particular company for their labour practices constitute an act of political participation? Some may deem this to be a 'political' act whereas for others it is not. Therefore, how survey questions are understood is likely to differ by respondent. This is true of many survey questions but poses particular problems in regards to the Internet.

And this all relates to a broader point of the blurring barrier between electoral politics and lifestyle politics. Post-industrialization theory sees the bypassing of traditional institutions in which 'individual political identity derives not from relatively fixed, collective institutional sources but is increasingly a matter of self-expression and lifestyle choice' so that politics is now intertwined with activities that were not regarded as political in the past (Chadwick, 2006, 29). All of these points suggest that tying down activity on the Internet conceptually is very difficult in relation to how we have understood political participation in the past. Studying these questions is important because young people are at the vanguard of new types of participation that the Internet allows (as this chapter with its brief sketch has suggested).

Participatory inequalities and a further shift to non-electoral participation

This chapter has suggested that the participatory inequalities which have been highlighted in the previous chapters are even more prevalent in regards to participation and communication on the Internet. It is difficult, at this early stage, to disagree that the Internet 'is a wonderful vehicle for citizens who are already interested in politics' (Margolis and Resnick, 2000, 22). The previous chapter showed that those activities in which the young are more engaged in are precisely those that require greater resources. The same seems true of the Internet. Online forms of political engagement may worsen political inequality by making those who are already engaged more effective, while leaving others on the sidelines (Levine, 2007, 97). Participatory inequalities seem likely to be exacerbated in the future and this is concerning as it regards political equality which has been raised as on ongoing concern throughout this book.

The Internet also seems likely to signal a greater shift to non-electoral participation, as spelt out in the previous chapter. For example, very few social movements on the Internet are aimed at traditional party political concerns such as redistribution. Therefore, the Internet is likely to exacerbate the trend in non-electoral politics of single issues becoming more important. Electoral politics is centred on issues of importance to a wide range of people (such as the health and welfare systems) and it is unlikely that these sorts of issues are going to lose their salience. However, the Internet, by creating an avenue for more single-issue groups, may expand the political space in which more groups are competing for the same amount of resources. If those active on the Internet are able to achieve their goals then others (who are less active) may get less of whatever they got from the political process in the first place. This may diminish the power of electoral politics to serve collective interests.

The Internet does have the ability to complicate governance in the future. Margolis and Resnick (2000, 211) argue that 'so far there is little evidence that initiatives organized through the Internet to have government adopt significant new policies or alter existing ones have been successful.' However, if Internet participation becomes more common this may change. But new strategies will likely be targeted at new issues which may not serve collective interests. Because of minute levels of personalization that the Internet allows 'This creates a radically individualized environment in which it is more difficult for policy makers to count on a coherent national, or even local, political community that it can assume has been exposed to broadly similar media content' (Chadwick, 2006, 8). Will the Internet weaken or reinforce existing power structures? The answer to that question will have important implications.

Conclusion

The conclusion of this chapter is slightly unsatisfactory because we have to end on the note of: 'we'll wait and see.' The evidence we have in regards to the Internet means any statements made must remain tentative. It is clear that the Internet is being used more by the young as a tool for political participation, communication and mobilization and that this trend reflects generational effects. But beyond that any conclusions are difficult to make. 'Thus, the micro-level data on the Internet's impact on participation, while it is abundant and growing, is at present, somewhat inconclusive' and it is too early to assess the long term impacts of the Internet (Gibson *et al.*, 2004, 5). This is compounded by the fact that 'Internet politics is a fast-moving field characterized by uncertainty, paradox, overstatement and understatement' (Chadwick, 2006, 326). While the optimism about Internet mobilization in the 1990s has been replaced by pessimism in the 2000s (partially confirmed by this chapter which found low levels of activity in political participation and discussion on the Internet by the young) this chapter has pointed to new types of organizations like the EDF which are both novel and successful (Chadwick, 2006, 142). In the next chapter I will make some suggestions as to how the Internet (among other things) may be used to better engage the young in the political process.

Part IV
What can be done?

This final chapter offers some policy recommendations in terms of better engaging young people in the political process by evaluating the potential effectiveness of civic education reforms, elite mobilization, easing registration requirements and changing the electoral system, as well as briefly considering other possible reforms. I pay particular attention to voting as this has been argued to be the most important aspect of political engagement.

7 Policy reforms

This chapter turns to what is often one of the hardest questions in political science: what can be done? In this chapter I examine the potential effectiveness of four reforms aimed at increasing political engagement among the young: civic education reforms, elite mobilization, easing registration requirements and changing the electoral system, as well as briefly considering other possible reforms. The reforms suggested all come from different positions in regards to how citizens may become more politically engaged. Civic education programmes are based on individuals gaining greater efficacy and appreciation of democracy through education programmes. Elite mobilization is based on young citizens being mobilized by political elites who use mobilization as a strategic resource. Registration reforms on a very basic level make it easier for individuals to vote by lowering any administrative hurdle that may prohibit young people from voting. Electoral system reforms change the calculus of political participation.

The follow up question to 'what can be done?' may be: 'about what?' This chapter will pay particular attention to electoral politics. This focus is based on young people's low level of attachment to electoral politics as expressed through volatile voting patterns, low civic duty, declining levels of party identification and declining levels of party membership. Particular attention is paid to increasing voter turnout because voting is the *sine qua non* of political activity in aggregating interests in a democratic way, as well as reducing participatory inequalities. Even in countries such as the US where turnout has recovered in recent years increasing turnout should be at the top of the list of priorities in terms of policy interventions. This chapter also considers the possible effect of reforms on political engagement more broadly.

The aim of this chapter is to both evaluate and categorize various policy reforms thus giving form to what is a rather unwieldy literature. Regardless of overall levels of political engagement among the young, finding out more about what reforms may increase young people's political engagement should be an important priority for social scientists. This chapter will examine whether policy makers can pull certain levers to increase young people's political engagement or whether the means to do this are outside

122 *What can be done?*

of their control. In doing these things this chapter will provide a more coherent way to think about policy reforms as well as analysing how feasible these reforms are.

Policy reforms aimed at the young

Civic education: will increasing knowledge increase political engagement?

One of the most common explanations for young people's low level of political engagement is young people's lack of knowledge about and therefore appreciation of democracy and the right to vote (i.e. young people are not politically engaged because they are not informed about politics) (see Milner, 2010). Civic education programmes in schools are seen as an essential component in addressing this. It is believed that 'Increased attention to civic education in schools particularly as it pertains to social and political participation will convey a political message about the benefits of interacting with others in the fulfilment of civic duties' (Pammett and LeDuc, 2003, 73). Civic education programmes are based then on enhancing young people's knowledge and efficacy. This belief in the efficacy of civic education programmes has been empirically verified and there is now clear evidence that civic education programmes result in higher levels of political knowledge among participants (for review see Galston, 2007).

Civic education programmes are based on a widespread perception that young people lack political knowledge which therefore depresses political engagement (see Milner, 2010). Therefore, it is expected that increasing young people's political knowledge will increase turnout. There is empirical support for this proposition. Blais *et al.* (2002) find that differing levels of knowledge and interest are clearly part of the explanation for generational differences in turnout in Canada (see also Rubenson *et al.*, 2004). In the US Green and Gerber (2008, 118) find that 'Seminars that convey information about how to vote and why voting is important increase turnout among young voters.' Similarly, a 2002 British report (Russell *et al.*, 2002, 8) also found that 'Voter information and awareness campaigns could play an important role in increasing turnout.' The literature suggests that increasing political knowledge through civic education classes will be a key factor in driving up turnout among the young.

The findings above are in line with a widespread belief in and significant public support for the introduction of civic education programmes (see White *et al.*, 2000; Pammett and LeDuc, 2003; Levine, 2007, 100). The literature cited above gives us good reasons to think that increasing young people's political knowledge through civic education programmes would drive up turnout. But this literature should not be accepted uncritically. For older generations who have higher levels of civic duty political knowledge may act as an extra and complementary stimulant which has the effect of increasing turnout. Among young people—who have lower levels of civic duty (see Chapter 1; Wattenberg, 2007)—increasing political knowledge may not result in stronger feelings of civic duty and therefore may not result in higher turnout. If young people don't see candidates and party positions as attractive then many young people may decide not to vote regardless of their political knowledge. We can see evidence of this in the US in turnout rates among the young in the 2000 election versus the 2004 and 2008 elections where political knowledge would not have changed (or changed very marginally) but turnout increased significantly.

There also remains a larger problem with assuming that increasing political knowledge through civic education programmes will increase turnout. While making information more easily available to young people through civic education programmes may make young people more likely to access it motivational problems among some young people may confound this effect—it is probably for this reason that increased education levels have not resulted in higher levels of political knowledge among today's well educated young. If political knowledge is currently a proxy for political interest then it does not necessarily follow that improving the level of knowledge among young people with low levels of political interest will lead to higher turnout.

This might lead some to argue that there is little use in putting resources into introducing civic education into what, in many countries, is an already crowded curriculum. Yet, while the arguments cited above should alert us to possible confounding effects, the significant potential that civic education could play in increasing political engagement among the young should not be dismissed. Rather, the more negative findings should highlight the care with which civic education classes should be introduced into the curriculum so that civic education is designed in a way that makes it interesting to students. Milner (2010, 185) points out that when Ontario introduced compulsory civic education there was little evidence of administrators and teachers trying to successfully implement this programme. 'The teachers generally complained that the course was too short and expressed dissatisfaction with the curriculum and textbooks' and school principals often dumped poor performing teachers into this course (Milner, 2010, 186). Thus, many students saw the new courses as an unwelcome intrusion into their curriculum. Even students who were politically interested expressed a negative view of the civic classes (Milner, 2010, 186). Similarly, in Britain evaluations have suggested that civic education was the worst taught subject in the curriculum (Fahmy, 2006, 147).

So, how may these problems be dealt with? One way would be to develop civic education classes in consultation with administrators and teachers as well as coordinating civic education programmes with universities where teachers could be trained in civic education (as is the case in many Scandinavian countries (see Milner, 2010, 207)). But what is most important is that civic education classes are interesting to students. An obvious way to do this that has been proposed by many experts is to design classes in which important historical events are tied to contemporary problems. Talking about current affairs in class has been found to be one of the most important factors in increasing knowledge (Levine, 2007, 128). Experts have also suggested that civic educations classes work best when they are experiential (Levine, 2007, 125). The 'chalk and talk' approach that civic education lessons have involved in the past is probably less attractive to today's young who are less deferential.

Simulations are another way to excite young people's political interest. Simulations where students are invited to play a leadership role in a historical or hypothetical situation or participate online in a model UN simulation could improve young people's interest and efficacy (see Levine, 2007, 141). Simulations could also be designed so that young people become more appreciative of the various pressures legislators face. For example, in one 'classroom experiment with an imaginary society, students became more tolerant when they observed the unfair effects of simple majority rule' (Levine, 2007, 140). Furthermore, students could be encouraged to develop their own computer-based simulations aimed at other young people which could then be used by others. There is significant potential for the Internet to be used here. Online material has the 'advantage that it can be incorporated into modules of civic education courses irrespective of location' (Milner, 2010, 214). Online materials that are interactive (and collaborative) are likely to be more attractive to the young.

Another way to stimulate students' interest might be to move from the tradition of conveying neutral information to bringing partisan politics into the classroom. Milner (2010, 206, 212) recommends making civic education courses more political by inviting politicians into the classroom and argues that 'The very notion of keeping politics out of the classroom is wrongheaded in a mature democracy.' Milner (2010, 213) believes that school visits could 'also make the entire political system more legitimate in the eyes of young people' and students could prepare and question politicians as if they were journalists at a press conference. This strategy has been found to be successful in the past and civic courses that have included a partisan element have been found to increase knowledge and, to a lesser extent, political participation (Milner, 2010, 190). Introducing partisan politics into the classroom is likely to be more successful than trying to create a neutral environment in which important issues are not discussed. However, while this seems like a sensible idea it is always going to be difficult to get administrative bodies which may be coordinating civic education to sign off on any initiatives with partisan undertones. The challenge then is to introduce partisan politics in a way that gives equal voice to all the important parties and be as transparent about this as possible so that allegations of bias are less salient.

I have argued in this section that civic education has significant potential to increase turnout among the young and in the process increase political interest. Although there has been very little research done in this area civic education reforms may also have an effect on other forms of political engagement such as party identification and party membership by instilling participatory values in young people. Civic education may also have an effect on political trust by which young people become more appreciative of the work politicians and parties do. Therefore, civic education may have indirect forms of influence which increase young people's political engagement more broadly.

While I have concentrated on the utility of civic education up to this point it should be added that education programmes should also be aimed at achieving normative goals and not just be seen in purely instrumental terms in regards to increasing turnout or political interest. Even if civic education programmes do not increase, for example, turnout immediately—because of confounding motivational problems—this does not mean they have failed (although funding bodies are likely to view things this way). A better informed citizenry is a key component to a healthy democracy. As Levine (2007, 99) argues: 'Civic education (defined as preparation for responsible and effective participation in politics and civil society) is a public good. If most people become good citizens, everyone benefits.' And when political events do arise that capture young people's attention they will be better informed to evaluate party platforms and leaders. This should be an important goal for civic education programmes in terms of governments remaining accountable.

Another normative goal of civic education should be to make students appreciative of the fact that politics involves conflict. Studies have found that those who disliked government and politics classes didn't like disagreement as reported through the media and 'Other research has found that many Americans do not acknowledge that there are real public disagreements' and see them as artificial and motivated by partisan interests (Levine, 2007, 126). Levine (2007, 126) argues that 'This resistance to conflict alienates people from participating in politics. It would therefore be helpful if students learned about disagreement and practiced taking sides without demonizing opponents.' Civic education can help achieve this. Therefore, civic education programmes should be aimed at satisfying practical and normative goals.

Elite mobilization: can politicians and parties mobilize young people?

Rather than the bottom-up approach of civic education whereby individuals gain political knowledge and efficacy the elite mobilization model involves a top-down approach by which elites mobilize young people into participation (i.e. young people are not politically engaged because parties and politicians do not mobilize them). Chapter 4 showed that in the US, Canada and Britain young people have become less likely to be contacted by a political party (relative to older people) over time (see also Levine, 2007, 50). We also saw that young people have become less likely to join political parties and less likely to identify with a party over time. This evidence points to the waning influence of party mobilization. Elite mobilization therefore is seen as a way to counter these trends.

This feeds into the work of Rosenstone and Hansen (1993, 5) who argue that mobilization has been overlooked by scholars concentrating on the personal resources that are so essential to civic education reforms. They argue that 'citizens participate in elections and government both because they go to politics and politics comes to them' (Rosenstone and Hansen, 1993, 6). Therefore, leaders can mobilize various groups into political participation. This is dependent not on the individual's level of knowledge about politics or their motivation to participate but rather on the mobilization abilities of elites. According to Rosenstone and Hansen (1993, 23) mobilization subsidizes the cost of obtaining political information and underwrites the cost of political participation. This should be even more applicable to the young who are more distracted by life events than other age groups.

While young people from an individual standpoint may decide that the cost of voting or becoming politically informed is too high, from an elite standpoint there is a clear incentive structure for parties and politicians to mobilize young people. Rosenstone and Hansen (1993, 25) argue that 'Citizen participation is a resource that political leaders use in their struggles for political advantage.' There are incentives for politicians and political parties to do this, particularly as it relates to young people. On the one hand young people are often mobile, distracted by life events and lack firm party attachments. This means that the cost of mobilizing young people may be higher than for mobilizing more stable, established and settled age groups. However, the pay-off could be quite significant in terms of mobilizing a disenfranchised cohort. Young people are 'up for grabs,' so to speak. The advantage in electoral terms could be significant for politicians and parties who attract support from young people, as seen in the 2008 US election.

There is empirical support for this type of mobilization in the literature. Green and Gerber show that personal contact has a large impact on getting people to the polls in the US (see also Rosenstone and Hansen, 1993, 210). Green and Gerber (2008, 10) found that 'the more personal the interaction between campaign and potential voter, the more it raises a person's chances of voting.' They found door-to-door canvassing to be most effective, followed by chatty unhurried phone calls. By contrast they found that prerecorded 'get-out-the-vote' phone calls to be completely ineffective (Green and Gerber, 2008, 10). In Britain a study showed that telephone canvassing or a personal home call by an independent, non-partisan organization could increase turnout by about 7 per cent (Stoker, 2006, 172). Roger Creedon (former Chief Executive at the Electoral Commission in

Britain) states that 'research shows that when parties engage voters, turnout increases' (Electoral Commission, 2004).

However, whether the effect of elite mobilization is larger or smaller for the young is not well established. Franklin (2004, 216) argues that 'a serious attempt by parties to engage young voters could have a dramatic effect on turnout.' But there is little empirical data to directly support this proposition. Evidence presented in Chapter 4 did show that more young people were contacted during the 2004 and 2008 elections which did seem to have an effect on turnout. There seem to be good reasons to think that elite mobilization would be very important to young people but there is also likely to be a group of people who are 'un-gettable' no matter how great the mobilization effort is (as found by the Electoral Commission, 2004). However, it is reasonable to assume that a greater effort by parties and politicians to mobilize young people would increase young people's political engagement. Furthermore, experiments by CIRCLE have shown that the cost of mobilizing young people is much less expensive than many leaders and consultants assume (Levine, 2007, 209).

These expectations are consistent with Green and Gerber's (2008, 10) observation that 'the more personal the interaction between campaign and potential voter, the more it raises a person's chances of voting.' But this raises a paradox. As the population grows and mass communication media technologies become a more important channel for politicians and parties there is less and less personal contact between politicians and parties. Paradoxically, this is the very thing that is likely to increase turnout and political engagement more generally! Given the trend towards mass communication—that is likely to become more pronounced in the future—this may temper our expectations about what exactly personalized contact can achieve.

Given all of this, mass communication technologies may be seen by parties as a more attractive (if less effective) tool for mobilizing the young as opposed to personalized contacting. There is potential for the Internet to play a significant role here. For example, in the lead-up to the 2008 election Barack Obama had 2.4 million people on Facebook signed up as supporters while John McCain had only 624,000 (Falcone, 2008). Research in Australia by Gibson and McAllister (2006) has found that the quality of the candidate's personal website was positively related to their vote-share. In the future the Internet may be used as a tool for politicians to mobilize young people. If, as argued, grass roots political party organization is breaking down the Internet may help politicians more easily contact young people and mobilize them into voting. Although direct contacting is more effective the Internet is a tool through which young people could be mobilized at a cost that is likely to be deemed more affordable by politicians and parties.

It is clear that elite mobilization (in person and online) will mobilize more young people to vote (how many more it is difficult to say). Furthermore, in the very act of politicians and parties trying to connect with young people young people's electoral engagement and political interest may increase also. Attempts at trying to mobilize young people (either in person or online) may be seen positively by young people and lessen the distance many citizens feel exists between themselves and politicians and parties thereby increasing trust.

But how might we measure such effects? The 2008 US campaign is instructive in this regard. Obama clearly mobilized young people to vote in 2008. But did this mobilization effort have any effect on trust and interest? Despite Obama mobilizing the young in 2008 trust actually decreased in 2008 (no doubt due to other confounding factors). In regards to interest this increased in 2004 and actually decreased slightly in 2008. Therefore, the wider milieu of politics likely has an effect on factors such as political trust and interest which makes measuring the effect of mobilization on other factors like trust and interest problematic. While we may assume that mobilization may affect such political engagement variables as interest and trust sorting out causation here is, and will remain, difficult. Furthermore, a more long term question arises about whether parties and politicians may attempt to mobilize the young in the way Obama did in 2008. Therefore, elite mobilization may have direct and indirect effects but it will always be difficult to measure the indirect effect as opposed to the direct ones such as mobilization increasing voter turnout.

Registration effects: will making it easier to register increase turnout?

There are other incentives which may encourage or discourage young people from becoming politically engaged, and to vote or not vote in particular. Aside from the reasons mentioned above there are other more mundane factors that may have an effect on political engagement. Chief among these are registration requirements (i.e. young people don't vote because it is too hard to get to the polls). It is well established in the literature that young people are less likely to be registered to vote. In Britain, 'young people are less likely to register to vote than other age groups: 20 per cent of 18–25 year olds were not registered in 1995' (Ballington, 2001, 11). Russell *et al.* (2002, 8) argue that 'Non-registration constitutes a significant barrier to improving turnout. It is therefore essential to improve registration procedures and increase levels of registration.' Research outside of Britain has also shown that young people are less likely to be registered. As noted earlier, prior to the 2010 election the Australian Electoral Commission (2010) reported that there were 1.4 million people missing from the electoral roll and one-third of these people were aged 18–24 and 70 per cent were aged 18–39. This is tied to the fact that, like in many other countries, many young people are unenthusiastic about registering therefore freeing themselves of the need to vote.

There are good reasons to think that registration reforms would increase turnout among the young. Registration reforms would decrease the cost of voting thereby helping overcome some of the distractions of early adulthood which keep young people away from the polls. For example, in a Canadian report (Pammett and LeDuc, 2003, 18) being too busy with school, work or family was mentioned as a reason for not voting by 23 per cent of respondents aged 18–25 but only 5 per cent of those aged 65 and over. Registration reforms which have been shown to be effective should be considered. Election day registration (which has been available in Canada since 2001 and in some US states) has had an effect on turnout among the young (Milner, 2010, 168) and has boosted turnout in the US (Eisner, 2004, 102). Other reforms such as mailing campaigns to let people know where polling booths are or extending voting hours have also shown some capacity to increase turnout (Levine, 2007, 208). However, the National Voter Registration Act of 1993 (known as Motor Voter) was introduced in the US with the aim of making it easier for young people to register to vote when they got their licence but this significant reform did not have the effect of increasing turnout (Levine, 2007, 208). In Britain, Denver (2005, 46) also argues that making voting easier does not appear to have had a large effect on turnout. Therefore, while registration reforms do seem promising there is some mixed evidence in this regard.

The Internet could also play a role by making registration easier for young people. In their study of non-voters in Canada, Pammett and LeDuc (2003, 74) concluded that 'the predominance of reasons for not voting in this study relating to lack of time and absence from the constituency lead to the observation that new technologies could help provide solutions to these problems.' They find high levels of public support for Internet registration, information modification and Internet voting, particularly among young non-voters. Pammett and LeDuc (2003, 58) predict that Internet voting could lift voter turnout by almost 3 per cent and Internet registration could lift voting by almost 1.5 per cent. The Australian Election Study also found much stronger support for Internet voting among the young than the old.

Related to this is whether it is desirable to mobilize voters (via Internet voting, for example) with low levels of political interest and, presumably, low levels of political knowledge. Wattenberg (2002, 165) notes that because of the cumbersome electoral process in the US mobilizing citizens with low levels of political knowledge may result in citizens treating voting like picking lottery numbers. There is therefore a tension between making voting easier and having people with very low levels of interest and knowledge voting. There is however the possibility that making voting easier may increase interest by ensuring more and more people participate in the electoral process, a process through which they main gain more political knowledge. Levine (2007, 208) also argues that allowing citizens to enrol on election day benefits young people and makes it more likely that parties will contact them and there is some evidence that this can 'set off a virtuous cycle of higher turnout and more attention' (Levine, 2007, 208). This may also have an effect on political trust by lessening the distance between young people and politicians and parties that attempt to mobilize young people.

Electoral system reforms: will changing the electoral system increase political engagement?

The previous policy reforms would be relatively easy to implement by policy makers if there existed the political will to do so (which, admittedly, is a big if). The institutional reforms suggested below seem much less likely to be implemented in the foreseeable future given that a modest referendum proposing a shift from first-past-the-post to the alternative vote (optional preferential voting) was rejected in Britain and that there has been little to no discussion of radical electoral system change in the US and Australia (for the Canadian case see LeDuc et al. 2010, 524; Milner 2010, 141). There has however been significant electoral reform in another Anglo-American democracy that is not included in this book (New Zealand) so the cause is not a hopeless one. All of that said, it is worth discussing electoral system reform as it might tell us something about the mechanisms by which young people become politically engaged.

Whereas the previous recommendations have looked at the role of individuals and elites, electoral system reform involves factors exogenous to the individual that influence turnout in important ways. Electoral system reform is premised on increasing young people's political engagement by framing young people's political choices differently (i.e. young people are not politically engaged because the electoral system provides no incentive for them to vote). Many of these institutional effects relate to the cost of participation that may either provide incentives or disincentives for citizens to participate in politics. Therefore, particular electoral systems are structured to increase the costs and decrease the benefits of voting and becoming politically engaged (Teixeira, 1992, 17).

The two most important institutional factors are electoral system type and compulsory voting. Proportional representation (PR) systems may act to increase turnout in contrast to majoritarian/plurality systems. For example, turnout may be higher in a proportional system because citizens are more likely to find a party that is aligned with their interests and concerns. PR systems allow for parties that can better represent minorities and 'new politics' cleavages. Crepaz (1990, 188) notes that since the early 1980s European politics has been altered by the emergence of 'Green' and 'Alternative' parties representing new political dimensions such as women's rights, participatory democracy and anti-nuclear energy. This is relevant to the young because if the young lack representation (as suggested in Pammett and LeDuc, 2003) then turnout among the young may be higher in PR systems which better accommodate young people's diverse interests. Therefore, environmental and alternative parties may mobilize the young into voting.

Evidence suggests that voter turnout can be influenced by the electoral system (Russell *et al.*, 2002, 8). Turnout has been found to be higher in PR systems with Lijphart (1994, 6) predicting that turnout is about 9 percentage points higher in PR systems (see also Milner, 1997, 90; Blais and Dobrzynska, 1998, 251; Milner, 2002, 75; Wattenberg, 2002, 18). In other research (Crepaz, 1990, 200), the existence of a postmaterial party in particular electoral systems has been found to increase turnout. This evidence would lead us to expect that young people would be more likely to vote in PR systems.

PR would also increase competitiveness although this could be achieved without the introduction of PR. For example, in the US electoral boundaries are drawn in a way that makes many electoral districts uncompetitive. For example, in 2004 none of California's 153 legislative seats changed hands (Levine, 2007, 211). One way to increase competition is to create non-partisan commissions (at the state or federal level) and have electoral maps drawn by a computer (Levine, 2007, 212). This is particularly important to the young because youth turnout is higher in the US states that are more competitive (Levine, 2007, 211).

Electoral rules also affect participation and the changing of these rules could drive up turnout among the young. Of particular importance is compulsory voting. There is strong support for compulsory voting increasing turnout (in countries where it is enforced). Australia is the most obvious case here where compulsory voting has resulted in high turnout rates (although registration rates among the young remain a problem as seen in Chapter 1). Compulsory voting is typically found to increase turnout by 10–15 percentage points (Blais, 2007, 625; see also Lijphart, 1997, 8; Blais and Dobrzynska, 1998, 246). Compulsory voting compels people to vote, in particular the young who may be distracted by life events. If motivation is a problem for young people then compulsory voting gets rid of certain motivational barriers (Teixeira, 1992, 151). An expression of this was found in the Youth Electoral Study which found that only 50 per cent of young people said they would vote if voting were not compulsory (Print *et al.*, 2004, 2). Whatever the merits of compulsory voting it is difficult to see the introduction of compulsory voting in the near future in any of the Anglo-American democracies unless turnout dropped to seriously low levels.

Other reforms

There are a number of other reforms that (while not the focus of this chapter) could be considered: one of these is reducing the voting age to 16. There are good arguments for doing this including the fact that reducing the voting age would allow voting to be integrated into civic education in schools (before the more competitive later years in high school) and would better allow students to be made aware of registration procedures. However, the Electoral Commission in the UK recently looked closely at this issue and decided against recommending 16-year-old voting (see Milner, 2010, 157) and the Australian Election Study found low support for changing the voting age, even among young people! While the Austrian government recently introduced 16-year-old voting this reform does not seem likely in the Anglo-American democracies at present. Devolution is another initiative that the Blair government in particular pursued although this does not seem to have affected political engagement in Britain. Voting advice applications (VAAS) in which users give their opinion on certain issues and then the party that is most suited to these views is listed also show potential promise and have been used extensively in Sweden proving very popular among the young (Milner, 2010, 135). Information campaigns and concerts promoting enrolment (such as Rock the Vote in the US) are also worthy of consideration, as are fixed election dates (see Milner, 2010, 160–7) and deliberative polls (Milner, 2010, 134).

Discussion

Of these reforms civic education is probably the most important. Milner (2010, 97) argues that 'Getting the Internet generation to participate politically entails, first and foremost, instilling in them the habit of paying attention to public affairs.' Similarly, O'Neill (2007, iv) argues that 'Civics education stands as an effective, if not the most effective, mechanism for addressing deficiencies in political knowledge and understanding of the public responsibilities associated with citizenship.' The most promising way to do this is by designing a civic education curriculum that is attractive to administrators, teachers and, most importantly, students. This could be achieved by making civic education more interactive and connected to contemporary political problems. Civic education is attractive to many and will likely be considered in the future as a possible policy reform to better engage the young. In terms of increasing turnout among the young, increasing young people's electoral engagement more generally and making young people more interested in politics there is no match for the potential reach and scope that civic education has in both empirical and normative terms.

Civic education reforms are largely based on the presumption that 'the problems are located (so to speak) inside the heads of young people' (Levine, 2007, xiv). The elite mobilization model shifts the blame from citizens to politicians and parties. There is clear evidence that parties and politicians are not mobilizing young people. For example, in 1999 Dane Strother, a consultant who worked for the Democrats said: 'I help sell politicians and young adults don't participate in the political process.

Whenever we buy television and target our advertising spots we just completely ignore anyone under 30' (cited in Levine, 2007, 204). In a survey of Democratic and Republican party leaders the young were not mentioned as an important target group (Levine, 2007, 204). The same is no doubt true of the other Anglo-American democracies. But the 2008 campaign in the US showed how young people can be mobilized in an effective way. Green and Gerber's (2008) research also shows that concerted efforts to mobilize young people in the US work. Elite mobilization shows significant potential for mobilizing the young to vote which may in turn improve young people's political interest, trust and electoral engagement.

Making registration easier (particularly in the US) would also pay dividends. Making registration easier is not a gargantuan task. Relatively simple measures such as election day registration or extending the time polling booths are open have been shown to have an effect on youth turnout. These reforms may also have an indirect effect in that politicians and parties make more of an effort to mobilize the young. No doubt there will remain a group of young people who will not register no matter how low the registration barrier. However, by making registration easier it is likely that at least some young people with low levels of interest will register because of these reforms.

Institutions also matter: 'The more institutions are able to simplify the relationship between voters' actions and political outcomes, and to foster party identification—both of which reduce the cost of political knowledge—the lower the portion of political dropouts' (Milner, 2010, 138). Introducing PR is the best way to achieve this. However, this does not seem likely at present. Nor does the introduction of compulsory voting. Nevertheless, it should still be on the menu of reforms that may be considered in the future and the New Zealand case shows how politicians can lose control of the electoral reform process whereby significant electoral reform was achieved (see Renwick, 2010). While major electoral system reform seems unlikely at present the New Zealand case gives at least some cause for optimism.

The importance of these reforms should be underscored because there exists a considerable ability for political inequality to be reduced through these reforms. Chapter 5 showed that non-electoral forms of participation that exacerbate participatory inequalities seem to be becoming more common among the young. In contrast, many of the reforms listed above would equalize participation by improving access to what is still the most important form of political activity: voting. If more young people register and vote, or find out more about politics through civic education campaigns then this will improve the quality of democracy in the Anglo-American democracies by giving voice to the otherwise voiceless and improving political engagement among the young more generally.

But given the focus of this book and the wide range of political engagement indicators covered it is worth asking how any intervention may be measured. Legislators are likely to push for standardized measurement of any policy intervention. In the case of turnout we have an easily identifiable variable although proving causation is never easy. But in the case of political trust and interest the effect of policy interventions are harder to measure. This raises the question of what exactly the goal should be in introducing the reforms mentioned above. Do we want reforms to achieve utility (and therefore be measurable) or to improve norms which are much less amenable to quantification? In this chapter I have argued that reforms should be aimed at both practical and normative concerns although any reform that is introduced will need to be sensitive to policy makers' understandable wish for quantification.

Conclusion

This chapter has provided us with a more coherent way to think about policy reforms aimed at increasing political engagement (and turnout in particular) among the young. This chapter has suggested a number of reforms that should be given careful consideration by policy makers. Pammett and LeDuc (2003, 73) argue that political engagement will not be increased with short term, small scale reform measures. Furthermore, because of the multifaceted nature of young people's engagement with politics 'Youth engagement won't be boosted in a single stroke. There is no simple solution to apply, no magic tonic to administer' (Zukin *et al.*, 2006, 138). This chapter has suggested that the biggest reforms, such as compulsory voting and electoral system change, are very unlikely to be introduced. However, many other more easily implementable reforms such as introducing civic education are more likely to be adopted. Other reforms such as easing registration requirements and elite mobilization also show considerable promise. This chapter has shown that there are various reforms available to policy makers which could have the effect of increasing political engagement among the young. It has been suggested here that increasing political engagement is not out of policy makers' control and there are various levers which can and perhaps will be pulled to increase political engagement (voting in particular) among the young.

Conclusion

Political engagement is commonly said to be in a state of chronic decline. A frequent claim made in recent academic discussion of political engagement in 'Western democracies has been that public involvement in politics is in decline and democracy is in crisis … the apparent evidence of malaise in the Western body politic also extends to worries about public attitudes towards the political system' (Pattie et al., 2004, 224). Because of the perceived gravity of this problem concern is not confined to the academy but 'has also been expressed in numerous public speeches, editorial columns, and policy forums' (Norris, 2011, 221). These claims are thought to be especially salient to young people. Young people are often alleged to be disengaged from politics on a number of levels. The common view is that young people don't vote (and are disengaged from electoral politics more generally), do not trust politicians and have low levels of political interest. This book tested these claims and found confirmation of some claims but challenged the conventional wisdom in a number of areas. This conclusion outlines the most important findings of this book and highlights the book's central themes.

The findings

Part I: voter turnout

Central to concerns about young people's lack of political engagement is voter turnout. Book titles such as *Is Voting for Young People?* (Wattenberg, 2006) are typical of much of the literature on voter turnout among the young. In this literature 'the half empty ballot-box is taken as the most common symptom of democratic ill-health' (Norris, 2011, 220). Part I of this book showed that although the gap between young and old has been widening in some countries turnout is not in secular decline among the young. Recent years have seen significant increases in youth turnout. This is especially true of the United States whereby turnout among the young increased significantly in the 2004 and 2008 elections. This is consistent with a broader trend of young people's turnout patterns becoming increasingly erratic in recent decades. Thus, generational effects play out in terms of young people being volatile rather than absent voters. This volatility seems to be linked to young people's lack of civic duty, as expressed through the ISSP importance of vote question. Young people, it seems, have not inherited their parents' strong feelings of civic duty and for this reason are less likely to consistently vote. If true, this explains why young people's turnout has become more volatile in recent years. However, while the increase in voting among the young in recent years provides some cause for optimism the degree of volatility in young people's voting patterns means that in some elections young people are markedly absent (such as in the US in 1988 and 2000 and Britain in 2005). Combined with young people's low level of civic duty this should be concerning because voting is the most important element of young people's political engagement.

Part II: political attitudes

Part II turned to political attitudes in terms of political trust and political interest. Political attitudes are important because 'How citizens view politics tells us much about the health of a political system' (McAllister, 2011, 85). In regards to political trust Chapter 2 showed that while overall levels of trust were very low among the general population, young people were not found to be particularly distinct in this regard. Trust has declined quite steeply in the US and Britain (among young and old alike). In Canada the data prevents us from making any definite conclusions and in Australia political trust is very volatile and seems to follow the electoral cycle rather than being in secular decline. In the countries where we have consistent data young and older people do not differ greatly in their levels of political trust over time. Nor do low levels of trust among the young (and old) found in all of the Anglo-American democracies signal a 'crisis of democracy' as the young are still overwhelmingly supportive of democracy as the best form of government. Overall, young people are best characterized as 'dissatisfied democrats.' It seems that the young are supportive of democracy but dissatisfied with the performance of politicians and parties.

In regards to political interest concern has been expressed about low levels of political interest among the young in the Anglo-American democracies (Gidengil et al., 2003; Pattie et al., 2004, xvi; Levine, 2007, 202). Chapter 3 showed that, as with political trust, patterns of political interest over time are quite varied. In the US political interest among the young was not found to be in secular decline. Rather, levels of political interest among the young were found to be very volatile. That said, an age gap between the young and old has opened up over time. The Canadian data is less consistent but shows that an age gap between the young and old has opened up over time as well. In Britain levels of political interest have been quite static among young and old alike over the last few decades and in Australia political interest is trending upwards among the young (although this upwards trend is even more pronounced among older age groups).

These varied findings are at odds with young people in advanced democracies being depicted as chronically disinterested in politics.

Part III: political participation beyond voting

Part III examined political participation beyond voting. In this section I distinguished between electoral engagement and non-electoral participation. In regards to electoral engagement 'the conventional wisdom arising from a substantial scholarly literature suggests that during recent decades, many post-industrial societies have experienced a tidal wave of public withdrawal from the traditional channels of conventional political activism' (Norris, 2011, 220). This is said to be especially true of young people across the Anglo-American democracies (see Putnam, 2000; Blais *et al.*, 2002, 8; Fahmy, 2006, 1; Zukin *et al.*, 2006, 189). Chapter 4 showed that party identification and party membership has been declining over time among the young. These findings reflect generational effects and in this regard the socialization process seems to be breaking down. Young people are also less likely to have contacted a politician. Therefore, on the electoral front (beyond voting) young people were found to be very disengaged. Broadly speaking 'Representative government is no longer as compelling a proposition as it once was' (Dahrendorf cited in Dalton, 2006, 267). This is especially true of the young.

However, to get a more complete picture of political participation Chapter 5 and Chapter 6 examined non-electoral participation in terms of attending a demonstration, signing a petition, boycotting consumer products and participating in politics on the Internet. While 'there has been a steady secular erosion of the traditional avenues of political engagement' the late twentieth century saw an expanding array of political activity that citizens are engaged in such as attending a demonstration and boycotting consumer products for political reasons (Norris, 2002, 215). Norris (2002, 222) argues that while young people are disengaged from traditional channels of participation, such as parties, young people are more likely to channel their energies through non-electoral forms of participation. Similarly, Zukin *et al.* (2006, 3) argue that citizens in the US 'are participating in a different mix of activism from in the past, and that is due largely to the process of generational replacement' (see also Vromen, 2003; Pattie *et al.*, 2004, 110; O'Neill, 2007). The findings of Chapter 5 generally supported this research while acknowledging that we lack data to test the claims above in a systematic way.

In particular, Part III allowed us to test the expectations informed by the work of Putnam and Inglehart and Welzel. In *Bowling Alone* Putnam (2000, 31) argues that 'the character of Americans' involvement with politics and government has been transformed over the past three decades.' Putnam (2000, 35) states that:

declining electoral participation is merely the most visible symptom of a broader disengagement from community life. Like a fever, electoral abstention is even more important as a sign of deeper trouble in the body politic than as a malady itself.

Putnam attributes much of this change to generational change.

In contrast, Inglehart and Welzel (2005, 44) argue:

> New forms of political self-expression extend the boundary of politics from the narrow domain of elite-led electoral campaigns into increasingly autonomous forms of public self expression.... Contrary to often-repeated claims that social capital and mass participation are eroding, the publics of postindustrial societies are intervening in politics more actively today than ever before; however, they are changing the ways in which they participate. Elite-led forms of participation are dwindling. Mass loyalties to long-established hierarchical political parties are weakening. No longer content to be disciplined troops, the public has become increasingly autonomous and elite challenging.

One of the most unequivocal findings of this book is that while young people have low levels of civic duty and have become less likely to identify with and join political parties young people are uniformly more likely than older people to be engaged in non-electoral forms of political participation such as signing a petition and attending a demonstration. Electoral forms of activity and engagement are becoming *less* popular among the young while non-electoral forms of engagement seem to be becoming *more* popular. Through the process of generational replacement it is quite likely that these forms of activity will increase in the future. In this regard Part III found support for the predictions made by Inglehart and Welzel.

However, while these findings present a brighter picture it should not distract us from the wider problem which is young people's lack of engagement in electoral politics, expressed through low civic duty and a lack of party identification in particular. No matter how widespread non-electoral forms of participation are they are not and never will be a substitute for electoral politics. For many, elections are 'the defining feature of the democratic process. They are the critical juncture where individuals take stock of their various political attitudes and preferences and transform them into a single vote choice' (Dalton and Weldon, 2005, 4). Voting, for many citizens, is the one opportunity they get every few years to 'have their say.' Elections and the parties that contest them matter.

Inglehart (1997, 230) argues that 'voting turnout largely reflects the parties' ability to mobilize their supporters, and it is a misleading indicator of real interest and involvement.' However, this view greatly underplays the essential role elections play in determining political life. While it could be argued that young people's greater level of non-electoral participation is arguably 'consistent with an honest appraisal regarding where power increasingly lies in the contemporary world' (Zukin et al., 2006, 189) it is difficult to dispute that elections remain the most important mechanism through which preferences are aggregated. Given the centrality of parties to political society it is concerning that so 'many analysts downplay the role of political parties and other traditional types of political organizations' (Milner, 2010, 5). Politics is essential to our daily lives and young people's lack of engagement in electoral politics is worrying in this regard (Zukin et al., 2006, 192). Young people do have different preferences from older people (Zukin et al., 2006, 166; Milner, 2010, 25) so young people's lack of connection to electoral politics does have implications in terms of what is expressed to government. As Milner (2010) argues: 'the need and interests of those unable to participate effectively in political life fall to the bottom of the political agenda.'

Furthermore, that relatively low numbers of young people are engaged in non-electoral activity should be concerning because this means that a subsection of young people are disengaged from politics altogether (see Milner, 2010). Hay (2008, 26) argues that 'A mounting body of recent research suggests that, far from being apathetic politically, a significant proportion of those who regard themselves as having disengaged entirely from formal politics are actively engaged in modes of informal yet collective political conduct.' In so far as I was able to measure informal participation in Chapter 5 and Chapter 6 it is difficult to sustain this proposition. While young people are more engaged in non-electoral participation than older people the number of people involved (especially for more demanding forms of activity such as attending a demonstration) is very small and does not make up for the shortfall in electoral engagement.

A central claim in this book is that participatory distortions are/and will arise from the changing nature of young people's political engagement. Electoral politics seems to be losing its primacy. Inherent in the changing nature of political participation are participatory inequalities which should be a real concern. These have been largely overlooked by the likes of Inglehart and Welzel. In *Voice and Equality* Verba et al. (1995, 11) show that 'The propensity to take part is not randomly distributed across relevant categories' and that 'participatory inequalities have implications for politics.' Therefore, while many types of political participation seem to be increasing 'ironically, overall increases in political involvement may mask a growing social-status bias in citizen participation and influence, which runs counter to democratic ideals' (Dalton, 2006, 74). In Part III I described this as the dark side of modernization theory.

Part IV: what can be done?

Given the findings above it is perhaps unsurprising 'that concerns about young people's electoral non-participation, and their wider disengagement from conventional politics, have increasingly begun to exercise the minds of policy makers' (Fahmy, 2006, 2). For example, the Blair government's 'program of constitutional and parliamentary reforms was initiated with the explicit goal of restoring public faith in government and revitalising democracy' (Fahmy, 2006, 2). Part IV examined possible policy reforms aimed at increasing young people's political engagement and argued that there are a number of avenues through which young people may become more engaged in the political process. All too often there is a tendency to say that young people are ignorant, too hard to reach and too distracted by other life events to ever become politically engaged. This is consistent with a long line of thinking that sees the young as corrupted and selfish. In Chapter 7 I examined the potential of four reforms aimed at increasing political engagement (and voting in particular) among the young: civic education reforms, elite mobilization, easing registration requirements and changing the electoral system as well as briefly considering other possible reforms. In Chapter 7 I argued that, in particular, increasing political knowledge through well designed and well taught civic education programmes could increase political engagement as could politicians and parties making more of an effort to mobilize young people.

Citizenship in the twenty-first century

The findings in this book go to the heart of questions about what it means to be a citizen in the twenty-first century. Partly as a result of concerns expressed about young people's political engagement there has been a renewed focus on citizenship. 'Citizenship—broadly understood as a relationship between an individual and a state in which the individual owes loyalty to the state and is entitled to its protection—has behavioral, attitudinal, and normative aspects' (Van Deth, 2009, 402). Tied up with being a 'good citizen' is being active in political and public life. In 431–430 BC Pericles stressed the obligations of a 'good citizen' by arguing that:

> An Athenian citizen does not neglect the state because he takes care of his own household; and even those of us who are engaged in business have a fair idea of politics. We alone regard a man who takes no interest in public affairs, not as a harmless, but as a useless character; and if few of us are originators, we are all sounds judges of policy.
> (cited in Van Deth, 2009, 402)

This view is echoed by democratic theorists who value a participatory citizenry (Pateman, 1970, 1985; Macpherson, 1977; Barber, 1984). For example, Barber (1984) compares 'thin democracy' to 'strong democracy' whereby the citizenry are engaged and attentive to public affairs. 'This sense of duty towards "public affairs" is characteristic for most conceptualizations of citizenship' (Van Deth, 2009, 405).

The data cited throughout this book suggests that young people are not habitually engaged in politics. While young people's political engagement is more complex than much of the literature would lead us to believe there remains a large segment of young people who are disengaged, from electoral politics in particular. Carmines and Huckfeldt (1996, 250) argue that

> a revised model of citizenship has emerged—a model of the citizen as a cost-conscious consumer and processor of political information who, while taking her duties seriously, has successfully reduced the impulse to be consumed by politics and political affairs.
>
> (cited in Van Deth, 2009, 415)

The data cited in the various chapters of this book supports this view.

This is particularly true in regards to electoral forms of participation. For example, large N surveys in Europe have shown that while there is widespread support for voting as a part of citizenship very few people mention being active beyond voting as an obligation of citizenship (Van Deth, 2009, 414). However, young people (as shown in Chapter 1) have a lower level of civic duty but are more likely than older people to participate in non-electoral forms of participation. This seems to signal a shift in citizenship norms in which young people value non-electoral participation over electoral participation (see Dalton, 2008). Electoral participation seems not to be a norm of citizenship for many young people. But exactly how this will play out in the future is not clear. The idea of the 'good citizen' is being questioned by the young and therefore reshaped.

All of this relates to where the rights of citizenship are exercised in the twenty-first century. Schudson (1998, 8) argues that the expansion of rights-consciousness has made the polling place less central to governing political life. Politics is now everywhere, according to Schudson. 'For example, dietary matters have become part of congressional debate, laws against tobacco are in legislation, and sexual harassment ruled on by the Supreme Court' (Schudson, 1998, 241). As a result, ownership of the political sphere has shifted:

> ...in the eighteenth century, political activity was set in motion and controlled by gentleman; in the nineteenth century, it was organized by parties; in the twentieth century, after democratization had reduced the authority of social class and reforms had seriously weakened the parties, claimants compete to set the standards of political life.
>
> (Schudson, 1998, 8)

While Schudson is arguing this point in relation to the US the same process has occurred (albeit in a much more moderate form) in the other Anglo-American democracies. Furthermore, the general process that Schudson sees as happening in the US, with influence being shifted from electoral participation to non-electoral participation, seems especially true of the young as found in this book. This raises further concomitant measurement issues. If politics goes on everywhere how do we measure this? In this book I have tried to consider a very broad range of political participation by looking at non-electoral participation (including participation on the Internet). However, if Schudson is right then some facets of political engagement may be missed by surveys (although Schudson acknowledges that he does not have better measurements than the existing ones). Part III of this book made us aware of these problems and suggests that 'We need to renovate our research methods to make them more sensitive to new trends in political participation' (Fields, 2011, 60).

To conclude...

Declining political engagement is deemed to be a pressing problem facing the Anglo-American democracies. Accordingly, concerns about this problem have been expressed in many different forms outside of the academy (Norris, 2011, 221). For example, Former Home Secretary David Blunkett expressed concern about 'worrying signs that people are retreating from active citizenship' (cited in Pattie *et al.*, 2004, 107). Mr. Blunkett is not alone in expressing these concerns (see Wattenberg, 2002, 102; Blair, 2010, 106). This book has examined this problem specifically as it relates to the young. By separating out the different facets of political engagement this book conducted a 'stock-take' of young people's political engagement in the Anglo-American democracies.

Are young people politically disengaged? In regards to political attitudes young people do not differ significantly from the old in regards to their levels of political trust. Young people's political interest is varied across the Anglo-American democracies but was not found to be in secular decline. In terms of their attachment to electoral politics (as measured by the importance of vote response, party identification and party membership) young people are clearly less politically engaged. This does not mean that turnout is in secular decline among the young as there have been increases in turnout among the young in recent years. But young people's weaker attachment to electoral politics seems to result in more volatile turnout patterns. Young people are also much more likely to engage in non-electoral forms of participation (providing some support for the work of Inglehart and Welzel) although the extent and meaningfulness of this participation should not be overstated. An acknowledgement of what I have called the dark side of modernization theory is missing from much of the literature.

Scholars will likely lament young people's lack of political engagement, as they have been doing for centuries. In providing a 'stock-take' of young people's political engagement this book has tried to enlighten this discussion by putting some parameters around the debate. While it may be more emotionally satisfying to say young people are chronically disengaged from politics and this problem is getting worse, this book has shown that the intellectually honest answer to whether young people are politically engaged or not is: 'it's complicated.' This book has shown trends that have the potential to have an extremely corrosive effect on the quality of democracy in the future. However, the overall conclusion must be that citizenship among the young is 'closed for renovations.'

Appendix
Note on data sources and analysis

This book relies predominantly on the national election studies from each country. The American National Election Study (ANES) was accessed through www.electionstudies.org. The Canadian Election Study was accessed through the Canadian Opinion Research Archive and Interuniversity Consortium for Political and Social Research (ICPSR). The British Election Study was accessed through the ICPSR, the UK Data Archive and the British Election Study website. The Australian Election Study (and the Australian National Political Attitudes Surveys) were accessed through the Australian Social Science Data Archive.

For the sake of simplicity several data sources are referred to as single studies (i.e. the British Election Study and the Australian Election Study) even when they have incorporated a few different components. For example, the predecessor to the first British Election Study was called Political Change in Britain (1963–1970). The predecessor to the Australian Election Study was the Australian National Political Attitudes Surveys (1967–1979).

This book relies on the post-election components of the national elections studies (unless otherwise stated). The exception is the Australian National Political Attitudes Surveys (1967–1979) which were not strictly speaking election surveys (see McAllister, 2011, 266). The Political Change in Britain 1963 survey has not been included however as that was conducted outside of an election and the next data-point (1964) on an election year was a better place to start the British analysis. The US analysis is of presidential election years only.

This book relies on cross-sectional data with the exception of the Political Change in Britain 1970 survey and the Canadian Election Study in 1980 which are comprised of panel respondents only. No new respondents were added to these surveys. The British Election Study and Canadian Election Study have also included panel respondents in various years but these surveys were 'topped up' so as to constitute cross-section data sets. Panel respondents in the 2006 and 2008 Canadian Election Studies were excluded from the analysis.

In order to make sure that data from the British Election Study was comparable over time I filtered out respondents who were not registered to vote as of 1997 because the pre-1997 surveys only targeted registered voters before the BES changed their sampling frame to the Postal Address File which includes targeting those who are not registered. This is likely to introduce some biases but is the best way to ensure comparability across the data sets.

Weights (where available) have been added to all the national election studies as advised in the codebooks.

Sources for the non-national election study data sources are as follows:

> The ISSP Citizenship survey was accessed through the GESIS—Leibniz-Institute for the Social Sciences archive.
>
> The Georgetown Citizenship, Involvement, Democracy (CID) survey was accessed through the Georgetown University CID website http://www8.georgetown.edu/centers/cdacs/cid/data.htm.
>
> The ANUpoll Internet survey was accessed through the Australian Social Science Data Archive.

Notes

Introduction

1 New Zealand is not included in this study because we have very little across-time data for New Zealand.
2 The Anglo-American democracies are quite homogenous in terms of their institutions with Australia and Canada inheriting the Westminster system of government from the British. The US is more unique with a presidential system of government. None of the Anglo-American democracies has proportional representation. It is for this reason that this book concentrates on micro-factors.
3 Australia is slightly anomalous here in not developing a national elections study on par with other international studies until 1987 (see McAllister, 2011, xii). However, the Australian National Political Attitude Surveys were run in 1967, 1969 and 1979 that this book also draws from although these are not strictly speaking national election studies.
4 I use the term electoral engagement to refer to political actions related directly to voting (and electoral politics) such as joining a political party or identifying with a party. The term non-electoral is used to refer to political actions not directly linked to electoral politics such as signing a petition or boycotting a consumer product for political reasons as well as participating in politics on the Internet.

1 Is turnout declining among the young?

1 See also Wolfinger and Rosenstone, 1980, 102; Lyons and Alexander, 2000; Putnam, 2000, 34; Wattenberg, 2002, 86; Blais *et al.*, 2004; Wattenberg, 2006; Galston, 2007, 631.
2 This gap is likely inflated given the problems associated with a change in question wording in 2008.
3 It should however be noted that the 1995 Quebec referendum saw 94 per cent of eligible voters turn out to vote (Le Duc *et al.*, 2010, 443).
4 The reported turnout in 2008 should be treated with some scepticism (due to the problem of overreporting outlined in this chapter) and more reliable evidence suggests turnout among the young fell in 2008 (see Barnes, 2010; Milner, 2010, 91).
5 However, this should not contaminate the findings in Chapter One to too greater extent. Research shows that there are few cross-sectional differences within countries between reported and actual turnout and that the magnitude of this problem does not increase over time (Shaffer, 1981, 71; Abramson and Aldrich, 1982, 503; Abramson, 1983, 292; Highton and Wolfinger, 2001, 202).

2 Political trust: the not particularly less trusting young

1 For a harsher critique of the measurement of political trust see Schudson (1998, 306).
2 See also Inglehart, 1997; Norris, 1999a; Nye *et al.*, 1997; Pharr and Putnam, 2000; Newton, 2001; Milner, 2002.
3 That is, it was not included in the 2010 survey with comparable coding.

3 Political interest among the young

1 There are also debates as to what political interest means to different people. Some researchers have criticized the narrow nature of previous research and suggested young people are interested in politics but just not as researchers frame it (Henn *et al.*, 2002, 168; see also O'Toole *et al.*, 2003b; Marsh *et al.*, 2007). This argument relates to the point that, broadly conceived, young people are interested in politics. However, when asked in surveys whether they are interested in politics the way young people tend to see this is as relating to parliament, politicians and other political institutions that they may feel estranged from. This book does not engage in these debates in any substantial way as I am dealing with large-N quantitative data that does not allow me to penetrate the subtleties of the way young people conceive of political interest. Rather, political interest is taken as a general interest in politics. This entails a cognitive engagement rather than a behavioural engagement. As such, it is tricky to measure in a definitive way. Nevertheless, interest in politics suggests a cognitive engagement and interest in the political world and a willingness to obtain and retain information which will likely inform political choices.

4 Electoral engagement: a disengaged youth

1 This may be because parties do not address the issues that young people are interested in (Wattenberg, 2002, 90). There is a concern that the major political parties and politicians do not represent the concerns of young people and the issues they are interested in. When Wattenberg and Gray in the US asked people in four Californian counties in their post-2000 election survey: 'some of the issues discussed during the campaigns for the November election directly related to policies affecting people of your generation. Do you think that politicians pay too much attention to these issues, about the right amount or too little?' 62 per cent of respondents under the age of 30 said 'too little,' 21 per cent said 'about the right amount,' and 9 per cent said 'too much.' The percentages for those 65 and over were 33, 41 and 11 per cent respectively (Wattenberg, 2002, 90).
2 Yet, while contact does seem to have decreased over this period this does not preclude other forms of contact (via mail and the Internet, for example) increasing over the same period. Unfortunately, we lack consistent across-time data to test this.

5 Non-electoral forms of participation: a brighter picture?

1 In regards to her not giving up her seat Rosa Parks later said:

> I had not thought about it and I had taken no previous resolution until it happened, and then I simply decided that I would not get up. I was tired, but I was usually tired at the end of the day, and I was not feeling well, but then there had been many days when I had not felt well. I had felt for a long time, that if I was ever told to get up so a white person could sit, that I would refuse to do so.
>
> (cited in Schudson, 1998, 253)

6 The Internet: emerging new forms of participation

1 The ANUpoll is a poll conducted by researchers at the Australian National University. The poll was done via telephone with an N of 1,200. The CID survey was conducted by the Center for Democracy and the Third Sector at Georgetown University via in-person interviews and had an N of 1,001.
2 However, as regards across-country comparisons we can say little about this because of the time lapse between the two surveys in which Internet use would have changed a great deal.
3 There is some ambiguity in regards to how this question is worded and 'political activities' could be taken to mean different things by different respondents and the young and the old in particular.
4 In using this example Chadwick draws from Bimber, 2003.

Bibliography

Aberbach, J.D. and Walker, J.E. (1970) 'Political Trust and Racial Ideology,' *American Political Science Review* 64(4): 1199–219.

Abramson, P.R. (1983) *Political Attitudes in America: Formation and Change*, San Francisco: W.H. Freeman and Company.

Abramson, P.R. and Aldrich, J.H. (1982) 'The Decline of Electoral Participation in America,' *American Political Science Review* 76(3): 502–21.

Abramson, P.R. and Inglehart, R. (1986) 'Generational Replacement and Value Change in Six Western European Societies,' *American Journal of Political Science* 30(1): 1–25.

Achen, C. (2002) 'Parental Socialization and Rational Party Identification,' *Political Behavior* 24(2): 151–70.

Adsett, M. (2003) 'Change in Political Era and Demographic Weight as Explanations of Youth "Disenfranchisement" in Federal Elections in Canada, 1965–2000,' *Journal of Youth Studies* 6(3): 247–64.

Aitkin, D. (1982) *Stability and Change in Australian Politics*, Canberra: Australian National University Press.

Almond, G.A. and Verba, S. (1963) *The Civic Culture: Political Attitudes and Democracy in Five Nations*, Princeton, NJ: Princeton University Press.

Almond, G.A. and Verba, S. (1989) *The Civic Culture: Political Attitudes and Democracy in Five Nations*, Newbury Park, CA: Sage.

Anderson, C.J. (2007) 'Structure and Voting Behavior,' in R.J. Dalton and H.D. Klingemann (eds) *Oxford Handbook of Political Behavior*, New York: Oxford University Press.

Andersson, H.E. and Granberg, D. (1997) 'On the Validity and Reliability of Self-Reported Vote: Validity without Reliability,' *Quality and Quantity* 31(2): 127–40.

ANES Guide to Public Opinion and Electoral Behavior, Available at: www.electionstudies.org/nesguide/toptable/tab6a_2.htm (accessed 5 August 2011).

Australian Electoral Commission (2010) Radio Interview Transcript: Famous People Vote Too. Online. Available at: www.aec.gov.au/About_AEC/publications/speeches/interview-famous-people.htm (accessed 10 September 2011).

Ballington, J. (2001) 'Youth and Political Participation: Tuned In or Tuned Out?' *International IDEA*: 11–13.

Barber, B.R. (1984) *Strong Democracy: Participatory Politics for a New Age*, Berkeley: University of California Press.

Barnes, A. (2010) 'Youth Voter Turnout in Canada: 1. Trends and Issues,' Library of Parliament (Canada): 1–7.

150 Bibliography

Barnes, S.H. and Kaase, M. (1979) *Political Action: Mass Participation in Five Western Democracies*, Beverly Hills, CA: Sage.

Bean, C. (1991) 'Are Australian Attitudes to Government Different?: A Comparison with Five Nations,' in F.G. Castles (ed.) *Australia Compared: People, Policies and Politics*, North Sydney, NSW: Allen and Unwin.

Bean, C. (2003) 'Citizen Confidence in Social and Political Institutions in a Changing World,' paper presented at the Conference on Social Change in the 21st Century, Centre for Social Change Research, Queensland University of Technology.

Bean, C. (2005) 'Is There a Crisis of Trust in Australia?' in S. Wilson, G. Meagher, R. Gibson and D. Denmark (eds), *Australian Social Attitudes: First Report*, Sydney, University of New South Wales Press.

Beck, P.A. and Jennings, K.M. (1982) 'Pathways to Participation,' *American Political Science Review* 76(1): 94–108.

Bell, S. and Hindmoor, A. (2009) *Rethinking Governance: The Calamity of the State in Modern Society*, Melbourne: Cambridge University Press.

Bennett, S.E. (1998) 'Young Americans' Indifference to Media Coverage of Public Affairs,' *PS: Political Science and Politics* 31(3): 535–41.

Bimber, B. (2003) *Information and American Democracy: Technology in the Evolution of Political Power*, New York: Cambridge University Press.

Bimber, B., Stohl, C. and Flanigan, A.J. (2009) 'Technological Change and the Shifting Nature of Political Organization,' in A. Chadwick and P. Howard (eds) *Routledge Handbook of Internet Politics*, London: Routledge.

Birch, A.H. (1993) *The British System of Government*, 9th edn, London and New York: Routledge.

Blair, T. (2010) *A Journey*, London: Hutchison.

Blais, A. (2000) *To Vote or Not to Vote*, Pittsburgh: University of Pittsburgh Press.

Blais, A. (2006) 'What Affects Voter Turnout?' *Annual Review of Political Science* 9: 111–25.

Blais, A. (2007) 'Turnout in Elections,' in R.J. Dalton and H.D. Klingemann (eds) *Oxford Handbook of Political Behavior*, New York: Oxford University Press.

Blais, A. (2010) 'Political Participation,' in L. LeDuc, R. Niemi and P. Norris (eds) *Comparing Democracies 3: Elections and Voting in the 21st Century*, Thousand Oaks, CA: Sage.

Blais, A. and Dobrzynska, A. (1998) 'Turnout in Electoral Democracies,' *European Journal of Political Research* 33(1): 239–61.

Blais, A. and Loewen, P. (2011) 'Youth Electoral Engagement in Canada,' Working Paper Series, Elections Canada.

Blais, A. and Young, R. (1999) 'Why Do Young People Vote? An Experiment in Rationality,' *Public Choice* 99(1): 39–55.

Blais, A., Gidengil, E., Nevitte, N. and Nadeau, R. (2002) 'Generational Change and the Decline of Political Participation: The Case of Voter Turnout in Canada,' paper presented at Citizenship on Trial: Interdisciplinary Perspectives on Political Socialization of Adolescents Conference, McGill University, Montreal, Canada.

Blais, A., Gidengil, E., Nevitte, N. and Nadeau, R. (2004) 'Where Does Turnout Decline Come From?' *European Journal of Political Research* 43(2): 221–36.

Brady, H., Verba, S. and Shlozman, K.L. (1995) 'Beyond SES: A Resource Model of Political Participation,' *American Political Science Review* 89(2): 271–94.
Brundidge, J. and Rice, R.E. (2009) 'Political Engagement Online: Do the Information Rich Get Richer and Like-minded More Similar?' in A. Chadwick and P. Howard (eds) *Routledge Encyclopedia of Internet Politics*, London: Routledge.
Burden, B. (2000) 'Voter Turnout and National Election Studies,' *Political Analysis* 8(4): 389–98.
Butler, D. (1995) *British General Elections Since 1945*, 2nd edn, Oxford, UK: Blackwell.
Cain, B.E., Dalton, R.J. and Scarrow, S.E. (2003) *Democracy Transformed?: Expanding Political Opportunities in Advanced Industrial Democracies*, New York: Oxford University Press.
Campbell, A., Converse, P.E., Miller, W.E. and Stokes, D.E. (1960) *The American Voter*, New York: John Wiley & Sons, Inc.
Campbell, A., Converse, P.E., Miller, W.E. and Stokes, D.E. (1966) *Elections and the Political Order*, New York: John Wiley & Sons, Inc.
Campbell, A., Gurin, G. and Miller, W.E. (1954) *The Voter Decides*, Evanston, IL: Row, Peterson and Company.
Cassel, C.A. and Lo, C.C. (1997) 'Theories of Political Literacy,' *Political Behavior* 19(4): 317–35.
Catterberg, G. and Moreno, A. (2005) 'The Individual Bases of Political Trust: Trends in New and Established Democracies,' *International Journal of Public Opinion Research* 18(1): 31–48.
Chadwick, A. (2006) *Internet Politics: States, Citizens and New Communication Technologies*, New York: Oxford University Press.
CIRCLE (2008) Youth Voting. Available at: www.civicyouth.org/quick-facts/youth-voting/ (accessed 21 August 2009).
Citrin, J. (1974) 'Comment: The Political Relevance of Trust in Government,' *American Political Science Review* 68(3): 973–88.
Clarke, H.D., Sanders, D., Stewart, M.C. and Whiteley, P.F. (2004) *Political Choice in Britain*, New York: Oxford University Press.
Converse, P.E. (1964) 'The Nature of Belief Systems in Mass Publics,' in D.E. Apter (ed.) *Ideology and Discontent*, New York: Free Press of Glencoe.
Cox, G.W. (1999) 'Electoral Rules and the Calculus of Mobilization,' *Legislative Studies Quarterly* 24(3): 387–419.
Crepaz, M.M.L. (1990) 'The Impact of Party Polarization and Postmaterialism on Voter Turnout,' *European Journal of Political Research* 18(2): 183–205.
Crozier, M., Huntington, S. and Watanuki, J. (1975) *The Crisis of Democracy: Report on the Governability of Democracies to the Trilateral Commission 1975*, New York: New York University Press.
Dalton, R.J. (1984) 'Cognitive Mobilization and Partisan Dealignment in Advanced Industrial Democracies,' *Journal of Politics* 46(1): 264–84.
Dalton, R.J. (1996) 'Political Cleavages, Issues, and Electoral Change,' in L. LeDuc, R.G. Niemi and P. Norris (eds) *Comparing Democracies: Election and Voting in Global Perspective*, London: Sage.
Dalton, R.J. (1999) 'Political Support in Advanced Industrial Democracies,' in P. Norris (ed.) *Critical Citizens: Global Support for Democratic Government*, New York: Oxford University Press.

Dalton, R.J. (2000a) 'Citizen Attitudes and Political Behavior,' *Comparative Political Studies* 33(6): 912–40.
Dalton, R.J. (2000b) 'Value Change and Democracy,' in S.J. Pharr and R.D. Putnam (eds) *Disaffected Democracies: What's Troubling the Trilateral Countries?* Princeton, NJ: Princeton University Press.
Dalton, R.J. (2002) 'The Decline of Party Identification,' in R.J. Dalton and M.P. Wattenberg (eds) *Parties Without Partisans: Political Change in Advanced Industrial Democracies*, New York: Oxford University Press: 19–36.
Dalton, R.J. (2004) *Democratic Challenges, Democratic Choices: The Erosion of Political Support in Advanced Industrial Democracies*, New York: Oxford University Press.
Dalton, R.J. (2005) 'The Myth of the Disengaged American,' *Public Opinion Pros*: 1–5.
Dalton, R.J. (2006) *Citizen Politics: Public Opinion and Political Parties in Advanced Industrial Societies*, Washington, DC: CQ Press.
Dalton, R.J. (2008) *The Good Citizen: How a Younger Generation is Reshaping American Politics*, Washington, DC: CQ Press.
Dalton, R.J. (2011a) 'Introduction: The Debate over Youth Participation,' in R.J. Dalton (ed.) *Engaging Youth in Politics: Debating Democracy's Future*, New York and Amsterdam: international debate education association: 1–15.
Dalton, R.J. (2011b) 'Participation Beyond Elections,' in R.J. Dalton (ed.), *Engaging Youth in Politics: Debating Democracy's Future*, New York and Amsterdam: international debate education association: 112–31.
Dalton, R.J. and Klingemann, H.D. (2007) 'Citizens and Political Behavior,' in R.J. Dalton and H.D. Klingemann (eds) *Oxford Handbook of Political Behavior*, Oxford, UK: Oxford University Press.
Dalton, R.J. and Wattenberg, M.P. (2002) 'Unthinkable Democracy: Political Change in Advanced Industrial Democracies,' in R.J. Dalton and M.P. Wattenberg (eds) *Parties Without Partisans: Political Change in Advanced Industrial Democracies*, New York: Oxford University Press.
Dalton, R.J. and Weldon, S. (2005) 'Is the Party Over? Spreading Antipathy Towards Political Parties,' *Public Opinion Pros*: 1–5.
Dalton, R.J., Flanagan, S.C. and Beck, P. (eds) (1984) *Electoral Change in Advanced Industrial Democracies: Realignment or Dealignment?* Princeton, NJ: Princeton University Press.
Dalton, R.J., McAllister, I. and Wattenberg, M.P. (2002) 'The Consequences of Partisan Dealignment,' in R.J. Dalton and M.P. Wattenberg (eds) *Parties Without Partisans: Political Change in Advanced Industrial Democracies*, New York: Oxford University Press.
Dalton, R.J., Scarrow, S.E. and Cain, B.E. (2004) 'Advanced Democracies and the New Politics,' *Journal of Democracy* 15(1): 124–38.
Delli Carpini, M.X. and Keeter, S. (1996) *What Americans Know About Politics and Why it Matters*, New Haven, CT: Yale University Press.
Dennis, J. (1970) 'Support for the Institution of Elections by the Mass Media,' *American Political Science Review*, 64(3): 819–35.
Denver, D.T. (2003) *Elections and Voters in Britain*, New York: Palgrave Macmillan.
Denver, D.T. (2005) *Elections and Voters in Britain*, 2nd edn, New York: Palgrave Macmillan.

Dorling, D., Pattie, C., Rossiter, D. and Johnston, R. (1996) 'Missing Voters in Britain, 1992–1996: Where and with What Impact?' in D.M. Farrell, D. Broughton, D. Denver and J. Fisher (eds) *British Elections and Parties Yearbook 1996*, London: Frank Cass.

Downs, A. (1957) *An Economic Theory of Democracy*, New York: Harper Collins.

Dye, T.R. and Zeigler, L.H. (1970) *The Irony of Democracy: An Uncommon Introduction to American Politics*, Belmont, CA: Wadsworth Pub. Co.

Easton, D. (1965) *A System Analysis of Political Life*, New York: J. Wiley.

Easton, D. (1975) 'A Re-Assessment of the Concept of Political Support,' *British Journal of Political Science* 5(4): 435–57.

Easton, D. (1990) *The Analysis of Political Structure*, New York: Routledge.

Easton, D. and Dennis, J. (1969) *Children in the Political System: Origins of Political Legitimacy*, New York: McGraw-Hill.

Eisner, J. (2004) *Taking Back the Vote: Getting American Youth Involved in Our Democracy*, Boston: Beacon Press.

Electoral Commission (2004) News Release: Party Campaign Drive Record Turnout. Available at: www.electoralcommission.org.uk/news-and-media/news-releases/electoral-commission-media-centre/news-releases-corporate/party-campaigns-drive-record-turnout (accessed 14 June 2009).

Elklit, J., Svensson, P. and Togeby, L. (2005) 'Why is Turnout Not Declining in Denmark?' paper presented at 2005 Annual American Political Science Association, Washington, DC.

Erikson, R.S., MacKuen, M. and Stimson, J.A. (2002) *The Macro Polity*, New York: Cambridge University Press.

Fahmy, E. (2006) *Young Citizens: Young People's Involvement in Politics and Decision Making*, Aldershot: Ashgate.

Falcone, M. (2008) 'Youth Turnout Up by 2 Million From 2004.' Available at: http://thecaucus.blogs.nytimes.com/2008/11/05/youth-turnout-up-by-2-million-from-2004/ (accessed 15 July 2008).

Fieldhouse, E., Tramner, M. and Russell, A. (2007) 'Something About Young People or Something About Elections? Electoral Participation of Young People in Europe: Evidence from a Multilevel Analysis of the European Social Survey,' *European Journal of Political Research* 46(6): 797–822.

Fields, A.B. (2011) 'The Youth Challenge: Participating in Democracy,' in R.J. Dalton (ed.) *Engaging Youth in Politics: Debating Democracy's Future*, New York and Amsterdam: international debate education association.

Finkel, S.E. (1985) 'Reciprocal Effects of Participation and Political Efficacy: A Panel Analysis,' *American Journal of Political Science* 29(4): 891–913.

Flanigan, W.H. and Zingale, N.H. (1994) *Political Behavior of the American Electorate*, Washington, DC: CQ Press.

Franklin, M.N. (1999) 'Electoral Engineering and Cross-National Turnout Differences: What Role for Compulsory Voting?' *British Journal of Political Science* 29(1): 205–16.

Franklin, M.N. (2004) *Voter Turnout and the Dynamics of Electoral Competition in Established Democracies Since 1945*, New York: Cambridge University Press.

Freie, J.F. (1997) 'The Effects of Campaign Participation on Political Attitudes,' *Political Behavior* 19(2): 133–56.

154 Bibliography

Fuchs, D. (2007) 'The Political Culture Paradigm,' in R.J. Dalton and H.D. Klingemann (eds) *Oxford Handbook of Political Behavior*, Oxford, UK: Oxford University Press.

Fuchs, D. and Klingemann, H.D. (1995a) 'Citizens and the State: A Changing Relationship?' in H.D. Klingemann and D. Fuchs (eds) *Citizens and the State*, New York: Oxford University Press.

Fuchs, D. and Klingemann, H.D. (1995b) 'Citizens and the State: A Relationship Transformed?' in H.D. Klingemann and D. Fuchs (eds) *Citizens and the State*, New York: Oxford University Press.

Fuchs, D., Guidorossi, G. and Svensson, P. (1995) 'Support for the Democratic System,' in H.D. Klingemann and D. Fuchs (eds) *Citizens and the State*, New York: Oxford University Press.

Galston, W.A. (2001) 'Political Knowledge, Political Engagement, and Civic Education,' *Annual Review of Political Science* 4: 217–34.

Galston, W.A. (2007) 'Civic Knowledge, Civic Education and Civic Engagement: A Summary of Recent Research,' *International Journal of Public Administration* 30: 623–42.

Garrett, G. (1998) *Partisan Politics in the Global Economy*, Cambridge, UK: Cambridge University Press.

Gauthier, M. (2003) 'The Inadequacy of Concepts: The Rise of Youth Interest in Civic Participation in Quebec,' *Journal of Youth Studies* 6(3): 265–76.

Gibson, R. and McAllister, I. (2006) 'Does Cybercampaigning Win Votes?: Online Political Communication in the 2004 Australian Election,' *Journal of Elections, Public Opinion and Parties* 16(3): 273–88.

Gibson, R., Lusoli, W., Römmele, A. and Ward, S. (2004) 'Introduction: Representative Democracy and the Internet,' in R. Gibson, A. Römmele and S. Ward (eds) *Electronic Democracy: Mobilization, Organization and Participation via New ICTs*, London: Routledge.

Gidengil, E., Blais, A., Everitt, J., Fournier, P. and Nevitte, N. (2005) 'Missing the Message: Young Adults and Election Issues,' *Electoral Insight*: 1–6.

Gidengil, E., Blais, A., Nevitte, N. and Nadeau, R. (2003) 'Turned Off or Tuned Out?: Youth Participation and Politics,' *Electoral Insight*: 1–7.

Gidengil, E., Nadeau, R., Nevitte, N. and Blais, A. (2010) 'Citizens,' in W. Cross (ed.) *Auditing Canadian Democracy*, Vancouver: UBC Press.

Goot, M. (2002) 'Distrustful, Disenchanted and Disengaged? Public Opinion on Politics, Politicians and Parties: An Historical Perspective,' in D. Burchell and A. Leigh (eds) *The Prince's New Clothes: Why Do Australians Dislike Their Politicians?* Sydney: University of New South Wales Press.

Gordon, S.B. and Segura, G.M. (1997) 'Cross-National Variation in the Political Sophistication of Individuals: Capability or Choice?' *Journal of Politics* 59(1): 126–47.

Graetz, B. and McAllister, I. (1994) *Dimensions of Australian Society*, 2nd edn, South Melbourne, Vic.: Macmillan.

Granberg, D. and Holmberg, S. (1991) 'Self-Reported Turnout and Voter Validation,' *American Journal of Political Science* 35(2): 448–59.

Granberg, D. and Holmberg, S. (1992) 'The Hawthorne Effect in Election Studies: The Impact of Survey Participation on Voting,' *British Journal of Political Science* 22(2): 240–48.

Gray, M. and Caul, M. (2000) 'Declining Voter Turnout in Advanced Industrial

Democracies, 1950 to 1997: The Effects of Declining Group Mobilization,' *Comparative Political Studies* 33(9): 1091–122.
Green, D.P. and Gerber, A.S. (2008) *Get Out the Vote: How to Increase Voter Turnout*, Washington, DC: Brookings Institution Press.
Green, D.P. and Shachar, R. (2000) 'Habit Formation and Political Behaviour: Evidence of Consuetude in Voter Turnout,' *British Journal of Political Science* 30(4): 561–73.
Greenstein, F.E. (1970) 'A Note on the Ambiguity of "Political Socialization": Definitions, Criticisms, and Strategies of Inquiry,' *Journal of Politics* 32(4): 969–78.
Gronlund, K. and Milner, H. (2006) 'The Determinants of Political Knowledge in Comparative Perspective,' *Scandinavian Political Studies* 29(4): 386–406.
Haerpfer, C., Wallace, C. and Spannring, R. (2002) 'Young People and Politics in Eastern and Western Europe,' *Sociological Series* 54: 1–33.
Halman, L. (2007) 'Political Values,' in R.J. Dalton and H.D. Klingemann (eds) *Oxford Handbook of Political Behavior*, New York: Oxford University Press.
Hay, C. (2008) *Why We Hate Politics*, Cambridge, UK: Polity Press.
Hayes, B. and McAllister, I. (1999) 'Generations, Prejudice and Politics in Northern Ireland,' in L. Dowds, R. Breen and C.T. Whelan (eds) *Ireland North and South: Perspectives from the Social Sciences*, Oxford, UK: Oxford University Press.
Held, D. (1996) *Models of Democracy*, Stanford, CA: Stanford University Press.
Hellevik, O. (2002) 'Age Differences in Value Orientation—Life Cycle or Cohort Effects?' *International Journal of Public Opinion Research* 14(3): 290–310.
Henn, M. and Weinstein, M. (2006) 'Young People and Political (In)activism: Why Don't Young People Vote?' *The Policy Press* 34(3): 517–34.
Henn, M., Weinstein, M. and Hodgkinson, S. (2007) 'Social Capital and Political Participation: Understanding the Dynamics of Young People's Political Disengagement in Britain,' *Social Policy and Society* 6(4): 467–79.
Henn, M., Weinstein, M. and Wring, D. (2002) 'A Generation Apart? Youth and Political Participation in Britain,' *British Journal of Politics and International Relations* 4(2): 167–92.
Hetherington, M.J. (1998) 'The Political Relevance of Political Trust,' *American Political Science Review* 92(4): 791–808.
Heywood, A. (1997) *Politics*, London: Macmillan.
Hibbing, J.R. and Theiss-Morse, E. (2002) *Stealth Democracy: Americans' Beliefs About How Government Should Work*, Cambridge, UK: Cambridge University Press.
Highton, B. and Wolfinger, B.E. (2001) 'The First Seven Years of the Political Life Cycle,' *American Journal of Political Science* 45(1): 202–9.
Hirczy, W. (1995) 'Explaining Near Universal Turnout: The Case of Malta,' *European Journal of Political Research* 27(2): 255–72.
Holmberg, S. (1999) 'Down and Down We Go: Political Trust in Sweden,' in P. Norris (ed.) *Critical Citizens: Global Support for Democratic Government*, New York: Oxford University Press.
Holmberg, S. (2007) 'Partisanship Reconsidered,' in R.J. Dalton and H.D. Klingemann (eds) *Oxford Handbook of Political Behavior*, Oxford, UK: Oxford University Press.
Hooghe, M. (2004) 'Political Socialization and the Future of Politics,' *Acta Politica* 39: 331–41.

Howe, P. (2006) 'Political Knowledge and Electoral Participation: Comparisons with the Canadian Case,' *International Political Science Review* 27(2): 137–66.

Howe, P. (2010) *Citizens Adrift: The Democratic Disengagement of Young Canadians*, Vancouver: UBC Press.

Huntington, S.P. (1981) *American Politics: The Promise of Disharmony*, Cambridge, MA: Belknap Press.

Inglehart, R. (1977) *The Silent Revolution: Changing Values and Political Styles among Western Publics*, Princeton, NJ: Princeton University Press.

Inglehart, R. (1981) 'Post-Materialism in an Environment of Insecurity,' *American Political Science Review* 75(3): 881–99.

Inglehart, R. (1990) *Culture Shift in Advanced Industrial Society*, Princeton, NJ: Princeton University Press.

Inglehart, R. (1997) 'Postmaterial Values and the Erosion of Institutional Authority,' in J.S. Nye, P.D. Zelikow and D.C. King (eds) *Why People Don't Trust Government*, London: Harvard University Press.

Inglehart, R. (2000) 'Globalization and Postmodern Values,' *The Washington Quarterly* 23(1): 215–28.

Inglehart, R. (2007) 'Postmaterialist Values and the Shift from Survival to Self Expression Values,' in R.J. Dalton and H.D. Klingemann (eds) *Oxford Handbook of Political Behavior*, New York: Oxford University Press.

Inglehart, R. and Klingemann, H.D. (1979) 'Ideological Conceptualization and Value Priorities,' in S.H. Barnes and M. Kaase (eds) *Political Action: Mass Participation in Five Western Democracies*, Beverly Hills, CA: Sage.

Inglehart, R. and Welzel, C. (2005) *Modernization, Cultural Change, and Democracy: The Human Development Sequence*, New York: Cambridge University Press.

Jackman, R.W. (1970) 'A Note on Intelligence, Social Class, and Political Efficacy in Children,' *Journal of Politics* 32(4): 984–89.

Jackman, R.W. (1987) 'Political Institutions and Voter Turnout in the Industrial Democracies,' *American Political Science Review* 81(2): 405–24.

Jackman, R.W. and Miller, R.A. (1995) 'Voter Turnout in the Industrial Democracies during the 1980s,' *Comparative Political Studies* 27: 467–92.

Jackman, S. (1999) 'Non-compulsory Voting in Australia?: What Surveys Can (and Can't) Tell Us,' *Electoral Studies* 18(7): 29–48.

Jennings, K. (2007) 'Political Socialization,' in R.J. Dalton and H.D. Klingemann (eds) *Oxford Handbook of Political Behavior*, New York: Oxford University Press.

Jennings, M.K. and Niemi, R.G. (1974) *The Political Character of Adolescence: The Influence of Families and Schools*, Princeton, NJ: Princeton University Press.

Jennings, M.K. and Niemi, R.G. (1981) *Generations and Politics: A Panel Study of Young Adults and Their Parents*, Princeton, NJ: Princeton University Press.

Jennings, M.K. and Stoker, L. (2004) 'Social Trust and Civic Engagement Across Time and Generations,' *Acta Politica* 39: 342–79.

Kaase, M. (2007) 'Perspectives on Political Participation,' in R.J. Dalton and H.D. Klingemann (eds) *Oxford Handbook of Political Behavior*, Oxford, UK: Oxford University Press.

Kaase, M. and Marsh, A. (1979a) 'Political Action: A Theoretical Perspective,' in S.H. Barnes and M. Kaase (eds) *Political Action: Mass Participation in Five Western Democracies*, Beverly Hills, CA: Sage.

Kaase, M. and Marsh, A. (1979b) 'Distribution of Political Action,' in S.H. Barnes and M. Kaase (eds) *Political Action: Mass Participation in Five Western Democracies*, Beverly Hills, CA: Sage.

Kavanagh, D. (1983) *Political Science and Political Behaviour*, London: Allen & Unwin.

Keane, J. (2011) 'Monitory Democracy? The Secret History of Democracy since 1945,' in B. Isakhan and S. Stockwell (eds) *The Secret History of Democracy*, New York: Palgrave Macmillan.

Key, V.O. (1949) *Southern Politics in State and Nation*, New York: Alfred A. Knopf.

Klingemann, H.D. (1999) 'Mapping Political Support in the 1990s: A Global Analysis,' in P. Norris (ed.) *Critical Citizens: Global Support for Democratic Government*, New York: Oxford University Press.

Kornberg, A. and Clarke, H.D. (1992) *Citizens and Community: Political Support in a Representative Democracy*, New York: Cambridge University Press.

Kurklinski, J.H. and Peyton, B. (2007) 'Belief Systems and Political Decision Making,' in R.J. Dalton and H.D. Klingemann (eds) *Oxford Handbook of Political Behavior*, New York: Oxford University Press.

Lane, J.E. and Ersson, S. (1990) 'Macro and Micro Understanding in Political Science: What Explains Electoral Participation?' *European Journal of Political Research* 18: 457–65.

Larcinese, V. (2007) 'Does Political Knowledge Increase Turnout? Evidence from the 1997 British General Election,' *Pubic Choice* 131: 387–411.

LeDuc, L., Pammett, J.H., McKenzie, J.I. and Turcotte, A. (2010) *Dynasties and Interludes: Past and Present in Canadian Electoral Politics*, Toronto: Dundurn Press.

Leigh, A. (2010) *Disconnected*, Sydney: University of New South Wales Press.

Leighley, J.E. (1995) 'Attitudes, Opportunities and Incentives: A Field Essay on Political Participation,' *Political Research Quarterly* 48(1): 181–209.

Levine, P. (2007) *The Future of Democracy: Developing the Next Generation of American Citizens*, Medford, MA: Tufts University Press.

Lijphart, A. (1994) 'Democracies: Forms, Performance, and Constitutional Engineering,' *European Journal of Political Research* 25(1): 1–17.

Lijphart, A. (1997) 'Unequal Participation: Democracy's Unresolved Dilemma,' *American Political Science Review* 91(1): 1–14.

Lijphart, A. (1999) *Patterns of Democracy: Government Forms and Performance in Thirty-six Countries*, New Haven, CT: Yale University Press.

Lipset, S.M. and Schneider, W. (1983) *The Confidence Gap: Business, Labor, and Government in the Public Mind*, London: Free Press.

Listhaug, O. (1995) 'The Dynamics of Trust in Politicians,' in H.D. Klingemann and D. Fuchs (eds) *Citizens and the State*, New York: Oxford University Press.

Listhaug, O. and Gronflaten, L. (2007) 'Civic Decline? Trends in Political Involvement and Participation in Norway, 1965–2001,' *Scandinavian Political Studies* 30(2): 272–99.

Listhaug, O. and Wiberg, M. (1995) 'Confidence in Political and Private Institutions,' in H.D. Klingemann and D. Fuchs (eds) *Citizens and the State*, New York: Oxford University Press.

Löfgren, K. and Smith, C. (2003) 'Political Parties and Democracy in the Information Age,' in R. Gibson, N. Paul and S. Ward (eds) *Political Parties and the Internet: Net Gain?* London: Routledge.

Lyons, W. and Alexander, R. (2000) 'A Tale of Two Electorates: Generational Replacement and the Decline in Voting in Presidential Elections,' *Journal of Politics* 62(4): 1014–34.

MacManus, S.A. (1996) *Young v. Old: Generational Combat in the 21st Century*, Boulder, CO: Westview Press.

Macpherson, C.B. (1977) *The Life and Times of Liberal Democracy*, New York: Oxford University Press.

Mair, P. (1989) 'Continuity, Change and Vulnerability of Party,' *West European Politics* 12(4): 169–87.

Margolis, M. (2009) 'E-Government and Democracy,' in R.J. Dalton and H.D. Klingemann (eds) *Oxford Handbook of Political Behavior*, Oxford, UK: Oxford University Press.

Margolis, M. and Resnick, D. (2000) *Politics as Usual: The Cyberspace 'Revolution'*, Thousand Oaks, CA: Sage.

Marsh, A. (1977) *Protest and Political Consciousness*, Beverly Hills, CA: Sage.

Marsh, A. and Kaase, M. (1979a) 'Measuring Political Action,' in S.H. Barnes and M. Kaase (eds) *Political Action: Mass Participation in Five Western Democracies*, Beverly Hills, CA: Sage.

Marsh, A. and Kaase, M. (1979b) 'Background of Political Action,' in S.H. Barnes and M. Kaase (eds) *Political Action: Mass Participation in Five Western Democracies*, Beverly Hills, CA: Sage.

Marsh, D., O'Toole, T. and Jones, S. (2007) *Young People and Politics in the UK: Apathy or Alienation?* New York: Palgrave Macmillan.

McAllister, I. (1992) *Political Behaviour: Citizens, Parties and Elites in Australia*, Melbourne: Longman Cheshire.

McAllister, I. (1998) 'Civic Education and Political Knowledge in Australia,' *Australian Journal of Political Science* 33(1): 7–34.

McAllister, I. (2011) *The Australian Voter: 50 Years of Change*, Sydney: University of New South Wales Press.

McDonald, S.P. and Popkin, S.L. (2001) 'The Myth of the Vanishing Voter,' *American Political Science Review* 95(4): 963–74.

Merriam, C.E. and Gosnell, H.F. (1924) *Non-Voting: Causes and Methods of Control*, Chicago: University of Chicago Press.

Milbraith, L.W. and Goel, M.L. (1977) *Political Participation: How and Why do People Get Involved in Politics?* Chicago: Rand McNally College Pub. Co.

Miller, A. (1974a) 'Political Issues and Trust in Government: 1964–1970,' *American Political Science Review* 68(3): 951–72.

Miller, A. (1974b) 'Rejoinder to "Comment" by Jack Citrin: Political Discontent or Ritualism,' *American Political Science Review* 68(3): 989–1001.

Miller, A. and Listhaug, O. (1999) 'Political Performance and Institutional Trust,' in P. Norris (ed.) *Critical Citizens: Global Support for Democratic Governance*, Oxford, UK: Oxford University Press.

Miller, W.E. and Shanks, J.M. (1996) *The New American Voter*, Cambridge, MA: Harvard University Press.

Milner, H. (1997) 'Electoral Systems, Integrated Institutions and Turnout in Local and National Elections: Canada in Comparative Perspective,' *Canadian Journal of Political Science* 30(1): 89–106.

Milner, H. (2002) *Civic Literacy: How Informed Citizens Make Democracy Work*, Hanover, NH: University Press of New England.

Milner, H. (2010) *The Internet Generation: Engaged Citizens or Political Dropouts*, Medford, MA: Tufts University Press.

Mossberger, K. (2009) 'Toward Digital Citizenship: Addressing Inequality in the Information Age,' in A. Chadwick and P. Howard (eds) *Routledge Handbook of Internet Politics*, London, Routledge.

Newton, K. (2001) 'Trust, Social Capital, Circle Society and Democracy,' *International Political Science Review* 22(2): 201–14.

Newton, K. (2007) 'Social and Political Trust,' in R.J. Dalton and H.D. Klingemann (eds) *Oxford Handbook of Political Behavior*, Oxford, UK: Oxford University Press.

Newton, K. and Norris, P. (2000) 'Confidence in Public Institutions: Faith, Culture or Performance?' in S.J. Pharr and R.D. Putnam (eds) *Disaffected Democracies: What's Troubling the Trilateral Countries?* Princeton, NJ: Princeton University Press.

Nie, N.H., Junn, J. and Stehlik-Barry, K. (1996) *Education and Democratic Citizenship in America*, Chicago: University of Chicago Press.

Nie, N.H., Verba, S. and Petrocik, J.R. (1984) 'The Decline of Partisanship,' in R.G. Niemi and H.F. Weisberg (eds) *Controversies in Voting Behavior*, Washington, DC: CQ Press.

Niemi, R.G. and Junn, J. (1998) *Civic Education: What Makes Students Learn*, New Haven, CT: Yale University Press.

Norris, P. (1997) *Electoral Change Since 1945*, Cambridge, UK: Blackwell.

Norris, P. (1999a) 'Introduction: The Growth of the Critical Citizen,' in P. Norris (ed.) *Critical Citizens: Global Support for Democratic Government*, New York: Oxford University Press.

Norris, P. (1999b) 'Conclusions: The Growth of Critical Citizens and its Consequences,' in P. Norris (ed.) *Critical Citizens: Global Support for Democratic Government*, New York: Oxford University Press.

Norris, P. (2001) *Digital Divide: Civic Engagement, Information Poverty, and the Internet Worldwide*, New York: Cambridge University Press.

Norris, P. (2002) *Democratic Phoenix: Reinventing Political Activism*, New York: Cambridge University Press.

Norris, P. (2003) 'Young People and Political Activism: From the Politics of Loyalties to the Politics of Choice?' Keynote Address at the Council of Europe Symposium 'Young people and democratic institutions: from disillusionment to participation,' Council of Europe, Strasbourg.

Norris, P. (2011) *Democratic Deficit: Critical Citizens Revisited*, New York: Cambridge University Press.

Nye, J.S. (1997) 'Introduction,' in J.S. Nye, P.D. Zelikow and D.C. King (eds) *Why People Don't Trust Government*, London: Harvard University Press.

Nye, J.S. and Zelikow, P.D. (1997) 'Conclusion: Reflections, Conjectures, and Puzzles,' in J.S. Nye, P.D. Zelikow and D.C. King (eds) *Why People Don't Trust Government*, London: Harvard University Press.

Nye, J.S., Zelikow, P.D. and King, D.C. (eds) (1997) *Why People Don't Trust Government*, London: Harvard University Press.

O'Neill, B. (2007) 'Indifferent or Just Different? The Political and Civic Engagement of Young People in Canada,' Canadian Policy Research Networks, *CPRN Research Report*.

O'Toole, T., Lister, M., Marsh, D. and McDonagh, A. (2003a) 'Tuning Out or Left Out? Participation and Non-participation among Young People,' *Contemporary Politics* 9(1): 45–64.

O'Toole, T., Marsh, D. and Jones, S. (2003b) 'Political Literacy Cuts Both Ways: The Politics of Non-participation among Young People,' *Political Quarterly* 74(3): 349–60.

Orren, G. (1997) 'Measuring the Performance of Government,' in J.S. Nye, P.D. Zelikow and D.C. King (eds) *Why People Don't Trust Government*, London: Harvard University Press.

Owen, D. (2006) 'The Internet and Youth Civic Engagement in the United States,' in S. Oates, D. Owen and R. Gibson (eds) *The Internet and Politics: Citizens, Voters and Activists*, London: Routledge.

Pammett, J. and LeDuc, L. (2003) 'Explaining the Turnout Decline in Canadian Federal Elections: A New Survey of Non-Voters,' *Elections Canada*.

Papadakis, E. (1999) 'Constituents of Confidence and Mistrust in Australian Institutions,' *Australian Journal of Political Science* 34(1): 75–93.

Pateman, C. (1970) *Participation and Democratic Theory*, Cambridge, UK: Cambridge University Press.

Pateman, C. (1985) *The Problem of Political Obligation: A Critique of Liberal Theory*, Cambridge, UK: Polity in association with Blackwell.

Patterson, T.E. (2002) *The Vanishing Voter: Public Involvement in an Age of Uncertainty*, New York: Alfred A. Knopf.

Pattie, C., Seyd, P. and Whiteley, P. (2004) *Citizenship in Britain: Values, Participation and Democracy*, Cambridge, UK: Cambridge University Press.

Pew Research Center for the People and the Press (2006) 'Who Votes, Who Doesn't, and Why: Regular Voters, Intermittent Voters and Those Who Don't,' Pew Research Center for the People and the Press.

Pew Research Center for the People and the Press (2007a) 'Trends in Political Values and Core Attitudes,' Pew Research Center for the People and the Press.

Pew Research Center for the People and the Press (2007b) 'Public Knowledge of Current Affairs Little Changed by News and Information Revolutions,' Pew Research Center for the People and the Press.

Pharr, S.J. and Putnam, R.D. (eds) (2000) *Disaffected Democracies: What's Troubling the Trilateral Countries?* Princeton, NJ: Princeton University Press.

Phelps, E. (2005) 'Young Voters at the 2005 British General Election,' *The Political Quarterly* 76(4): 482–7.

Pirie, M. and Worcester, R.M. (1998) *The Millennial Generation*, London: Adam Smith Institute/MORI.

Plutzer, E. (2002) 'Becoming a Habitual Voter: Inertia, Resources, and Growth in Young Adulthood,' *American Political Science Review* 96(1): 41–56.

Pomper, G. (1978) 'The Impact of the American Voter on Political Science,' *Political Science Quarterly* 93(4): 617–28.

Powell, B. (1984) 'Voting Turnout in Thirty Democracies: Partisan, Legal and Socio-Economic Influences,' in R.G. Niemi and H.F. Weisberg (eds) *Controversies in Voting Behavior*, Washington, DC: CQ Press.

Powell, B. (1986) 'American Voter Turnout in Comparative Perspective,' *American Political Science Review* 80(1): 17–43.

Print, M. (2007) 'Citizenship Education and Youth Participation in Democracy,' *British Journal of Educational Studies* 55(3): 325–45.

Print, M., Saha, L. and Edwards, K. (2004) 'Youth Electoral Study (YES)—Report 1: Enrolment and Voting,' *Youth Electoral Study*: 1–12.

Bibliography

Putnam, R.D. (1995) 'Bowling Alone: America's Declining Social Capital,' *Journal of Democracy* 6(1): 65–78.

Putnam, R.D. (2000) *Bowling Alone: The Collapse and Revival of American Community*, New York: Simon & Schuster.

Putnam, R.D., Pharr, S.J. and Dalton, R.J. (2000) 'Introduction: What's Troubling the Trilateral Democracies,' in S.J. Pharr and R.D. Putnam (eds) *Disaffected Democracies: What's Troubling the Trilateral Countries?* Princeton, NJ: Princeton University Press.

Rahn, W.M. and Transue, J.E. (1998) 'Social Trust and Value Change: The Decline of Social Capital in American Youth, 1976–1995,' *Political Psychology* 19(3): 545–65.

Rawnsley, G.D. (2005) *Political Communication and Democracy*, New York: Palgrave Macmillan.

Renwick, A. (2010) *The Politics of Electoral Reform: Changing the Rules of Democracy*, Cambridge, UK: Cambridge University Press.

Rose, R. (2007) 'Perspectives on Political Behavior in Time and Space,' in R.J. Dalton and H.D. Klingemann (eds) *Oxford Handbook of Political Behavior*, New York: Oxford University Press.

Rosenstone, S.J. and Hansen, J.M. (1993) *Mobilization, Participation, and Democracy in America*, New York: Macmillan.

Rubenson, D., Blais, A., Fournier, P., Gidengil, E. and Nevitte, N. (2004) 'Accounting for the Age Gap in Turnout,' *Acta Politica* 39: 407–21.

Rucht, D. (2007) 'The Spread of Protest Politics,' in R.J. Dalton and H. D. Klingemann (eds) *Oxford Handbook of Political Behavior*, New York: Oxford University Press.

Russell, A. (2004) 'The Truth about Youth? Media Portrayals of Young People and Politics in Britain,' *Journal of Public Affairs* 4(4): 347–55.

Russell, A., Fieldhouse, E., Purdam, K. and Kaira, V. (2002) 'Voter Engagement and Young People,' The Electoral Commission: London. Available at: www.electoralcommission.org.uk/about-us/voterengageyounggppl.cfm (accessed 1 June 2008).

Saha, L., Print, M. and Edwards, K. (2005) 'Youth Electoral Study (YES)—Report 2: Youth, Political Engagement and Voting,' *Youth Electoral Study*: 1–6.

Sapiro, V. (2004) 'Not Your Parents' Political Socialization: Introduction for a New Generation,' *Annual Review of Political Science* 7: 1–23.

Schmitt, H. and Holmberg, S. (1995) 'Political Parties in Decline?' in H.D. Klingemann and D. Fuchs (eds) *Citizens and the State*, New York: Oxford University Press.

Schudson, M. (1998) *The Good Citizen: A History of American Civic Life*, New York: The Free Press.

Shaffer, S.D. (1981) 'A Multivariate Explanation of Decreasing Turnout in Presidential Elections, 1960–1976,' *American Journal of Political Science* 25(1): 47–56.

Stoker, G. (2006) *Why Politics Matters: Making Democracy Work*, New York: Palgrave Macmillan.

Stokes, D.E. (1962) 'Popular Evaluations of Government: An Empirical Assessment,' in H. Cleveland and H.D. Laswell (eds) *Ethics and Bigness: Scientific, Academic, Religious, Political, and Military*, New York: Conference on Science, Philosophy and Religion in their Relation to the Democratic Way of Life, Inc.

Bibliography

Stolle, D. and Hooghe, M. (2004) 'The Roots of Social Capital: Attitudinal and Network Mechanisms in the Relation between Youth and Adult Indicators of Social Capital,' *Acta Politica* 39: 422–41.

Stolle, D. and Hooghe, M. (2005) 'Review Article: Inaccurate, Exceptional, One-sided or Irrelevant? The Debate About the Alleged Decline in Social Capital and Civic Engagement in Western Societies,' *British Journal of Political Science* 35(1): 149–68.

Strate, J.M., Parrish, C.J., Elder, C.D. and Colt, F. (1989) 'Life Span Civic Development and Voting Participation,' *American Political Science Review* 83(2): 443–64.

Tanguay, A.B. (2009) 'Reforming Representative Democracy: Taming the "Democractic Deficit,"' in J. Bickerton and A.G. Gagnon (eds) *Canadian Politics*, 9th edn, Toronto: University of Toronto Press.

Teixeira, R.A. (1992) *The Disappearing American Voter*, Washington, DC: Brookings Institution.

Thomassen, J. (1995) 'Support for Democratic Values,' in H.D. Klingemann and D. Fuchs (eds) *Citizens and the State*, New York: Oxford University Press.

Tingsten, H.L.G. (1963) *Political Behavior: Studies in Election Statistics*, Totowa, NJ: Bedminster Press.

Topf, R. (1995a) 'Electoral Participation,' in H.D. Klingemann and D. Fuchs (eds) *Citizens and the State*, New York: Oxford University Press.

Topf, R. (1995b) 'Beyond Electoral Participation,' in H.D. Klingemann and D. Fuchs (eds) *Citizens and the State*, New York: Oxford University Press.

Torney-Purta, J., Barber, C.H. and Richardson, W.K. (2004) 'Trust in Government-related Institutions and Political Engagement among Adolescents in Six Countries,' *Acta Politica* 39: 380–406.

Torney-Purta, J., Lehmann, R., Oswald, H. and Schultz, W. (2001) *Citizenship and Education in Twenty-eight Countries: Civic Knowledge and Engagement at Age Fourteen*, Amsterdam: International Association for the Evaluation of Educational Achievement (IEA).

Tranter, B. (2007) 'Political Knowledge and its Partisan Consequences,' *Australian Journal of Political Science* 42(1): 73–88.

Van Deth, J.W. (2009) 'Norms of Citizenship,' in R.J. Dalton and H.D. Klingemann (eds) *Oxford Handbook of Political Behavior*, New York: Oxford University Press.

Verba, S. (1999) 'Representative Democracy and Democratic Citizens: Philosophical and Empirical Understandings,' Tanner Lectures on Human Values, Brasenose College, Oxford University, UK.

Verba, S. (2003) 'Would the Dream of Political Equality Turn out to Be a Nightmare?' *Perspectives in Politics* 1(4): 663–79.

Verba, S. and Nie, N. (1972) *Participation in America: Political Democracy and Social Equality*, New York: Harper & Row.

Verba, S., Kim, J. and Nie, N. (1978) *Participation and Political Equality: A Seven-Nation Comparison*, Cambridge, UK: Cambridge University Press.

Verba, S., Schlozman, K.L. and Brady, H.E. (1995) *Voice and Equality: Civic Voluntarism in American Politics*, Cambridge, MA: Harvard University Press.

Vromen, A. (2003) '"People Try to Put Us Down...": Participatory Citizenship of "Generation X,"' *Australian Journal of Political Science* 38(1): 79–99.

Vromen, A. (2005) 'Three Political Myths about Young People,' *The Establish Review*: 1–14.

Vromen, A. (2008) 'Building Virtual Spaces: Young People, Participation and the Internet,' *Australian Journal of Political Science* 43(1): 79–97.
Vromen, A. and Gelber, K. (2005) *Powerscape: Contemporary Australian Political Practice*, Crows Nest, NSW: Allen and Unwin.
Ward, S. and Gibson, R. (2009) 'European Political Organizations and the Internet: Mobilization, Participation and Change,' in A. Chadwick and P. Howard (eds) *Routledge Handbook of Internet Politics*, London: Routledge.
Ward, S., Gibson, R. and Nixon, P. (2003) 'Introduction,' in R. Gibson, N. Paul and S. Ward (eds) *Political Parties and the Internet: Net Gain?* London: Routledge.
Wass, H. (2007) 'Generations and Socialization into Electoral Participation in Finland,' *Scandinavian Political Studies* 30(1): 1–19.
Wattenberg, M.P. (2002) *Where Have all the Voters Gone?* Cambridge, MA: Harvard University Press.
Wattenberg, M.P. (2007) *Is Voting for Young People?* New York: Pearson/Longman.
Western, J.S. and Wilson, P.R. (1973) 'Politics: Participation and Attitudes,' in H. Mayer and H. Nelson (eds) *Australian Politics: A Third Reader*, St. Kilda, Vic.: Cheshire.
Western, M. and Tranter, B. (2005) 'Are Postmaterialists Engaged Citizens?' in S. Wilson, G. Meagher, R. Gibson and D. Denmark (eds) *Australian Social Attitudes: First Report*, Sydney: University of New South Wales Press.
White, C., Bruce, S. and Ritchie, J. (2000) *Young People's Politics: Political Interest and Engagement Amongst 14–24 Year Olds*, York, UK: Joseph Rowntree Foundation.
Whittier, N. (1997) 'Political Generations: Micro-Cohorts, and the Transformation of Social Movements,' *American Sociological Review* 62(5): 760–78.
Wilson, S., Meagher, G., Gibson, R. and Denemark, D. (eds) (2005) *Australian Social Attitudes: First Report*, Sydney: University of New South Wales Press.
Wolfinger, R.E. and Rosenstone, S.J. (1980) *Who Votes?* New Haven, CT: Yale University Press.
Wright, T. (2003) *British Politics: A Very Short Introduction*, New York: Oxford University Press.
Wuthnow, R. (1976) 'Recent Pattern of Secularization: A Problem of Generations?' *American Sociological Review* 41(5): 850–67.
Young, L. and Cross, W. (2007) 'A Group Apart: Young Party Members in Canada: Charting the Course for Youth Civic and Political Participation,' *Canadian Policy Research Networks Research Report*.
Zaller, J. (1992) *The Nature and Origins of Mass Opinion*, New York: Cambridge University Press.
Zukin, C., Keeter, S., Andolina, M., Jenkins, K. and Delli Carpini, M.X. (2006) *A New Engagement? Political Participation, Civic Life, and the Changing American Citizen*, New York: Oxford University Press.

Index

Abramson, P.R. 4, 40, 42, 46, 54, 85
Adsett, M. 24
advantaged groups, non-electoral participation 97–9
age groups, study of 8–9
Aitkin, D. 75
Alexander, R. 12, 55
Almond, G.A. 7, 11, 12, 39, 54, 55
American National Election Study (ANES) 25–6, 45–6, 53, 58–60, 71–3, 82, 89, 144
American President's Commission for a National Agenda for the Eighties 40, 54
Anglo-American democracies, rationale for studying 9–10
ANUpoll, Australia 14, 103, 104, 108–9, 145
Australia: boycotting consumer products 93–4; candidate and party website visits 108–9; civic duty 32–4; contacting civil servants or politicians 80–1; electoral system 131; elite mobilization 127; Internet as tool for participation 103–5, 113–14; membership of political forums and discussion groups 106–7; party identification 75–7; party membership 79–80; petition signing 92–3; political Internet messages forwarded 107–8; political support 62–4; political trust 49–52; protesting 91–2; support for democracy 52–3; voter registration 128; voter turnout 30–2
Australian Election Study (AES) 30–1, 49–51, 62, 75–7, 129, 132, 144
Australian Survey of Political Attitudes 42

authority: erosion of respect for 5, 7, 51, 72–3; trust in 44, 53–4
autonomy 34, 48, 97–8
Avaaz.org 112

Ballington, J. 128
Barber, B.R. 114, 140
Barnes, S.H. 14, 70, 88, 98
Bean, C. 42, 51
Bell, S. 96
Bimber, B. 105, 113, 115–16
Birch, A.H. 29, 42, 95
Blair, T. 1, 142
Blais, A. 12, 13, 23, 24, 33, 34, 55, 57, 71, 88, 99, 122, 131, 137
book plan 10–16
Bowling Alone (Putnam) 4–5, 52, 57, 137–8
boycotting consumer products 88, 93–4
Bradley, B. 40
Britain: boycotting consumer products 93–4; civic duty 32–4; civic education 123; contacting civil servants or politicians 80–1; electoral reform 130; membership of political forums and discussion groups 106–7; mobilization by parties and politicians 83–4; non-electoral participation 88; party identification 74–5; party membership 70–1, 79; petition signing 92–3; political interest 57, 61, 62–4; political trust 42, 48–9, 51–2; protesting 91–2; support for democracy 52–3; voter registration 128, 129; voter turnout 28–30, 31–2
British Election Study (BES) 28–30, 48–9, 60–1, 74–5, 79, 83–4, 144–5
Brundidge, J. 113

Bush, G.W. 45–6
Butler, D. 4, 22, 28–9

Campbell, A. 8, 70, 85
Canada: boycotting consumer products 93–4; civic duty 32–4; contacting civil servants or politicians 80–1; membership of political forums and discussion groups 106–7; mobilization by parties and politicians 82–3; party identification 73–4; party membership 71, 78; petition signing 92–3; political interest 57, 60–1, 62–4; political trust 42, 43, 45–7, 51–2; protesting 91–2; support for democracy 52–3; voter registration 129; voter turnout 26–8, 31–2
Canadian Election Study (CES) 26–8, 45–7, 60–1, 73–4, 78, 83, 144
candidate websites 108–9
Carter, J. 10, 11, 39–40
Catterberg, G. 40, 42
causal links, identification of 10
Chadwick, A. 102, 105, 109, 110, 111, 112, 116, 117
Citizenship, Involvement, Democracy (CID) Survey 14, 103, 104, 107–9, 145
citizenship: in twenty-first century 140–3; shift in 100
Citrin, J. 53–4
civic duty: levels of 11, 15, 16, 21, 28, 32–4; political knowledge as complement to 122–3
civic education 122–5, 132
Civil Rights Act (1964), US 58
civil servants, contacting 80–1
civil society organizations, Internet as mobilization tool 110–13, 115
Clarke, H.D. 11, 23, 33, 37, 71
Clinton, B. 26, 45, 58, 59, 63, 112
Cold War, awareness of 53
Comparative Study of Electoral Systems (CSES) 52–3, 56
competitive elections 29, 131
compulsory civic education 123
compulsory voting 30, 130, 131, 133
Conservative Party, Britain 49
consuetude 24
consumer power, political use of 93–4
Crepaz, M.M.L. 130, 131
Crozier, M. 44, 54
current affairs lessons 124

Dahrendorf, R. 100
Dalton, R.J. 1, 11, 12, 13, 14, 15, 22, 23, 39, 40, 41, 42, 44, 45, 50, 52, 54, 55, 57, 70, 71, 85, 87, 88, 96, 98, 100, 101, 137, 138, 139, 141
data sources 6, 144–5
dealigned electorate 28, 74
Democratic Challenges, Democratic Choices (Dalton) 42
democracy, crisis of 24, 44, 53–4, 86, 135
democracy support 40, 53; data 52–3; erosion of 7; literature on 43–4
Democratic Phoenix (Norris) 88
Democrats, US 73
Dennis, J. 7, 42, 46, 47
Denver, D.T. 29, 30, 32, 74, 129
devolution 132
Digital Divide (Norris) 110–11
direct democracy 114–15
discussion groups 106–7, 114–15
'dissatisfied democrats' 44, 53
Dobrzysnka, A. 131
door-to-door canvassing 126–7
Dorling, D. 23
Downs, A. 34

Easton, D. 7, 42, 43, 46, 47
education effects: non-electoral participation 96–7; political equality 97–9; political interest 64; voter turnout 22; *see also* civic education
Eisner, J. 129
election day registration 129
Electoral Commission, UK 85
electoral engagement: data 71–84; defining political participation 69–70; discussion 84–6; literature on 70–1; non-electoral activity as supplement to 99; overview 12–13; research findings 137–9
electoral politics, future of 100
electoral system reform, effect on political engagement 130–1
electronic democracy disappointment with 109–10
elite mobilization 64, 81–4, 85–6; decline of 94–7; use of Internet 113–14; possibilities for 125–8, 132–3
elite-challenging forms of participation, rise of 94–6
Environment Defense Fund (EDF) 111, 115

Erikson, E.M. 1
Erikson, R.S. 12, 55
Europeans, support for democracy 44
experiential learning 124

face-to-face contact, importance of 109–10, 126–7
Fahmy, E. 2, 9, 11, 13, 37, 40, 42, 49, 123, 137, 140
Falcone, M. 26, 127
Fieldhouse, E. 5, 24
Fields, A.B. 16, 142
Franklin, M.N. 2, 24, 26, 34, 127
Fuchs, D. 37, 43, 44, 53, 95

Galston, W.A. 43, 46, 55, 57, 122
Garrett, G. 96
Gauthier, M. 88
generational effects: civic duty 34; electoral engagement 71, 73, 74–5, 76, 77, 78, 79–80, 85; identification of causal links 10; literature on 4–7; non-electoral participation 95, 96–7; political interest 57–8, 59–60, 61, 62, 63; political trust 42, 46, 47–8, 51–2; versus lifecycle effects 3–4; voter turnout 23–4, 26, 28, 31–2
Gerber, A.S. 122, 126, 127, 133
Gibson, R. 14, 102, 103, 105, 110, 111, 112, 113, 114, 115, 117, 127
Gidengil, E. 12, 43, 55, 57, 88, 114, 136
Global Exchange 112
global issues 110–13
globalization effects 95–6
Goot, M. 42, 51
Granberg, D. 32
Green, D.P. 23, 24, 122, 126, 127, 133
Greenstein, F.E. 7
Gronflaten, L. 88

Haerpfer, C. 44
Hansen, J.M. 41, 58, 64, 81, 126
Hawke, B. 76
Hay, C. 39, 53, 87, 90–1, 99, 139
Hellevik, O. 3
Henn, M. 42, 48, 57, 58, 71
Hetherington, M.J. 54
Highton, B. 3
Hindmoor, A. 96
Holmberg, S. 8, 32, 44, 52
Hooghe, M. 24, 71, 88
Howard John 51, 77
Howe, P. 2, 12, 43, 99
Human Rights Act (1998), US 49

Huntington, S.P. 44, 54
hybrid political organizations 112–13

Inglehart, R. 4–7, 34, 42, 44, 51, 52, 53, 57, 70, 85–6, 87, 88, 89, 94, 96, 97, 99, 100, 137–9
institutional effects 130–1, 133
international organizations, targeting 95–6, 111, 112, 115
International Social Survey Program (ISSP) Citizenship Survey (2004) 13, 21, 32–4, 77–8, 79–81, 89–90, 91–4, 103, 106–7, 136, 145
Internet: data 103; discussion 113–17; measurement issues 115–16; overview 14–15; participatory inequalities 116–17; political community 114–15; political participation 113–14; political mobilization 110–13, 115–16; research findings 137–9; as tool for political communication and political information 105–10; as tool for political participation 103–5; use in civic education 124, 127, 132; use in voter registration 129
Iran-Contra scandal 45
Iraq War 49, 63
Irvine, Derry 40, 49
Is Voting for Young People? (Wattenberg) 10, 21, 135
issue-based actions 95, 97
issue-based organizations 110–13, 117

Jackman, R.W. 8, 12, 51, 55
Jackman, S. 30–1
Jennings, M.K. 7, 8, 43, 85
Johnson, L.B. 72

Kaase, M. 14, 22, 69, 70, 88, 91, 95, 98
Keating, P. 76
Kennedy, J. 25
Kerry, J. 112
Klingemann, H.D. 12, 44, 54, 55, 95
Kornberg, A. 11, 37

Labor Party, Australia 51, 76
Labour Party, Britain 49, 74
LeDuc, L. 27, 28, 122, 129, 130–1, 134
Leigh, A. 42, 50, 70, 80
Levine, P.3, 34, 57, 90, 116, 122, 124, 125, 126, 127, 129–30, 131, 132–3, 136

Liberal Party, Australia 76–7
lifecycle effects: electoral engagement 80–1; party identification 73; political interest 57–8; political trust 42, 43, 46; versus generation effects 3–4; voter turnout 23–4, 31–2
lifestyle politics, blurred barriers with electoral politics 116
Lijphart, A. 9, 23, 131
Listhaug, O. 88
Loewen, P. 23
Lyons, W. 12, 55

McAllister, I. 11, 37, 39, 41, 42, 49, 51, 56, 75, 84, 127, 136, 144
McCain, J. 127
MacManus, S.A. 33, 42, 95
Mcpherson, C.B. 140
Margolis, M. 113, 116, 117
Marsh, A. 22, 42, 49, 69, 88, 90, 91, 95
Martin, P. 1–2, 55
mass communication, trend towards 127
measurement issues: Internet participation 113, 115–16; non-electoral participation 89–91, 96; policy reforms 133–4
middle-aged people: boycotting consumer products 93–4; candidate and party website visits 108–9; civic duty 32–4; contacting politicians or civil servants 80–1; definition of 9; Internet as tool for participation 103–5; membership of political forums and discussion groups 106–7; mobilization by parties and politicians 81–4; party identification 71–7; party membership 77–80; petition signing 92–3; political interest 58–64; political Internet messages forwarded 107–8; political trust 45–52; protesting 91–2; support for democracy 52–3; voter turnout 25–32
Miller, A. 53–4
Miller, R.A. 8, 51
Miller, W.E. 2, 4, 10, 23, 58, 71
Milner, H. 2, 9, 15, 22, 26, 33, 34, 55, 56, 58, 77, 85, 99, 100, 101, 109, 114, 122, 123, 124, 129, 130, 131, 132, 133, 139
minorities, representation of 130–1
mobilization: Internet as tool for 104–5, 110–13, 114, 115; *see also* elite mobilization
modernization theory 5–6; negative side of 97–9; positive side of 96–7
'monitorial citizens' 63–4, 97
Moreno, A. 40, 42
MORI polls 42
Mossberger, K. 113
motivation 64, 123, 125, 131
MoveOn 112–13, 115
multinational corporations, targeting 95–6, 112

National Voter Registration Act (1993), US 129
Netaction 112
New American Voter 23
New Zealand, institutional reform 133
Nie, N.H. 3, 15, 69–70, 109
Niemi, R.G. 7, 8, 43, 85
non-electoral participation: data 91–4; discussion 94–100; literature 5–6, 88–9; measurement and definition problems 89–91, 96; overview 13–14; reliance on resources and motivation 64; research findings 137–9; shift to 116–17
normative goals, civic education 125
Norris, P. 1, 2, 5, 6, 9, 10, 13, 14, 24, 39, 41, 42, 44, 52, 54, 70, 71, 74, 84, 87, 88, 89, 90, 92, 95, 98, 102, 105, 110–12, 114, 135, 137, 142
Nye, J.S. 40, 44, 46

O'Neill, B. 2, 13, 88, 132, 137
Obama, B. 59, 114, 127, 128
older people: boycotting consumer products 93–4; civic duty 32–4; candidate and party website visits 108–9; contacting politicians or civil servants 80–1; definition of 9; Internet as tool for participation 103–5; membership of political forums and discussion groups 106–7; mobilization by parties and politicians 81–4; party identification 71–7; party membership 77–80; petition signing 92–3; political interest 58–64; political Internet messages forwarded 107–8; political trust 45–52; protesting 91–2; support for democracy 52–3; voter turnout 25–32
Ontario, compulsory civic education 123

Orren, G. 43
overreporting problems, surveys 32
Owen, D. 14, 102, 103, 105, 110

Pammett, J. 122, 129, 130–1, 134
Papakadis, E. 42, 50
Parti Québécois 27
participatory inequalities 116–17
parties: downplaying role of 100; mobilization by 81–4, 85–6; possibilities for elite mobilization 125–8, 132–3; use of Internet-based mobilization 113–14; youth sections 71
partisan politics, in civic education programmes 124
party identification: effects of civic education 125; levels of 71–7, 84–5; literature 8; and social background 98
party membership: effects of civic education 125; levels of 77–80, 85
party websites 108–9
Pateman, C. 140
Patterson, T.E. 55, 57
Pattie, C. 12, 13, 14, 42, 48, 49, 55, 88, 92, 94, 95, 98, 135, 136, 137, 142
personalized political contact 126–7
petition signing 88, 92–3
Pew Research Center 105
Pharr, S.J. 11, 40, 46
Phelps, E. 24
Plutzer, E. 24
policy reforms: aimed at young people 122–32; discussion 132–4; overview 16; research findings 139–40
Political Action (Marsh/Kaase) 88
political communication, Internet as tool for 105–10
political community, Internet 114–15
political conflict, resistance to 125
political culture 7, 12, 41, 55
political engagement over time, examining 3–10
political equality: decline of 97–9; voting as device for 22–3
political events: effects on electoral engagement 72, 76–7; effects on political interest 58–9, 63–4; effects on political trust 45–6, 49, 50–1, 53; effects on voter turnout 25–6, 27–9
political forums 106–7, 114–15
political information, Internet as tool for 105–10

political interest: concept of 56–7; data 58–62; discussion 62–4; literature on 57–8; low levels of 129–30; overview 12; research findings 136–7
political Internet messages forwarded 107–8
political knowledge 56, 97–9; effect on political engagement 122–5; low levels of 129–30
political messages, forwarding 107–8, 115
political outcomes, effects of non-participation 23, 99, 117
political participation: changing styles of 94–6; concept of 2; defining 69–70, 115–16; effect of political knowledge 122–5; Internet as tool for 103–5; Internet as tool for equalizing 113–14; Internet forums as hindrance to 110–13
political reforms, Britain 49
political sphere, ownership of 141–2
political support, levels of 41, 54
political trust: data 45–51; defining 40–1; discussion 51–2; effects of civic education 125; implications of 53–4; literature 7, 8, 41–4; overview 11–12; research findings 136; and support for democracy 43–4, 52–3
politicians: contacting 80–1; mobilization by 81–4, 85–6; possibilities for elite mobilization 125–8, 132–3; use of Internet-based mobilization 114
politics: definition of 90–1; disengagement from 1–2
post-industrialization theory 116
Print, M. 31, 42, 51, 131
proportional representation (PR) systems 130–1
protest organizations 110–13
protesting 72, 88, 91–2; effectiveness of 95
Putnam, R.D. 3, 4–7, 11, 12, 13, 40, 41, 42, 43, 44, 46, 52, 55, 57, 70, 71, 85, 86, 87, 88, 109, 137–8

Rahn, W.M. 42
Rawnsley, G.D. 24, 42
Reagan, R. 45
reinforcement effect, Internet 104–5
Renwick, A. 133
Republicans, US 73
research findings 16–17, 135–40

research methodology 8–10
Resnick, D. 116, 117
resource model 15, 64, 97–9
Rice, R.E. 113
rights-consciousness, expansion of 141–2
Rosenstone, S.J. 34, 41, 58, 64, 81, 126
Rubenson, D. 122
Rucht, D. 88
Russell, A. 122, 128, 131

Schlesinger, A.M. 1
Schudson, M. 1, 63–4, 90, 96, 97, 141–2
segmented participation 110–13
Shachar, R. 23, 24
Shanks, J.M. 2, 4, 10, 23, 58, 71
simulations, use in civic education 124
single-issue groups 95, 110–13, 117
social capital: creation through Internet use 109–10 depletion of 4–5
social movements, Internet as mobilization tool 110–13, 115
social-status bias, citizen participation 97–9
socialization theory 7–8
socialization effects: Internet participation 103–5: party identification 72–3, 76, 85; political interest 63; political trust 51
socioeconomic development, effects of 5–6, 97–9
Spain, Internet participation 109
state power, erosion of 95–6
Stoker, G. 70, 87, 126
Stokes, D.. 11, 39, 40
Stolle, D. 24

Tanguay, A.B. 2, 42, 55
Teixeira, R.A. 32, 130, 131
telephone canvassing 126–7
Topf, R. 33
transient participation 110–13
transnational advocacy networks 111–12
transnational organizations 110–13
Transue, J.E. 42

US; boycotting consumer products 93–4; candidate and party website visits 108–9; civic duty 32–4; contacting civil servants or politicians 80–1; electoral system 131; elite mobilization 126–7, 128, 132–3;

generational effect 4–5; Internet as tool for participation 103–5, 113–14; membership of political forums and discussion groups 106–7; mobilization by parties and politicians 82; non-electoral participation 88; party identification 71–3; party membership 70, 77–8; petition signing 92–3; political interest 57, 58–60, 62–4; political Internet messages forwarded 107–8; political trust 41, 42, 43, 45–6, 51–2; protesting 91–2; support for democracy 52–3; voter registration 129; voter turnout 24–6, 31–2; voting age population 4

Van Deth, J.W. 140, 141
Verba, S. 3, 7, 11, 12, 14, 15, 22, 39, 54, 55, 56–7, 69–70, 98, 139
Vietnam War 29, 45, 72
Voice and Equality (Verba) 139
volatility: civic duty perceptions 34; party identification 74, 76; political interest 62; political trust 50–1; voter turnout 25–6, 27, 28, 30, 31–2, 34
Voter Decides 8
voter information and awareness campaigns 122
voter registration 31, 128–30, 133
voter turnout: and civic duty 32–4; effects of civic education 122–3; effects of registration reforms 128–30; generational and lifecycle effects 23–4; importance of 22–3; overview 10–11; research findings 135–6; summarising voting data 31–2; voting data 24–31
voting advice applications (VAAS) 132
voting age 25–6, 27, 29, 131–2
voting, importance of 100
Vromen, A. 2, 13, 88, 105, 114, 137

Ward, S. 14, 102, 105, 110, 111, 112, 113, 115
Watergate scandal 45, 58
Wattenberg, M.P. 10, 21, 23, 55, 57, 71, 123, 129, 131, 135, 142
Weinstein, M. 42, 48, 71
Weldon, S. 22, 138
Welzel, C. 4–7, 34, 42, 44, 51, 52, 53, 85–6, 87, 88, 89, 96, 97, 98, 99, 137–8
White, C. 42, 48, 122

Whitlam, G. 50
Whittier, N. 3
Wolfinger, R.E. 3, 34
World Trade Organization (WTO) 111, 112, 115
World Values Survey 89
World War I 53
Wright, T. 15, 49, 61, 71, 74, 100
Wuthnow, R. 4

young people: boycotting consumer products 93–4; candidate and party website visits 108–9; civic duty 32–4; contacting politicians or civil servants 80–1; definition of 9; Internet as tool for participation 103–5; membership of political forums and discussion groups 106–7; mobilization by parties and politicians 81–4; party identification 71–7; party membership 77–80; petition signing 92–3; policy reforms aimed at 122–32; political interest 58–64; political Internet messages forwarded 107–8; political trust 45–52; protesting 91–2; support for democracy 52–3; voter turnout 25–32
Youth Electoral Study, Australia 131

Zaller, R. 56
Zukin, C. 2, 9, 10, 12, 13, 24, 33, 43, 55, 57, 71, 86, 87, 88, 90, 92, 93, 95, 96, 99, 100, 103, 134, 137, 139

CPSIA information can be obtained
at www.ICGtesting.com
Printed in the USA
FFOW01n1946141116
29387FF